Also by James William Gibson

———————————

*Warrior Dreams: Paramilitary Culture*
*in Post-Vietnam America*

*The Perfect War: Technowar in Vietnam*

# A REENCHANTED WORLD

# A
# REENCHANTED
# WORLD

---

### THE QUEST
### FOR A NEW KINSHIP
### WITH NATURE

---

## JAMES WILLIAM GIBSON

METROPOLITAN BOOKS

Henry Holt and Company · New York

Metropolitan Books
Henry Holt and Company, LLC
*Publishers since 1866*
175 Fifth Avenue
New York, New York 10010
www.henryholt.com

Metropolitan Books® and **m**® are registered trademarks
of Henry Holt and Company, LLC.

Library of Congress Cataloging-in-Publication Data
Gibson, James William.
   A reenchanted world : the quest for a new kinship with nature / James William Gibson.—
1st ed.
      p. cm.
   Includes bibliographical references and index.
   ISBN-13: 978-0-8050-7835-0
   ISBN-10: 0-8050-7835-5
   1. Human ecology.   2. Nature—Effect of human beings on.   3. Political ecology.
I. Title.
   GF41.G53  2009
   304.2—dc22                                                          2008031695

Henry Holt books are available for special promotions
and premiums. For details contact: Director, Special Markets.

First Edition 2009
Designed by Victoria Hartman
Printed in the United States of America
1  3  5  7  9  10  8  6  4  2

*For Carol Mithers*

# Contents

Part III · HOPE RENEWED

# A REENCHANTED WORLD

# INTRODUCTION

# Call of the Wild

Like Special Forces commandos, the L.A. County Sheriff's Deputies and Firefighters came at 2:00 AM, when they knew their enemy would be asleep. Earlier that day, a force of two hundred had secured a perimeter around the camp, cutting off all sources of outside resupply, while a small reconnaissance team managed to steal most of the man's food and water. After a seventy-one-day siege, the lone warrior knew the end was coming and chained himself into place for one last stand.

The assault came off with military precision. A fire truck with a hydraulic-powered ladder moved in. Firefighters with metal cutters scrambled up and quickly cut the man's chains; sheriff's deputies read the charges against him and escorted him down the ladder to the ground. The public watched, mesmerized. The *Los Angeles Times* was there, its reporters putting out a metro section lead story, one of a dozen the paper had run during the long standoff. A local TV station canceled normal programming and spent two and a half hours providing live coverage, an action normally reserved for wars, assassinations, and extraordinary political scandals.

In fact, the drama was the arrest of a tree-sitter, who was charged with trespassing. For just over two months, forty-two-year-old John Quigley had lived amid the boughs of a four-hundred-year-old oak tree, trying to save it from a developer's bulldozer. The oak stood at the entrance to a new subdivision in the Santa Clarita Valley, north of Los Angeles. The Los Angeles County Board of Supervisors had ruled that the tree had to go because it blocked the planned expansion of a two-lane road into a four-lane thoroughfare. A developer was constructing several hundred homes nearby.

Locals had protested, contending that the road could be curved around the tree. The county officials said no. Their best offer was to move the oak, an act several arborists said would lead to its death. So on November 1, 2002, Quigley, a well-known environmentalist-about-town, climbed into the tree and refused to leave. Early on in the sit, he and his support crew took a lesson from an earlier tree-sitter, Julia Butterfly Hill, who had lived atop a giant northern California redwood for twenty-one months. Hill claimed that her tree, dubbed Luna by the Earth First! activists who organized the tree-sit, communicated with her, teaching her how to climb and helping her endure winter storms. Hill routinely called the tree by name in her many interviews with the news media. By the time she successfully negotiated an agreement to save the redwood from logging, even conservative newspapers and her opponents in the lumber industry were referring to Luna as if the tree were a sentient being. Although Quigley never claimed his oak spoke to him, he and his closest advisers began calling it Old Glory. (The name apparently was the invention of two local boys who told Quigley, "We call her Old Glory because she stands in all her glory for all the oaks that have been cut down.")[1]

The name stuck, successfully turning the oak into a patriotic emblem of America for the post–September 11 era. The media loved the story, showing pictures of Old Glory with updates about the confrontation almost daily. The publicity created a strange carnival under the old oak tree. Parents brought their children to bear witness.

Native American groups drummed and danced in solidarity. As posters, poems, and tributes collected at its base, Old Glory started to resemble a monument or memorial. Everyone—except maybe the recalcitrant supervisors—could see that to millions living in the suburban sprawl of Southern California, the oak had become far more than a tree. Just as Quigley and the boys who named it hoped, it had become a symbol of all the other trees, animal life, and open spaces lost to development.

Except in its particulars, this story was by no means unique. Through the 1990s and early 2000s, a new and striking kind of yearning was evident in the ways ordinary people felt and talked about nature. People were touched by stories of bears who befriended humans, enthralled by the fluid grace of whales, moved to the depths of their souls by majestic trees, dark mountains, and flowing rivers, newly alive to the sense of mystery, of a world larger than themselves. Some suburban residents came to feel deeply connected to the few remaining open spaces—slivers of forest, wetland, meadow—around them, dedicating years, even decades to trying to save them from development. Others restored degraded places such as polluted wetlands and rivers. Naturalist Freeman House describes the effort to revitalize the Mattole River in northern California (which suffered from denuded stream banks and muddy runoff) as providing a kind of time travel, a journey back to a lost stage of human history. "Working together, with our feet in the water, moving large rocks and logs to armor raw and bleeding stream banks, or on the dry slopes above, planting trees, seemed to carry from our muscles to our minds a buried memory of human communities deeply integrated with the wild processes surrounding."[2] House thought that through their work, the activists were "becoming *indigenous*," rooted in the land.[3]

Reported experiences of communing with animals were equally extraordinary. Scuba divers talked openly about the love they felt for the sea lions, octopuses, and manta rays they met face-to-face in the water. More adventurous souls even set out to reestablish what they saw as lost intimacy. In Russia, for example, Angelo d'Arrigo, a two-time world-champion hang glider, decided that it was his mission to lead the world's last remaining western Siberian cranes to safety by taking them on a 3,400-mile journey from the Oka River in Russia to a wildlife refuge in Iran near the Caspian Sea. The birds had become threatened with extinction from habitat loss, hunting, and a perilous migratory route that exposed them to fighting in Afghanistan and Pakistan when they made their annual trip from Siberia to India.

With the assistance of the U.S.-based International Crane Foundation, d'Arrigo raised ten cranes in captivity. The chicks nested under d'Arrigo's hang glider, were fed by him, and grew to consider him their mother. D'Arrigo dressed to resemble a crane; his glider was equipped with a small motor for help in taking off but had cranelike wings. At a press conference, he described the mission as part of his Metamorphosis project, a five-year program to become as close to being a bird as humanly possible. "I think inside any person, there remains one part of birds," he explained. "Maybe it is possible to find in my mind this little part."[4]

In 2002, Jacques Mayol, a pioneer in deep-sea "free diving," described his breath-holding efforts in similar terms. "I don't dive to conquer the elements," Mayol explained. "I melt into the ocean."[5] His goal was to become *Homo Delphinus*, to reawaken "the dormant dolphin within man" and rediscover humanity's lost spiritual connection to the sea.[6] D'Arrigo and Mayol and their fellow adventurers were part of a new avant-garde, artist-athletes who reimagined and dramatized relationships to nature through radical performance art.

Across the country, the prospect of seeing wolves return to their native lands filled yet another set of people with a transforming passion so great that it changed their lives. After thirty-four gray wolves were reintroduced to Yellowstone National Park in 1995–96, the Druid Peak pack, led by an alpha male named 21 and a female alpha called 42, became the favorites of scientists, documentary filmmakers, and a band of extraordinarily committed amateur naturalists. Forty-two was eventually nicknamed Cinderella, because her older sister, a female alpha, had attacked her and killed her pups. One year Cinderella fought back, killing her sister and becoming the dominant female. So intense was the wolf family drama that people began traveling each year to watch and photograph it. One couple even moved from Denver to be closer to the pack, saying, "The Druids have almost become family members." Then one day Cinderella disappeared. Twenty-one "howled his guts out," said one observer, and Cinderella's human friends launched an intensive search. When a wildlife technician found her body—she'd been killed by another pack—radiation therapist Carol Yates, one of the amateur naturalists, wept. "I guess we're glad we were here when it happened," said her husband, Richard. "It's the way of the wolf." The story, in effect an obituary for a wolf, ran on the front page of the *Los Angeles Times*.[7]

Even more strikingly, people began speaking up for the dignity of ordinary domestic animals such as cows and pigs. Eric Schlosser's bestselling *Fast Food Nation* (2001) went far beyond Upton Sinclair's *The Jungle* (1905), describing the suffering not only of the humans who worked in the fast-food and meat-packing industries, but also of the animals they butchered. The image of cattle spending their last days and flood-lit nights in feedlots, being stimulated around the clock to eat hormone- and antibiotic-laced grain while standing knee-deep in their own manure, was not easily forgotten. Equally important, Schlosser showed that the industry's manipulation of consumers, abuse of workers, and contempt for animals were all parts of the same process.[8]

A year later, a conservative speechwriter who sometimes worked for President George W. Bush further heightened public awareness of animal suffering. Matthew Scully's *Dominion* rejected the traditional Biblical interpretation that God gave humans the moral right to dominate all creatures. Humans are but part of God's creation, Scully argued, their sovereignty limited. And those limits, he claimed, were now routinely broken on factory farms, where animals spent their entire lives indoors, confined to crowded cages, lying on slatted floors without straw or grass or any kind of padding so that their wastes could be hosed down. On entering a building holding five hundred young pigs, Scully was deeply affected: "Eyes appear between the slats of the fences. . . . Some [piglets] are up on their hind legs, forelegs curled over the fences of their pens, ears half-erect, eyes filled with fear and life and what any man with eyes of his own to see will know as intelligence. . . . They are just like puppies."9 The old split between animals we name and love and the "nameless, faceless beasts we condemn in our farms and labs to lives of ceaseless misery" was no longer defensible, he concluded. "Factory farming isn't just killing. It is negation, a complete denial of the animal as a living being with his or her own needs and nature."10 Widely and positively reviewed, *Dominion* helped fuel increased moral reflection about humankind's ethical obligations to animals and the natural world.

HOW ARE WE to understand this upsurge of feeling? To some degree, it can be considered a product of contemporary environmentalism. The current movement was born in January 1969, when an oil well blew out off Santa Barbara, drenching the California coast in thick black crude. In the weeks that followed, the news media showed the corpses of hundreds of oil-covered birds and the struggle by volunteer rescue workers to save them and to rescue sea lions and other suffering creatures. A year later activists established Earth Day. During the 1970s, the movement—a loose coalition of counterculture types, concerned scientists, animal rights activists, bioregionalists, and public interest lawyers—achieved extraordinary political victories. President Richard Nixon created the Environmental Protection Agency, and Congress passed the nation's first major environmental laws: the National Environmental Policy Act, the Clean Water and Clean Air acts, the Marine Mammal Protection Act, and the Endangered Species Act.

Victories continued even during the administrations of presidents

Ronald Reagan and George W. Bush, which were actively unfriendly to environmentalism. Large national organizations such as the Sierra Club, The Wilderness Society, and the Natural Resources Defense Council recruited millions of members through direct-mail campaigns. Armed with new monies and mailing lists of members ready to write and phone politicians and officials, the big groups effectively lobbied Washington and state capitols, becoming "players" on the political scene. When federal, state, or local governments failed to uphold environmental laws, the movement went to court. Thousands of lawsuits were filed by environmental groups in the 1980s and 1990s, and though only a fraction were won, they served to heighten recognition of and respect for these groups. Anyone who followed public affairs knew that the environmental movement fought for its beliefs.

Outside the courts, the movement's radical wing, its direct action troops, also kept the issue at the top of the news. Greenpeace activists captured global attention in the 1970s as they skimmed across wavetops in fast, inflatable boats, positioning themselves between whales and Russian ships armed with harpoon-firing cannons. The action was captured on film, and shown around the world, vastly increasing pressures that led to a moratorium on legal commercial whaling. Rainforest Action Network climbers unfurled banners across oil company office buildings, demanding that firms stop drilling in South American tropical rain forests, successfully bringing attention to the plight of indigenous peoples trying to save their lands—struggles the tribes eventually won. In 1999, when the World Trade Organization (WTO) convened in Seattle to endorse a new worldwide regulatory framework that, among other depredations, permitted increased commercial exploitation of the environment (including the abrogation of national laws designed to protect places and species), activists countered with sit-down strikes across the city, blockading entrances both to the convention center and to local hotels. Out on the streets, television cameras captured what looked like a bizarre, wilderness-themed costume party. Some protesters came as redwood trees demanding an end to clear-cutting, others as sea turtles in favor of turtle-excluding devices on fishing nets. Every creature had its advocate. And anyone who watched TV, listened to radio news, or read the paper witnessed the demonstrators shutting down the WTO meeting.

By the 2000s, environmental awareness had permeated much of the country's institutions and everyday life. The nation's public schools made concern for the environment an integral part of the curriculum. Edenic murals showing mountains, oceans, and forests filled with wildlife came to grace school walls, and children learned to speak unself-consciously of Mother Earth. Recycling programs encouraged people to think about the impact of their way of life on the world around them. Organic food experienced a surge in popularity, appearing on the shelves of mainstream supermarkets. Concern for the environment had become a majority position. By the mid-1990s, a stunning 90 percent of Americans agreed that "Justice is not just for human beings. We need to be as fair to plants and animals as we are to people."[11]

BUT THE SPREADING influence of the environmental movement only partially explains the last two decades' fundamental change of consciousness. No political movement or platform can account for the intensity of feeling expressed by those who long to rediscover and embrace nature's mystery and grandeur, who experience an attachment to animals and places so overwhelming that they feel morally compelled to protect them, and who look to nature for psychic regeneration and renewal. More than an ideology, this quest for connection indicates a fundamental rejection of the most basic premises of modern thought and society.

Briefly stated, these premises centered on a view of nature as inert matter, void of spirit and consciousness. For an early scientist like René Descartes, writing in the first half of the seventeenth century, animals were simply unfeeling machines, incapable of emotions or pain. As the accomplishments of science earned it increasing prestige, this purely utilitarian view of nature became the dominant mode, further reinforced by the success of industrial capitalism founded on a scientific-technological paradigm. As Karl Marx and Friedrich Engels observed in *The Communist Manifesto*, the modern world was built largely through "the subjection of Nature's forces to man."[12]

This subjection was so complete it virtually eclipsed humankind's past, and, with it, the traditional unity between humans and the rest of creation typical of premodern societies. Among Native American tribes, for example, animal species were, like other tribes, deemed "nations," such as the buffalo nation or beaver nation. Premodern creation myths typically highlighted a tribe's moral relationships to animal and plant species important to its survival. On the Great Plains, the Lakota Sioux told how a powerful spirit, White Buffalo Calf Woman, brought the sacred pipe and the buffalo to them—and how both pipe and buffalo must be treated with profound respect. Along the coast of the Pacific Northwest, Native American tribal myths explained that the salmon they caught were actually the children of salmon-people who lived on the bottom of the sea; each year the salmon-people changed their young into salmon and sent them as a gift, a blood sacrifice bonding the two peoples. Beyond any particular group's connection to any particular creatures and places, the premodern cosmos possessed a kind of enchantment: Since animals and plants and places had spirits, people could communicate with them through rituals, prayers, and meditation. In an enchanted cosmos, humans were never alone: The crane flying overhead, the ground beneath one's feet, the great oak tree near the creek, the creek itself, could all be addressed as kin by those who knew the right words and rituals.

Modernity, as has been widely noted, drained the cosmos of that magic. In Max Weber's formulation, the West's elevation of "rational empirical knowledge" led to the "disenchantment of the world and its transformation into a causal mechanism."[13] Radical and utter isolation followed. Carl Jung, a contemporary of Weber, grasped that loneliness had its tragic implications: "Man feels himself isolated in the cosmos. He is no longer involved in nature and has lost his emotional participation in natural events, which hitherto had symbolic meaning for him. Thunder is no longer the voice of a god, nor is lightning his avenging missile. No river contains a spirit, no tree means a man's life, no snake is the embodiment of wisdom, and no mountain harbors a great demon. Neither do things speak to him nor can he speak to things, like stones, springs, plants and animals."[14]

THIS IDEA OF the human world as separate from the rest of nature never gained complete acceptance in the West. There were always a few mavericks and romantics who saw such isolation as wrong in substance and unbearable in spirit. Over generations, they repeatedly fought back, launching waves of protest, both cultural and political. Led by such diverse figures as Henry David Thoreau and Herman Melville, John Muir and his successors in the public lands movement, photographers such as Ansel Adams and Eliot Porter, and scientists like Rachel Carson, these protests have ebbed and flowed, risen in power and then become marginalized once again.

But the current wave of spiritual interest in nature is not simply another outburst of romanticism. For one thing, it is fueled by a new sense of urgency. Just how fast global warming is proceeding remains a legitimate scientific question, but there is no longer a question of its reality, or of the threat that it poses. Species extinction is accelerating to a thousand times beyond what fossil records indicate is a normal, evolutionary rate. Polar bears were listed as a threatened species by the U.S. Fish and Wildlife Service in 2008 because their icy habitat was thawing; reports of bears drowning while swimming between increasingly distant ice floes conjure up haunting images of what the future might bring.[15] Salmon have nearly vanished from the Northwest because dams impede their migrations. Ivory-billed woodpeckers have disappeared from southern swamps because of clear-cut logging; after years of habitat loss to development, some butterfly species in the Florida Keys are down to a few dozen members. Tropical rain forests in the Amazon and Indonesia, long renowned for their rich biodiversity, are losing thousands of square miles each year to logging and fires set by ranchers and farmers to clear their lands.

Moreover, the current change is much broader, deeper, and more varied than what has come before. Virtually every part of contemporary culture, from the highest realms of science, theology, art, and literature to the mundane world of commercial television programming, has experienced its revolutionary influence. Already, mainstream geneticists openly discuss the idea of human-animal kinship, while major Hollywood films such as *The Whale Rider* enthusiastically promote the idea of cross-species bonding. Even children's movies reflect a radical shift in the portrayal of human-animal relationships: Whereas coming-of-age classics like *The Yearling* (1946) and *Old Yeller* (1957) portrayed the killing of a beloved pet as a necessary step toward maturity, newer tales, like Disney's *Brother Bear* (2003), feature heroes that choose to remain forever in the animal kingdom. The ultimate goal of this sweeping change, which I call "the culture of enchantment," is nothing less than the reinvestment of nature with spirit. Flatly rejecting modernity's reduction of animals, plants, places, and natural forces to either matter or utilitarian resource, the culture of enchantment attempts to make nature sacred once again.

Of course, not all people touched by the culture of enchantment will devote their whole lives to it, in the style of Angelo d'Arrigo or Julia Butterfly Hill. But however dissimilar and partial their commitments, people respond to the culture of enchantment because it offers them something they need (and cannot find elsewhere in consumerist America): *transcendence*, a sense of mystery and meaning, glimpses of a numinous world beyond our own. The spiritual connections made to animals and landscapes almost invariably lead—often intentionally, sometimes not—to a new relationship to nature in general. And nature perceived as "sacred" is allowed to exist on its own terms, for its own sake, valuable simply because it is there. For nature to retain its mystery, it must retain its autonomy: While its products may be used by people, it is not to be exploited or perceived as a mere resource for human consumption. The culture of enchantment, then, alters the fundamental meanings that the West has given the natural world, imagining a new covenant between people, land, and creatures.

The implications of this shift are enormous. If first Luna and then Old Glory can be reenchanted, whole forests or entire mountain ranges or coastlines might come to command our love and respect. Even degraded and polluted landscapes—the kind often found in and around cities—might gain our compassion and be deemed worthy of care. In creating spiritual and moral reasons for reconceiving man's relation to nature, the culture of enchantment poses profound challenges to modern institutions, raising standards that few, if any, can now meet. But though no one knows what changes would have to follow from a conviction that nature is spiritually alive, the struggle for enchantment is a crucial part of the larger struggle over the kind of culture and society humanity will have. How that struggle began, the forms it has taken, and its prospects for success are the concerns of this book. The stakes could not be higher. Enchantment is the last remaining utopian dream.

# Part I

# FORMS OF
# ENCHANTMENT

# 1

## Modernity and Its Discontents

The achievements of industrial societies have been the subject of endless celebration, but there have always been those who saw the darker side of progress. The generations of discontented social critics, nature writers, conservationists, landscape photographers, Native American activists, and counterculture leaders who decried the destruction of lands, animals, and indigenous peoples form the intellectual tradition grounding the new culture of enchantment.

Even the earliest proponents of industrial society were not blind to its destructive capacity. Marx and Engels, who lauded the potential for unprecedented social change released by industrialization, also realized that the subjection of nature had a price. The best of the premodern world, including its beauty, was being devastated by the industrial revolution and the market, and, in the pair's famous phrase from *The Communist Manifesto* (1848), "all that is holy is profaned."[1] In the 1840s, when Engels visited England, his observations in *The Condition of the Working Class in England* (1845) included long passages detailing fouled air and water. The Irk River running through Manchester, for example, was "in dry weather, a long string of the most disgusting, blackish-green, slime pools . . . from the depths of which bubbles of miasmic gas constantly arise and give forth a stench unendurable even on the bridge forty or fifty feet above the surface of the stream."[2]

While Marx and Engels clearly saw the physical damages wrought by industrialism, Max Weber better understood its spiritual costs. Weber pointed to Protestantism's definition of God—a transcendent being who does not dwell in the natural world or its creatures and is concerned only with humans—as the motive force behind the "practical rational conduct" necessary for sustained capitalist development. Earlier religions, Weber notes in *The Protestant Ethic and the Spirit of Capitalism* (1920), had erected "spiritual obstacles" involving "magical and religious forces and the ethical ideas of duty based upon them," which created "serious inner resistance" to society's utilization of nature purely for its own practical purposes.[3] Although Weber did not elaborate, it's not difficult to infer the different consequences of the two theological visions. No one would cut down a grove of trees to build houses, for example, if forest spirits were believed to inhabit the woods. Conversely, in the absence of such spirituality, cutting is a rational act if it produces a profit.

Weber saw himself as a man of science, but these developments disturbed him greatly. He repeatedly bemoaned "the fate of our time, with its characteristic rationalization, intellectualization, and above all else, the disenchantment of the world."[4] The conclusion of *The Protestant Ethic* reads like an indictment:

> No one knows . . . whether at the end of this tremendous development entirely new prophets will arise, or there will be a great rebirth of old ideas and ideals, or, if neither, mechanized purification, embellished with a sort of convulsive self-importance. For of the last stage of this cultural development, it might well be truly said [quoting Goethe], "Specialists without spirit, sensualists without heart; this nullity imagines that it has attained a level of civilization never before achieved."[5]

In North America, the clash of the two visions was vividly expressed in the treatment of the natural world as the frontier moved west. Whereas the old Native American cultural norms generated "serious inner resistance" to the wanton killing of wildlife, Christianity contained no such prohibitions, and colonizing Europeans embarked on a vast slaughter and transformation of the landscape. Before contact, some thirty to one hundred million buffalo had ranged from the Rocky Mountains to the Atlantic.[6] Then, in 1800, Anglo-American traders reached the Great Plains. Buffalo kills escalated throughout the first half of the nineteenth century and accelerated radically after the Civil War. Hunters killed buffalo for meat to supply workers constructing the new transcontinental railroads, to ship hides and tongues to national and international markets, and to deprive Plains Indians of their principal food source.[7] By 1878 no herds remained on the southern plains of Texas, Oklahoma, and Nebraska. Within the next five years, the northern herds of the Dakotas and surrounding regions were gone as well. By 1887 no more than a few dozen buffalo remained, protected by assorted ranchers and Indian tribes, living in tiny herds scattered across the West.[8]

As the buffalo disappeared, the wolves of the Great Plains and Rockies found a new food source—the cattle herds arriving from Texas. Former buffalo hunters turned their attention to the wolves and, from 1865 to 1895, killed between one and two million, eliminating the animals entirely in most states and reducing the population to near-extinction in others.[9] Cattle ranching in turn led to the death of the tall-grass prairie, because the cows grazed far more intensely than their bison predecessors. America's tens of millions of beavers, which had thrived in virtually all waterways, were relentlessly hunted, their pelts turned into hats and fur coats; by the late nineteenth century, most were gone.[10] Without beaver dams and the wetlands that grew around them, American waterways increasingly became turbid and filled with silt. The moving frontier line also meant deforestation on a grand scale as first settlers and then business and industry sought lumber. No region was spared: New England, Mid-Atlantic, the South, the Midwest, the Rockies, and the West Coast all lost tens of millions of acres of forests.

Even ocean life fell prey to the conquest. On the Pacific coast, Russian and American fleets killed over two hundred thousand sea otters. By 1900 they were nearly extinct; only a tiny remnant population of three hundred to four hundred animals survived, hidden in the Big Sur region along California's central coast.[11] Millions of whales—right, humpback, fin, gray, Bryde's, bowhead, sei, blue, and sperm whale species—died from harpoons in the nineteenth century. Some 1.5 million died in the South Pacific alone.[12]

BY THE LATE 1840s, a culture of protest to the killing and ecological devastation arose in New England. Writers such as Ralph Waldo Emerson and Henry David Thoreau challenged both the Protestant concept of a God indifferent or even hostile to nature's creatures and the nation's dominant frontier-capitalist mentality. Emerson revered the mysteries and beauty of nature, even in the most ordinary forms: "Crossing a bare common, in snow puddles, at twilight, under a clouded sky, without having in my thoughts any occurrence of special good fortune, I have enjoyed a perfect exhilaration. I am glad to the brink of fear."[13] For Emerson, nature offered continual revelations of a unified divine realm, variously named the Universal Soul, Reason, Absolute Spirit, or God. Even the natural rhythms of day and night served as pathways to the absolute: "Not the sun or summer alone, but every hour and change yields its tribute of delight; for every hour and change corresponds to and authorizes a different state of the mind, from breathless noon to grimmest midnight."[14]

For Thoreau, on the other hand, animals and places had value in their own right, each with its own spirit and mystery. "Can he who has discovered the true use of whale-bone and whale oil be said to have discovered the true use of the whale?" he asks in an 1864 essay.[15] Rejecting the contemporary description of animals as soulless automata, he looked instead to naturalists of older generations, for whom animals were sensuous, sentient beings. He approvingly quotes a 1607 essay called "The History of Four-footed Beasts," in which certain antelopes are said to live near the river Euphrates and "delight much to drink of the cold water thereof." In contrast, Thoreau laments, the creatures depicted by modern naturalists "do not *delight* in anything, and their water is neither hot nor cold. . . . Surely the most important part of an animal is its *anima*, its vital spirit, on which is based its character and all the peculiarities by which it most concerns us. Yet most scientific books which treat of animals leave this out altogether, and what they describe are as it were phenomena of dead matter."[16] (Emerson's eulogy for Thoreau celebrated his intimacy with animals: "Snakes coiled round his legs; the fishes swam into his hand, and he took them out of the water; he pulled the woodchuck out of its hole by the tail, and took the foxes under his protection from the hunters."[17])

Among the contemporaries who shared Thoreau's sensibilities, Herman Melville stands out. Ishmael, the narrator of *Moby-Dick* (1851), points to the majesty, beauty, even divinity of whales. When the sperm whales navigate the globe, it's as if they were "guided by some infallible instinct—say rather, secret intelligence from the Deity. . . . No ship ever sailed her course, by any chart, with one tithe of such marvelous precision."[18] Captain Ahab, by contrast, personifies the human will to dominate nature, and his growing derangement points to flaws in the entire Western mentality. He describes to Starbuck, his first mate, "the madness, the frenzy, the boiling blood and the smoking brow, with which, for a thousand lowerings old Ahab has furiously, foamingly chased his prey—more a demon than a man!—aye, aye! What a forty years' fool—fool—fool—old fool, has old Ahab been!"[19]

Thoreau and Melville were joined by Frederick Law Olmsted, their editor and colleague. The designer of Central and Prospect parks in New York City, Olmsted also served as the de facto head of the federal government's Yosemite Valley commission, which in 1864 established Yosemite Valley and the nearby Mariposa Grove as a thirty-nine-square-mile reserve for "public use, resort, and recreation . . . inalienable for all time."[20] While not called a national park at the time, this was the beginning of the National Park System, and marks an early recognition of the threat that industrial depredation posed to the natural world.

Still, the influence of these writers and wilderness advocates was limited. Neither Thoreau nor Melville were widely read at the time. And when Congress moved to establish a national park at Yellowstone in 1871, supporters stressed that the land was unfit for agriculture rather than that it was a wilderness worthy of preservation: Saving it, they emphasized, would do "no harm to the material interests of the people."[21] Even those who promoted the splendor of natural landscapes often acted out of financial self-interest. Financier Jay Gould, having invested a fortune in the Union Pacific, Kansas Pacific, and Denver Pacific railroads, publicized Yellowstone and the West by hiring landscape photographer William Henry Jackson to create images that would attract tourists. As Jackson later explained his work for Gould, "Most of all, it was a matter of money."[22]

Similarly, New York's Adirondack Forest Preserve (initially 313 square miles), protected in the state constitution by an amendment that included the famous Forever Wild clause, was created in 1885 to address threats to New York City's water supply and Hudson River trade from excessive logging in the Adirondack forest watershed. Certainly the Adirondack region had many advocates who saw it as a majestic example of nature's intricate processes and a spiritual presence warranting protection—Verplanck Colvin, the Adirondacks' first major surveyor, claimed that in the forest "a grand and beautiful solemnity and peace makes its way into the soul, for human strife and discord seem here to have passed away forever"—but these were not as influential as the practical and economic concerns.[23]

Still, by the 1890s, the political and spiritual heirs of Emerson, Melville, and Thoreau began to exert greater pressure on national politics. John Muir, one of the founders of the Sierra Club, drafted legislation expanding Yosemite to nearly 1,200 square miles in 1900, and lobbied successfully to make it an official national park.[24] A perceptive scientist, Muir was the first to propose (accurately) that Yosemite Valley had been formed by glaciers scraping away rock and earth. Equally important, he made repeated efforts to sound the alarm about destruction of the West. In an extraordinary series of essays for the *Atlantic Monthly*, he assessed the damage: The magnificent five-hundred-mile-long bed of golden and purple flowers of California's Central Valley had been "ploughed and pastured out of existence," the "once divinely beautiful" ground in his beloved Sierras, "the noblest forests of the world," was now "desolate and repulsive, like a face ravaged by disease." This disease would spread across the whole Pacific Coast and throughout all the Rocky Mountain forests and valleys, he warned, "unless awakening public opinion comes forward to stop it."[25]

Muir reminded his readers of how much had already been lost. Calaveras Grove, inside what would later become part of Sequoia National Park in the eastern Sierras, once had trees three thousand to four thousand years old and over twenty-four feet in diameter. But settlers cut down the sequoias and danced on the stumps. At times Muir's writings reveal his admiration of the kind of premodern sensibility that would find a spiritual presence in each forest, valley, mountain, and desert: "So charming a fall and pool in the heart of so glorious a forest good pagans would have consecrated to some lovely nymph."[26] In other instances, he seems more transcendentalist, seeing each natural wonder as a manifestation of a universal God. As he reverently describes Yosemite: "The walls are made up of rocks, mountains in size, partly separated from each other by side canyons, and they are so sheer in front, and so completely and harmoniously arranged on a level floor, that the Valley, comprehensively seen, looks like an immense hall or temple lighted from above. But no temple made with hands can compare to Yosemite."[27] In every case, Muir clearly considered the land as sacred, and he used the language of religion as a rhetorical tool to influence public opinion. Early in the twentieth century, Muir fought to save Yosemite's Hetch Hetchy Valley from being dammed and drowned to provide drinking water for San Francisco. "These temple destroyers, devotees of ravaging commercialism, seem to have a perfect contempt for Nature, and, instead of lifting their eyes to the God of the mountains, lift them to the Almighty Dollar," he raged. "Dam Hetch Hetchy! As well dam for water-tanks the people's cathedrals and churches, for no holier temple has ever been consecrated in the heart of man."[28] Muir lost this battle, the dam was built, and Hetch Hetchy Valley disappeared under water. But the memory of Hetch Hetchy became a rallying cry for future struggles, and now, nearly a century later, a new movement proposes to tear down the dam and restore the valley.

Muir's writings exerted their influence in another way as well, setting up some fundamental rhetorical conventions that would inform generations of literary nature writers. First, he showed that the very act of writing could lead to a radical change in how something was perceived: Evoking the sanctity of a place prompted others to see it as sacred, too.[29] Some, affected by the poetic evocation of nature's spiritual presence, might experience immediate conversion, but even skeptics were exposed to a powerful suggestion that nature might be more than just an inert resource for human use.

Second, Muir popularized a kind of hybrid discourse, alternating lyrical descriptions with scientific references to geology and ecology.[30] Thus, he reveres the giant sequoia trees of California both in their own right and for their ecological contributions. At twilight, their "rosy, glowing countenances seemed to be hushed and thoughtful, as if waiting in conscious religious dependence upon the sun"; once the sun set, "the trees seemed to cease their worship and breathe free."[31] Yet in the same essay, writing of the trees' proximity to streams, he notes that "it is a mistake to suppose that the water is the cause of the groves being there. On the contrary, the groves are the cause of the water being there. The roots of this immense tree fill the ground, forming a sponge which hoards the bounty of the clouds and sends it forth in clear perennial streams instead of allowing it to rush headlong in short-lived destructive floods."[32] Muir's break with the accepted conventions separating science and poetry buttressed the idea of a nature that was neither inert nor dead, but on the contrary alive and awe-inspiring—in a word, *enchanted*.

Finally, Muir always included in his writings the personal element that would become vital to the contemporary culture of enchantment. His extensive, intimate experiences of the places he wrote about gave his writing special power and intensity. He climbed the mountain crests; he drank from the creeks; he smelled the flowers in Hetch Hetchy Valley; he personally saw the wrecked land and the tree stumps after timber harvests. In contrast to capitalism's treatment of land as an impersonal commodity and scientists' use of dry abstractions to describe and analyze nature, Muir conveyed to his readers a profound encounter with the landscape—whether aesthetic, spiritual, or moral—that was compelling, even life-changing.

MUIR'S WORK INSPIRED others, including Aldo Leopold, one of the founders of modern ecology—the study of the interrelationships among species living in a region—and Ansel Adams, America's preeminent landscape photographer. Building on Muir's approach, they introduced the creative mix of thought and feeling into new areas and disciplines. Leopold's story is particularly striking. As a young forester and specialist in game management working for the U.S. Forest Service, he was already an environmentalist, advocating wilderness preservation within federally owned lands and, in 1924, successfully persuading the service to designate nearly nine hundred square miles in Gila National Forest as a wilderness preserve.[33]

Initially, Leopold accepted traditional game management ideas about the need to kill "bad" predators that preyed on the "good" species that humans traditionally hunted for food. But eventually, he pushed the new science of ecology into broader, more holistic directions, abandoning these moral categories in favor of understanding the role of *every* creature in a region. Leopold attributed the change in his way of thinking to an encounter he had had with the prototypical "bad" animal—the wolf. Since the 1870s wolves had been considered vicious, indiscriminate predators, their killing rewarded with bounties and public acclaim. Leopold had participated in such killings; according to conventional thinking, fewer wolves meant more deer, and the Forest Service was charged with managing public lands for the benefit of hunters. But one day, on a mountain in the Southwest, a kill went badly. Leopold and his friends opened fire on an alpha female and her grown pups, then ran to find their bodies. "We reached the old wolf in time to watch a fierce green fire dying in her eyes," he wrote. "I realized then, and have known ever since, that there was something new to me in those eyes—something known only to her and to the mountain."[34]

Afterward, Leopold viewed the relationships among deer, wolves, and mountains differently. He saw that in places where the wolves had all been killed, deer populations at first soared. But then the deer changed the mountain ecology. "I have seen every edible bush and seedling browsed, first to anemic desuetude, and then to death," he observed. With the vegetation gone, the deer died. Unable to learn the lesson in the piles of bleached deer bones, ranchers continued to kill off the wolves rather than let the wolves do their job of "trimming the herd to fit the range." Those ranchers, Leopold concluded, were like him before he saw the green fire in the dying wolf's eyes. They have "not learned to think like a mountain," Leopold concluded. "Hence we have dustbowls, and rivers washing the future into the sea."[35]

In the late 1940s, toward the end of his life, Leopold elaborated the lesson from the mystical mountain into a systematic set of principles he called "The Land Ethic." In Leopold's understanding, ethical behavior required individuals to cooperate and recognize the interdependence of all community members. Modern society's restriction of membership in the community to only humans, its disregard of other creatures, he insisted, failed to recognize society's dependence on nature and was morally wrong. He instead advocated enlarging "the boundaries of the human community to include soils, waters, plants and animals, or collectively: the land."[36] It was a radical argument, for if the land and its creatures were regarded as part of the community, they, too, would have to be granted rights and moral worth. "A land ethic changes the role of *Homo sapiens* from conqueror of the land-community to plain member and citizen of it," Leopold argued. "It implies respect for his fellow-members, and also respect for the community as such."[37] Within these terms, human action would necessarily be judged in terms of its impact on nature. "A thing is right when it tends to preserve the integrity, stability, and beauty of the biotic community," he wrote. "It is wrong when it tends otherwise."[38]

Landscape photographer Ansel Adams saw it as his role to illuminate the divine presence within nature.[39] His photographs sought to capture the spirit of a place and its connection to the larger universe. Adams showed how landscapes had been shaped and created by natural forces such as wind, rain, and geological upheavals, thus connecting science to aesthetic beauty and transcendent spirituality. Like Leopold, Adams saw landscapes as sacred, and, like Muir, he sought to sway public opinion to help save parts of the American West for national parks and forests. He sent one of his first books of photography, the 1938 *Sierra Nevada*, to Secretary of the Interior Harold Ickes, who was working on a bill to establish Kings Canyon National Park in the Sierra Nevada of California. According to Adams, his photos helped garner congressional support, leading to the park's creation in 1940.[40] Twenty years later, in 1960, the Sierra Club sent copies of another Adams collection, *This Is the American Earth*, to every member of Congress to help create support for the Wilderness Bill, which sought to protect areas owned by the U.S. Forest Service, the Bureau of Land Management, and the U.S. National Park Service from road building. The bill was finally passed in 1964. Soul-stirring photographs have since become integral to the Sierra Club's strategy to save America's wild places. One of the club's "battle books," for example, featured Philip Hyde's photographs of the Grand Canyon and was instrumental in persuading Congress not to build a dam on the Colorado River there.[41]

THE RAPID EXPANSION of industrial capitalism during World War II brought with it the exploitation of vast tracts of undeveloped lands and the production of huge quantities of toxic wastes, greatly increasing the depredation of the natural world. Prior to the war, the U.S. economy had been relatively decentralized: Even as late as 1940, the hundred largest companies produced 30 percent of all manufactured goods, with the rest being made by some 175,000 smaller-scale operations. By 1944, the percentages had flipped, with a full 70 percent of the nation's manufactured goods coming from the top hundred firms while all the rest produced only 30 percent. Between 1941 and 1945 the gross national product increased from $91 billion to $166 billion.[42] This expansion of the economy and its dominance by large firms depended to a significant extent on scientific and technological innovation in the production process and the development of weapons. But the new techniques for manufacturing weaponry and industrial and consumer goods devoured land and resources to an unprecedented degree and often required the use of synthetic chemicals, producing large-scale toxic risks to people and the environment.

This change created what German sociologist Ulrich Beck calls "risk society." No longer was industrial society to be conceptualized as focused solely on the production and distribution of wealth and income, with owners and workers fighting over the spoils. Now industrial society also produced and distributed toxic risks, and new social conflicts erupted over just how dangerous these risks were and what the roles of science and government would be in understanding and managing them.[43] Splitting the atom gave the United States tremendous power, but uranium mining poisoned miners and contaminated lands with toxic wastes. Fallout from more than two hundred aboveground tests of nuclear weapons was responsible for an extra 11,300 to 212,000 cases of thyroid cancer over a thirty-five-year period and over 11,000 deaths, according to studies by the Centers for Disease Control and the National Cancer Institute.[44] (Plutonium remains lethally radioactive for over forty thousand years.)

Danger from more ordinary industries grew, too. By the 1950s, smog from car and truck exhaust covered major urban areas, and cities routinely issued air quality advisories, urging children, the aged, and the sick to remain indoors. Between 1940 and 1991, the annual production of synthetic organic chemicals (chemicals containing carbon atoms) grew from 2.2 billion to 214 billion pounds. Some seventy thousand chemicals were in routine commercial use, but fewer than 10 percent had been tested for their effects on the nervous system, and only a handful thoroughly evaluated.[45]

This shift from what Beck calls "simple" modernity to postwar risk society unleashed "boomerangs"—unintended, harmful effects that accompany technological advances—and it was one of these that Rachel Carson took as her subject in *Silent Spring* (1962).[46] Carson examined the effects of DDT and other insecticides and herbicides on the environment and demonstrated that DDT didn't just kill harmful insects but entire ecosystems. Birds that ate poisoned insects died. Runoff carried DDT into streams, then to lakes and oceans, where it accumulated in the fatty tissues of fish. Humans and animals with high DDT levels had reproductive problems and increased incidence of cancer.

Carson's work prompted others to take up the issue of pollution. Year after year, as the "latency period" of various toxic chemicals expired, the health problems they caused became visible in humans, animals, and plant ecosystems. The fact that scientists involved in the corporate, military, and industrial establishments continued to defend the harmlessness of known toxins made them, in Beck's words, "legitimizing patrons of a global industrial pollution and contamination of air, water, foodstuffs, etc., as well as the related generalized sickness and death of plants, animals, and people."[47] For Beck, the cavalier approach toward toxic risks taken by the mainstream of the scientific establishment meant that the sciences had "squandered until further notice their historic reputation for rationality."[48]

The crisis in the scientific-technological view was one of several factors that pushed the sixties generation toward a counterculture that saw nature as a source of goodness and meaning. However, the hippies did not find their way back to nature by themselves, nor was the counterculture purely their creation. Like other pilgrims before them, they had help from an unanticipated source—the Indians.

BEFORE THE MID-1960S, Indians were generally seen as degraded and marginal, a people whose time had passed. After all, the nation's core creation myth rested on the savagery of Indians, and the transformation of wilderness into civilization.[49] But as dissent against the Vietnam War grew, and radicals and counterculture rebels began to question American institutions and culture, it was natural that they challenged its Western mythology, too.[50] New research and recovered tribal histories proved that the death and destruction inflicted upon indigenous peoples had been far greater than previously thought. Demographers and scholars now estimate that as many as 4 to 12.5 million Native Americans lived in what is now the continental United States at the time of first contact with the Europeans, but by 1907 their U.S. population was only around 400,000, an extraordinary slaughter, comparable in scale to the elimination of buffalo, wolves, and sea otters, and other large animals as well.[51]

Indian lands were ravaged, too. Between 1871 and 1934, the Department of the Interior gave away two-thirds of the 234,000 square miles of Indian land once secured by treaties. The land went to railroads, the U.S. military, and federal and state parks and forests.[52] By 1934, demoralized and impoverished tribes and individual Indian families had sold 42,000 of the remaining 78,000 square miles to non-Indians.[53] From 1936 to 1974, federal dam-building took an additional 12,500 square miles of Indian land.[54] By the early 1970s, Indians were left with only about 23,400 square miles, roughly 10 percent of what they'd had in 1871.

The campaign of violence, land seizure, and cultural repression was nothing less than genocidal, the attempted eradication of Native Americans as a distinct people. But ironically, the coming of risk society stimulated a resurgence of Native American identity. In 1947, Chief Sackmasa of the Coyote Clan, part of the Hopi tribe in the Four Corners region of the Southwest, announced that the dropping of the atom bomb on Hiroshima and Nagasaki and the emerging threat of a global nuclear war fulfilled an ancient Hopi prophecy. He pointed to tribal stories that foretold a day when a "gourd of ashes fell from the sky" to burn the land—a portent of the destruction of the world.[55] The Hopi had been charged with preserving the Earth's natural balance by the Great Spirit Maasau'u, Guardian of the Earth. That guardianship required warning other Indians as well as whites of the impending danger and the need for peaceful changes. Hopi elders selected four "messengers" who would devote their lives to these tasks.

The messengers reached out to medicine men and spiritual leaders of other tribes, persuading them to participate in Hopi-sponsored conferences in the 1950s. The conferences in turn helped launch the Indian unity movement, which sought to resurrect traditional tribal cultures and lobby against the Bureau of Indian Affairs program of enforced Indian assimilation into white society.[56] As the movement grew, so did more formally structured organizations. The National Indian Youth Council participated in early 1960s protests in the Pacific

Northwest to preserve Native American fishing rights. United Indians of All Tribes led the occupation of Alcatraz Island in 1969 as a way to demonstrate Indian needs for land. The most radical organization, the American Indian Movement (AIM), demanded the restoration of broken treaties and Indian sovereignty.

Mindful that the Hopi prophecies warning of global destruction had also instructed the tribe to send messengers to whites, the elders decided the counterculture was most likely to be sympathetic. Messengers began to speak at rock concerts, rallies, and be-ins. One of them, a Mohawk named Craig Carpenter, became a principal organizer of the 1967 Hollywood Easter Love-In and the Monterey Pop Festival. Carpenter and the other messengers—Cherokee medicine man Rolling Thunder, Chumash medicine man Semu Haute, and the Hawaiian *kahuna* (shaman) David Bray—became known as charismatic leaders who could readily articulate Native American spirituality.[57] They brought with them a sign that in time became the very emblem of the youth movement: The upside-down *y* enclosed in a circle, meaning peace and unity, was derived from the footprint of the crane, a bird sacred to the Hopi.[58] They also brought a style that helped create the whole hippie look: long hair on men, which in Pilgrim days had been outlawed as a manifestation of sympathy for Indians, headbands, fringed buckskin jackets, jeans embroidered with geometric designs, and turquoise jewelry.

But their influence was hardly confined to symbols. The "back to the land" movement of the period drew much of its inspiration from the Indians, who were thought to have remained untouched by corruptions of urban America.[59] Indian myths and traditions seemed to answer a growing spiritual hunger among young whites for connection to a premodern cultural landscape. In works such as *Black Elk Speaks*, John G. Neihardt's 1932 interviews with Lakota (Sioux) medicine man Black Elk, and in Native American theologian-scholar-activist Vine Deloria Jr.'s *God Is Red* (1973), an analysis of the differences between Christian monotheism and Native American polytheism, readers were brought close to this nearly vanquished culture, in particular its harmonious vision of a natural world shared by humans and wild creatures and infused with spirit.

In the Native American cosmos humans and animals belong to the same family. Black Elk speaks of a time when "we were happy in our own country, for then the two-leggeds and the four-leggeds lived together like relatives, and there was plenty for them and for us."[60] There were practical consequences to this belief. When Native Americans hunted and fished, gathered food, or chopped down trees for canoes and firewood, their culture dictated respect and restraint toward creatures and plants; the resulting limits on how much humans could take helped preserve and sustain ecosystems. As one scholar surmised, "a belief in active, watchful, and potentially vengeful animal spirits was 'probably universal' among North American Indians. The Indians had to use them carefully and propitiate them for their sacrifice if they were to rely on their continued abundance."[61] Lame Deer, another Sioux holy man, noted the different mores of the white world. "For the white man each blade of grass or spring of water has a price tag on it. And that is the trouble, because look at what happens. . . . The prairie becomes a thing without life—no more prairie dogs, no more badgers, foxes, coyotes. The big birds of prey used to feed on prairie dogs, too. So you hardly see an eagle these days. The bald eagle is your symbol. You see him on your money, but your money is killing him. When a people start killing off their own symbols, they are in a bad way."[62]

In the Indian cosmos, land, too, was sacred, never a resource or commodity to be bought and sold. Massasoit, a chief of the Wampanoags who befriended the Pilgrims, found the idea of selling land preposterous. "What is this you call property? It cannot be the earth. For the land is our mother, nourishing all her children, beasts, birds, fish, and all men. The woods, the streams, everything on it belongs to everybody and is for the use of all. How can one man say it belongs only to him?"[63] Over a hundred years later, in 1805, Chief Tecumseh rallied tribes in what is now Indiana to resist white encroachment by arguing, "Let us unite as brothers, as sons of one Mother Earth. . . . Sell our land? Why not sell the air? . . . Land cannot be sold."[64]

Indian leaders never tired of trying to convey that their land held deep meaning, that it was the spiritual foundation of a tribe's existence. In 1854, Chief Seal'th, speaking of tribal lands lost in the region that bears his name (Seattle), proclaimed, "Every part of this soil is sacred in the estimation of my people. Every hillside, every valley, every plain and grove has been hallowed by some sad or happy event in days long vanished. Even the rocks, which seem to be dumb and dead as they swelter in the sun along the silent shore, thrill with memories of stirring events connected with the lives of my people."[65] Or, as Chief Curley of the Crow explained his refusal to cede more land to the federal government in 1912, "The soil you see is not ordinary soil—it is the dust of the blood, the flesh, and the bones of our ancestors. . . . The land as it is, is my blood and my dead; it is consecrated and I do not want to give up any portion of it."[66]

Ecological stewardship and the honoring of holy places were central religious obligations in a system that admitted of no anthropomorphic deity separate from creation.[67] As Lame Deer's uncle told him, the Great Spirit "is no old man with a beard."[68] Instead, the Great Spirit or Great Mystery was a power or life force that enveloped all of creation. When a holy man meditates, explained Lame Deer, "He talks to the plants and they answer him. He listens to the voices of the *wama kaskan*—all those who move upon the earth, the animals. He is one with them. From all living beings something flows into him all the time, and something flows from him. I don't know where or what, but it's there."[69] In this unified cosmos, there was no division between society and the wild. Indian cultures do not have a word for wilderness; a division between society and the wild simply does not exist. As Oglala (Sioux) author Luther Standing Bear recalled in his autobiography: "We did not think of the great open plains, the beautiful rolling hills, and winding streams with tangled growth as 'wild.' Only to the white men was nature a 'wilderness' and only to him was the land 'infested' with 'wild' animals and 'savage' people. To us it was tame. Earth was bountiful and we were surrounded with the blessings of the Great Mystery."[70]


THROUGH THE 1960s and into the '70s, these ideas moved through the counterculture, then into the intelligentsia, the universities, and, finally, into the wider world. Gary Snyder, who defined himself as a poet-shaman, called on the nation to follow Indian wisdom as the path to cultural renewal.[71] He declared that "where our civilization goes wrong is the mistaken belief that nature is something less than authentic, that nature is not as alive as man is, or as intelligent, that in a sense it is dead, and that animals are of so low an order of intelligence and feeling, we need not take their feelings into account. . . . What we must find a way to do, then, is incorporate the other people—what the Sioux Indians called the creeping people, and the standing people, and the flying people, and the swimming people—into the councils of government."[72] Hippies living on the land, Snyder argued, were not "some nostalgic replay of the nineteenth century" but "a generation of white people finally ready to learn from the Elders."[73] Unless the country moved in their direction, the power structure would lose its legitimacy. As he writes in *Turtle Island* (1974):

> *The USA slowly lost its mandate*
> *in the middle and later twentieth century*
> *it never gave the mountains and rivers,*
> *trees and animals,*
> *a vote.*
> *All the people turned away from it.*[74]

Snyder's call was one of many. Carlos Castaneda's *The Teachings of Don Juan: A Yaqui Way of Knowledge* (1968) enticed a generation of college kids to explore a different kind of enchanted Indian cosmos—mescaline-enhanced "nonordinary reality."[75] Dee Brown's pivotal history of the war against the Great Plains Indians, *Bury My Heart at Wounded Knee* (1970), helped create sympathy for Native American claims of sovereignty. Tom Laughlin's 1971 film, *Billy Jack*, declared that "the time is now for the red man to prevail; the whole spiritual wisdom of the great holy men of the Indian traditions is now what the young people of the world want."

By the mid-1970s, one hundred years after Custer died at Little Big Horn, there was, as Vine Deloria Jr. exclaimed, a "vast outpouring of good will" for Native Americans. "The stoic and heroic red man, who had somehow gotten along in an almost idyllic existence prior to the coming of the white man, seemed to hold the key to survival and any meaning that America would now find for itself."[76] So many hippies sought refuge on Indian reservations that Native Americans had to turn them away. But even if literally becoming an Indian was not an option, Indian myths and values, particularly their egalitarianism and their insistence that nature was alive, filled with spirits, with humans and animals connected by totemic family ties, retained intense appeal.

As whites searched for spiritual healing, traditional Native Americans, together with urban Indians and reservation Indians who had been influenced by the sovereignty movement, took the lead in struggles to preserve the ecological integrity of reservations, especially sacred areas, and to restore the sanctity and dignity of the land. Navajo and Hopi tribes in the Four Corners region fought against coal strip mining on Black Mesa, an area of profound spiritual significance. The Sioux and Cheyenne bitterly resisted a study calling for sustained coal and uranium mining and oil and gas drilling in the Black Hills of South Dakota. Mohawks living along the St. Lawrence River on the U.S.-Canadian border protested the fouling of twenty-two thousand square miles of reservation lands by PCBs and fluoride ash generated by General Motors and Reynolds Aluminum industrial plants.[77]

Seminoles in Florida battled to retain their historic rights to hunt and fish in parts of the Everglades (land they also held to be sacred); the Cherokee in Tennessee fought to stop a dam from being built on the Little Tennessee River; the Western Shoshone refused to accept repeated federal offers of money in exchange for giving up their claims to twenty-five thousand square miles in Nevada. And the Chumash living along the Southern California coast managed to stop the construction of a liquid natural gas depot at Point Conception—the "western gate" through which the spirits of the dead travel to the afterlife.

For a brief few years, the combination of political demands for sovereignty, assiduous defense of the environmental integrity of the land, and insistence upon the resurrection of Native American mythology seemed to cohere as a single movement offering a systematic critique of and alternative to risk society. But in 1973, in the aftermath of a monthlong battle between federal agents and American Indian Movement activists that took place at Pine Ridge, South Dakota, the federal government arrested much of the AIM leadership on various criminal charges.[78] Many were found innocent, but the ongoing court battles absorbed much of the movement's energy for years. Severe internal faction-fighting, together with alcohol and drug problems, made a difficult situation worse.[79] By the late 1970s, the political wing of the Indian movement had been seriously weakened.

The culture industry also played a part in depoliticizing the movement's radical core, often turning Native Americans into what anthropologist Victor Turner calls "liminal" figures who stand outside the dominant social order and move between different worlds in ways ordinary people cannot.[80] Native Americans frequently became cast as shamanlike figures who journeyed between society and a spiritually alive nature. For example, in *Free Willy* (1993) a Native American marine theme park worker befriends the film's young white hero and explains to him the sacredness of the orca whale. Then the Indian steps aside and the boy takes the lead in returning Willy the whale to the ocean. While casting Native Americans this way helped move the culture of enchantment forward, such films also made Indians subordinate to whites and completely ignored their movement to regain sovereign tribal rights and land claims negotiated in treaties.

Not surprisingly, such mass images enjoyed wider distribution than the more complicated and radical Indian religious myths and political movements. In 1971, when the Keep America Beautiful foundation launched an advertising campaign aimed at reducing littering and pollution, they centered it on an image of Native American actor Iron Eyes Cody with tears in his eyes. The caption at the top of the ad read: "Pollution: it's a crying shame."[81] Indian values, such images suggested, were not so different from those of the white world after all.

In 1971, Ted Perry, a professor of literature at Middlebury College in Vermont, rewrote Chief Seal'th's famous 1854 speech for a film called *Home*. In Perry's version, Chief Seattle says, "One thing we know: your God is also our God. The earth is precious to him and to harm the earth is to heap contempt upon its creator. Your destiny is a mystery to us. What will happen when the buffalo are all slaughtered? The wild horses tamed?" Seal'th's original speech had actually been a protest against the expropriation of his people's land by the government. He had bitterly noted that he did not believe the whites' Great Father in Washington would ever care for his people, because "your God is not our God! Your God loves your people and hates mine!"[82] No matter. Perry's rewrite was taken up with enthusiasm and circulated as authentic for decades, even among environmental activists. In 1991, Earth Day organizers put it in a children's book, *Brother Eagle, Sister Sky: A Message from Chief Seattle*, and started a campaign asking religious leaders to read it aloud to their constituencies.[83] As late as 1999, a candidate for the Oakland city council circulated Perry's version on the Internet in honor of the Seattle protests against the World Trade Organization.

Of course, the collapse of the Native American movement was not an isolated case. The antiwar movement, too, fell apart in the early 1970s. The counterculture (suffering from its own drug problems, among other ills) lost its edge, as mainstream media and marketing transformed its critical themes into pop fashions without any particular political or cultural message. But even as hopes for broad social change were shipwrecked, environmental concern grew. A modern movement emerged that considered caring for the land a necessity for material and spiritual well-being, as well as a moral obligation. This desire to connect with the spirit inherent in every part of creation drew upon the legacies of Thoreau, Muir, Leopold, Adams, Carson, and the recently recovered tradition of Native American spiritualism. Out of these shards of history came the new culture of enchantment.

# 2

## Animals Who Speak to Us

In the creation myths of many Native Americans and other hunter-gatherer peoples, humans and animals once spoke the same language. Indeed, before the "fall," when animals and humans went their separate ways, there was no rigid distinction between them. As the Inuit (Eskimo) woman Nalungiaq explained to ethnologist Knud Rasmussen nearly a century ago, "In the very earliest time when both people and animals lived on earth, a person could become an animal if he wanted to and an animal could become a human being. Sometimes they were people and sometimes animals and there was no difference."[1] Even after this golden age, many Indian tribes celebrated an intimate connection to particular species. When a Pawnee scout pulled a ceremonial wolf skin over his body, he was not putting on a costume, argues nature writer Barry Lopez. Rather, the wolf skin was "an outward sign to the man himself and others who might see him that he was calling on his wolf power. . . . What was actually present was an intimacy with the environment, a magic 'going in and out,' so that the line of distinction between a person and his animal helper was not always clear."[2]

Tribal shamans often changed into animals for journeys. The Yakuts in Siberia told Peter Matthiessen that their shamans sometimes transformed themselves into cranes: "Our shamans say that this world is actually three worlds. We live in the middle one. The world below belongs to the dark spirits, and to fly down there to obtain power in order to predict the future and deal with someone's fears, the shaman must become a hooded crane. The hooded crane is black, so people fear it, because seeing one may bring about a death. To fly to the upper worlds, the shaman must become the white crane, *kitalik*. Only the shaman can travel to the upper and lower worlds and describe what he learns from cranes and eagles on these journeys."[3]

Claude Lévi-Strauss, in his seminal work, *The Savage Mind*, used the term *totemism* to describe this mixing of human and animal realms.[4] In totemic or animistic cultures, people conceptualize animals not as beings different from themselves but as similar creatures with special physical and mental abilities and spiritual powers. Nature is an extension of human culture; even though humans and animals may no longer speak the same language, relationships between them are social and cultural and imbued with spiritual significance. James Cowan, in his work on the myths of Australian aborigines, argues that in totemic conceptions of the universe, animals and people are literally family; both humans and animals carry within their psyches links to former members of their shared tribe, all the way back to the tribe's origins. As Cowan says, "Totemic identity suggests that a person is both 'himself/herself' in one sense, but is also 'another' in the sense that he (or she) participates in an earlier, transitory form of existence."[5] What's more, that "other" self from an earlier lifetime might equally well have been either an animal or a human being.

The restoration of this human-animal connection—and with it the transformation of animals from profane to sacred—is a central theme in the culture of enchantment. While John Muir intuitively accomplished this transformation in his writings, sociologist Emile Durkheim provided a theoretical basis for the process. Durkheim argued that a culture comes to call certain places, creatures, and objects sacred not because of their intrinsic qualities but because of the intensity of emotions they evoke. These intense "feelings of sacredness" are readily communicated. As Durkheim put it, sacredness "transmits itself contagiously. What makes its reality is a special emotion; if it attaches itself to some object, it is because this emotion has found this object in its way."[6] Most efforts to make something sacred, what Durkheim calls "rites of consecration," depend upon this principle of contagiousness and are most effectively accomplished by hybrid discourses that mix the secular and the religious. As Rachel Carson said of her approach to writing *The Sea Around Us* (1958), "If there is poetry in my book about the sea, it is not because I deliberately put it there, but because no one could write truthfully about the sea and leave out the poetry."[7] Poetry acknowledges and tries to illuminate the mystery of the sea, its beauty, its abundance of animal life, and its ability to inspire awe. In short, it helps create what Durkheim called feelings of sacredness—and those feelings help its audience grasp the essence of a creature and form a connection with it.

THE SACRALIZATION OR consecration of animals can come about in a number of ways. It may result from deliberate efforts to reconnect people to the animal world; it may be the product of unexpected revelation; or it may combine elements of both. This mix is by no means unique. Major cultural changes and even religious movements invariably involve both conscious striving by innovators and haphazard or partial commitments.

The first step is often a powerful encounter with animals. Naturalist Alan Tennant happened to join a group of researchers on Texas's Padre Island who were capturing peregrine falcons to attach transmitters to their legs and track their migrations. He found himself completely entranced: "Padre's peregrines," he wrote, "were no longer simply beautiful raptors to be lured in for banding. They were part of something larger. Something ancient and powerful."[8] Learning that the falcons had become an endangered species after decades of decline from DDT contamination of their eggs, Tennant set out to track one falcon from Padre Island to its summer range on Alaska's North Slope. Along with pilot George Vose, Tennant followed "Amelia" for weeks in a small single-engine plane, flying up to eighteen hours per day. The journey created a feeling of deep connection. When they finally parted from Amelia, Tennant wrote, "Soon the swiftly winnowing speck Vose and I had hardly ever seen would be all we would ever know of her. Yet she'd not been just an abstraction. George and I had flown where she had flown, seen the land that she had raked all day with her binocular eyes. And we had felt through our own fragile flight surfaces the same air currents, peered into the same mist and storm and rain that Amelia had known in every nerve, hollow bone, and fairy feather of her hard-muscled body."[9]

Nature writer Dan O'Brien recalled a similarly transformative encounter in South Dakota's Black Hills. Entranced by the Black Hills on a childhood visit, O'Brien returned to the region as an adult and bought the Broken Heart ranch. But his plan to raise cattle there proved far more difficult than he'd anticipated—cattle died in the harsh South Dakota winters and those that survived routinely overgrazed the prairie, forcing him to buy grain for them. By the late 1980s, the stress and threat of financial ruin had destroyed his marriage and his health.

One afternoon O'Brien got in his truck and started driving aimlessly on backcountry roads. Somewhere near the Badlands National Monument he saw an enormous buffalo that had somehow escaped a nearby ranch known for its strong, high fences. O'Brien threw the truck into reverse, but before he could drive off, the buffalo raised his head and looked straight into O'Brien's eyes. "Like the wedding guest caught in the stare of the Ancient Mariner," he says, "I was frozen in place. We stared at each other for perhaps a minute, and for that minute all my business worries were dwarfed by this dose of reality lying in the road ahead. . . . I sensed that the buffalo signaled something profound."[10] The bull buffalo reminded O'Brien of the key role that buffalo hunts played in the American West, and of how "we, as humans, evolved eating wild meat, and our success as a species is, at least in part, a result of that evolution. Perhaps it is knowing that truth that consecrates such meat for me."[11] Within months of his vision O'Brien sold his cattle, began restoring the prairie grasses on his land, and started raising buffalo calves.

A buffalo also appeared to Canadian peace activist Paul Watson back in 1973, when he served as a medic to the American Indian Movement volunteers occupying Wounded Knee. After the siege ended, Watson underwent honorary initiation as a Lakota Sioux in a sweat lodge ceremony conducted by Wallace Black Elk (grandson of the legendary medicine man interviewed by Neihardt) and Leonard Crow Dog, leader of the Sioux who had invited the activists to the Pine Ridge Reservation.[12] Watson says that during the sweat, he had a vision in which spirit animals appeared and spoke to him. "I suddenly saw myself in a grassy, rolling field, gazing into the eyes of a wolf. The wolf looked at me, then into a pond, and walked away. When I told the Sioux what had happened, they gave me my Indian name, Gray Wolf/Clear Water. Then I went back into the vision, and saw a buffalo standing on a ridge. It began to speak to me, and as it told me that I must protect the buffalo of the sea, an arrow came and struck it in the back. Attached to the arrow was a cord, symbolic of a harpoon."[13]

Not long thereafter, Watson joined with Robert Hunter to found Greenpeace, whose first mission was to protect whales. In June 1975, Watson and a colleague tried to stop a Soviet whaler in the North Pacific from harpooning sperm whales. Their plan was to steer their inflatable boat between the whales and the whaling ship, thinking the Soviets wouldn't fire for fear of hitting them. But the scheme didn't work. The whalers shot a female whale, and when a bull, enraged by her death, turned and tried to ram the whaling ship, the Soviets shot him, too. As the whale died, Watson says, "he rose slowly out of the water, a quarter of his bulk towering above us. . . . He looked at us. It was a gentle, knowing, forgiving gaze. What had I seen? Was it understanding? . . . I no longer try to understand what happened between that dying sperm bull and me, I know only that I felt a commitment."[14]

Henceforth Watson saw whales as sacred beings. He subsequently founded Sea Shepherd Conservation Society, an organization that raised money to buy and refurbish old oceangoing vessels to patrol the seas against whale hunters. The International Whaling Commission had imposed a moratorium on commercial whaling in 1986, and Watson and his comrades saw whalers as "pirate ships" violating both the commission and the 1982 United Nations World Charter for Nature.[15] They rammed several pirate whalers, and destroyed others while the vessels were docked in harbors. "When we show up, whales don't die," Watson says proudly of his organization.[16]

The shocking power of touching wild animals has also pulled many people into the culture of enchantment. The fishers of San Ignacio Lagoon in Baja California, had long been taught to fear gray whales, which had earned a reputation as "the fish of the devil."[17] In the nineteenth century, the New England whaling fleet had hunted California gray whales in the lagoons of Baja, where they wintered and gave birth. In these hunts, whalers killed baby whales to bring their mothers in close; the gray whales fought back, smashing boats, and became known as ferocious fighters. By 1921 the grays had been hunted nearly to extinction, and only after the League of Nations issued the International Agreement for the Regulation of Whaling in 1937 did the population slowly increase. Still, the fishers remained fearful.

Then, in 1972, Francisco "Pachico" Mayoral, a fisher at San Ignacio Lagoon, broke with tradition. A gray whale came near Mayoral's panga, an open skiff, and he took a risk. "I don't know what finally compelled me to reach out my hand. The moment I touched the whale for the first time, I felt something incredible. I lost my fear. I was amazed. It was like breaking through some kind of invisible wall.

And I kept touching. That moment I compare with when my first child was born. It leaves a deep impression in my heart."[18]

Pachico Mayoral's story initiated gray whale enchantment. Soon he and other local fishers began to ferry handfuls of tourists out to meet the whales, and word spread. Hundreds of tourists began to make the pilgrimage to San Ignacio Lagoon each winter to see and try to touch whales. And the whales responded. Both adults alone and mothers with calves routinely approached boats to interact with humans. A quarter of a century later, the whales are still coming to the boats in San Ignacio Lagoon, and leaving people emotionally and spiritually transformed. Dick Russell, author of *Eye of the Whale*, says of his contact: "The look exchanged penetrates to my very depths. It feels as though I am being read by the whale, as though my entire life—for one endless moment—is an open book."[19]

These stories, the *Free Willy* and *Whale Rider* (2002) movies, and numerous television documentaries and news reports about whales have helped deepen their consecration. Every near-death of a whale now warrants rescue attempts and news coverage. Ice-breakers are sent to help whales caught in unexpected closure of arctic ice floes. The media show pictures of every sick and disoriented whale found struggling in the surf. Invariably rescuers surround the whales, touching them, pouring water over them, trying to move them back to the sea. The rescues are both literal, physical efforts to save the whales' lives, and also quasi-religious rituals—occasions to touch the creatures, to feel their life force, and, if the rescues fail, to give them last rites and companionship as they die. Whales have become kin.

THE CONSECRATION OF animals (or recognition of their sacredness) frequently comes as a result of their proximity to death, either as an individual animal or as an entire species. Their kinship is perhaps most recognized at the moment of dying. Death has always been a liminal experience of supreme import and mystery in the lives of humans.

The culture of enchantment extends that import and mystery to the death of wild animals.

Poet and nature writer Terry Tempest Williams tells the story of a World War II veteran, an infantryman with the 10th Mountain Division, who returned home to Wyoming eager to pursue his annual ritual of bear hunting. Not long after hunting season opened, the man spotted and shot a black bear in the mountains. But for the first time in his hunting career, the veteran heard the bear scream as it died. He shook with fright. Then, as he began to skin the bear, pulling "the fur coat away from the muscle, down the breasts and over the swell of the hips, he suddenly stopped. This was not a bear. It was a woman."[20] No doubt the veteran had seen many shattered human bodies during the war. We are gristle, meat, and blood beneath the skin, and so are bears. Without its fur, the bear appeared human. It was the veteran's last bear hunt.

Hugh Walker, a social worker and member of a Native American tribe in Alaska, told naturalist Peter Steinhart about the last time his uncle and father hunted wolves from an airplane: "The wolves were headed for the timber and they got almost halfway over and they realized the plane was going to catch them. They turned around and faced the airplane and were jumping off the ground at it. Over the sound of the engine, my father and my uncle could hear the wolves barking and screaming. They were barking and screaming because they knew it was over. My uncle did shoot them. But from that day, they could not do that anymore."[21] The wolves' show of intelligence, defiance, and courage shocked the hunters. They could no longer kill such animals for bounty and sport—it was too close to murder.

This is not to say that all hunting is taboo. On the contrary, hunting holds a special place in the culture of enchantment, tied to its significance to premodern cultures. As philosopher Paul Shepard points out, hunting and meat-eating were often not essential for nutrition in these societies; wild plants and roots, fruits, and nuts could have provided an adequate, if monotonous, diet. Shepard notes that the hunt was rather a fundamental religious ritual central to tribal cultures, "for in hunting they are immersed in their most deeply held spiritual and aesthetic conceptions."[22] Hunted animals were sacred game, and meat-eating at the end of a successful hunt was a sacramental meal.[23] Thus, when the whites killed off Native American food animals, they also provoked a spiritual crisis. As the Lakota medicine man Lame Deer explained in his 1972 autobiography, *Lame Deer: Seeker of Visions*, "you have even changed the animals, which are part of us, part of the Great Spirit, changed them in a horrible way, so no one can recognize them. There is power in a buffalo—spiritual, magic power—but there is no power in an Angus, in a Hereford."[24]

The hunt itself was not an act of domination, but a means of establishing a unique spiritual relationship with animals. Anthropologist Richard Nelson first went to Alaska as a graduate student in the early 1960s to study the sacred hunt among the Koyukon people who lived in northern Alaska. Over the next twenty years he became deeply immersed in Koyukon culture, and even took up hunting, both to feed his family and as a spiritual quest. From his mentor, Koyukon elder Grandpa William, Nelson learned that "the meeting of hunter and prey must be foreordained, a willful exchange of life, a manifestation of spiritual power."[25] If the hunter acted in harmony with the land and its animals, then he might be rewarded with an opportunity to participate in that exchange. "For an instant, everything is frozen, as if this winter morning is encased in ice. We could be discovered here a thousand years from now, a man with his rifle against a tree and a deer looking back, giving itself—the fusion of two lives."[26] Hunting allowed the hunter to travel back in time, as José Ortega y Gasset says, to "that early state in which, already human, he still lived within the orbit of animal existence."[27]

The sacred hunt does not only involve humans and animals, but extends to other predators and prey. For Barry Lopez, all predators engage their prey in what he calls the "conversation of death." Lopez explains: "When the wolf 'asks' for the life of another animal he is responding to something in that animal that says, 'My life is strong. It is worth asking for.' The death is mutually agreeable. The meat it produces has power, as though consecrated."[28] In hunting, then, humans acknowledge their status as predators, brothers to other predators like wolves and lions, inextricably tied to and dependent upon their prey.

Fishing, too, can be similarly sacred if conducted in ways that respect the fish and the sea. In 1999, Freeman House, a naturalist, writer, and former commercial salmon fisherman, published *Totem Salmon: Life Lessons from Another Species*. He describes the millions of salmon that once flooded the rivers of the Pacific Northwest every fall and spring and explores the various meanings the salmon held for Native Americans: gifts from the cosmos, source of food, and means of connecting people to one another and to their place on a river. For House, the advent of industrialized salmon fishing, in which boats with large nets harvest salmon for canning and sale on international markets, broke the human-salmon bond that had existed for thousands of years. Still, the sacred can be recovered, House found: On small salmon trollers (in states that have banned the use of nets on salmon, trolling is often the only legal way to fish commercially), something primordial took place. "Men and women working singly or in pairs were once more forced into an intimate relationship with their prey. And, in that the experience of fishing from a small boat radically alters perceptual experience and creates a set of nonnegotiable relationships with the moods of the sea, it could be said that the fishing technology had once again become sacralized." In such an intimate encounter, House says, "Each fish brought up from the deep carries with it implications of the Other, the great life of the sea that lies permanently beyond anyone's feeble strivings to control or understand it."[29] Such knowledge of the Other, House argues, is "information received and stored in the body," becoming a kind of reflex in the fisher, automatically orienting him or her to the sea and its creatures.[30] Fishing and hunting can create this knowledge, just as eating wild fish and game can generate a connection to a larger whole.

Richard Nelson's time with the Koyukon was life-changing in just that sense. One day while flying in a small plane on the Haida Strait, Nelson spotted an island and immediately felt a strong pull. He moved his family to the nearby mainland coast. The deer he hunted and the fish he caught for himself and his family all came from the island. He saw himself as part of nature. "I drink from the stream and it becomes me. Fiddleheads and cockles, lingcod and huckleberries, Dolly Varden trout and beach greens have all become me. I eat from this island; I eat from this ocean. The island and ocean flow through me."[31] In the culture of enchantment, hunting, fishing, and eating wild game are never simply ways of satisfying one's appetite, but spiritual processes of communion and resurrection.

SOMETIMES PEOPLE SACRALIZE animals by forming an actual human-animal family. In New Hampshire, a middle-aged, dyslexic gunsmith and naturalist named Benjamin Kilham decided in the spring of 1993 that he was ready for a new stage of life: motherhood. Kilham had long been fascinated by black bears and disturbed by the many cubs orphaned by hunters or by homeowners afraid of bears who had wandered onto their property. Kilham did not want to make pets of the bear cubs. His idea was "to walk with them and handle them without restraint, and to do so in an unfenced big-woods setting."[32] Like a good mother, he offered the cubs food and comfort. He allowed them to climb all over him and suckle his ears, even though they drew blood. It was his way of showing trust, and, in return, the bears bonded with him. Mother Kilham succeeded: Cub after cub grew up and, in time, left to find a mate in the New England woods. For every cub that left, a new orphan cub arrived, sent to him by the fish and game department. Kilham's wife and sister soon became bear mothers, too.

Nature writer Sy Montgomery, a friend of Kilham, fell in love with these cubs and soon began accompanying Kilham and wildlife biologists as they tracked black bears with radio transmitters. One day, Montgomery stuck her head in a cave, and came face-to-face with a mother bear and her two cubs: "Meeting her eyes, I recognized in her brown gaze an ancient knowing, a cognizance remarkably human-like, and yet more-than-human."[33] Moved by this quasi-mystical experience, Montgomery became increasingly fascinated by bears. She learned that in the mythologies of hunting and gathering peoples bears figure prominently as messengers between worlds. In Native American lore, many tribes think bears taught people how to use medicinal herbs—a story supported by an Alaskan hunting guide who watched a grizzly bear shred the bark of a willow tree and put it in his mouth. The guide shot the grizzly, and, upon examination, found the bark packed around an abscessed tooth.[34] (Willow bark contains salicylic acid, the active agent in aspirin.) Montgomery investigated speculation that early humans, having observed bears pass the winter in deathlike sleep and emerge alive in the spring, began to bury their dead in the hope of resurrection.[35] By revisiting old Native American myths about bears, and combining them with more contemporary research and observation on bear behavior, Montgomery helped consecrate the animals, and reestablish their ties with humans.

Once human-animal families are formed, it's possible for them to grow, expanding totemic kinship ties to include additional species. Dr. Gary J. Galbraith, professor of evolutionary biology at Northwestern University, argues that renewed interest in bears is rooted in the long human kinship with dogs: "It is impossible to look into the face of a bear and *not* see a dog because bears and dogs are such close relatives."[36] Galbraith explains that back in the Eocene, the Dawn Epoch of some fifty-five to thirty-four million years ago, there appeared a group of carnivores called Arctoids, who eventually gave rise to bears, wolves (and, from them, the nearly genetically identical dogs), weasels, raccoons, skunks, seals, and sea lions. "Bears," says Galbraith, "are, in a sense, giant dogs, and seals and sea lions are, in a sense, swimming bears."[37] In this way, the human-animal circle has widened from man's best friend to the "lost" bears, and from resacralized bears to seals and sea lions. The knowledge that seals and sea lions, mammals already popular with humans, are related to dogs brings them even closer to us, and helps consecrate them.

So great is the human acceptance of dogs as beings with intelligence and feelings that desperate marine biologists invoke their sacredness to help enchant fish. Technologically sophisticated fishing fleets have reduced the world's fish stocks to small fractions of what they were half a century ago. In a brave effort to change public opinion about lowly fish and promote conservation, Dr. Calum Roberts told the *New York Times:* "For me, they are as individual as dogs. They are incredibly varied. And quite intelligent. If you go underwater with a tank or a snorkel, you get to know them as individuals. When you look at tropical groupers on a reef, for instance, they have these big beautiful doleful eyes and they stare at you amid the coral."[38]

The individuality of animals is key to their acceptance into the human family. Thus animal rights groups have begun to stress the personalities and emotions of wild creatures. In the summer of 2003, Friends of Animals began a magazine advertising campaign to discourage the purchase of fur coats. Forty-five portraits of foxes were printed together in a block, with the title underneath reading, "ONE fur coat."[39] The foxes looked vividly distinct from one another. Some appeared alert, others angry or afraid. They held their ears and snouts in different positions. Together, the photographs resembled a collection of family portraits hanging in the hallway of a home, an illustration both of likeness and individual difference.

One obvious way to highlight the individuality of animals is to name them. As horse trainer, essayist, and literature professor Vicki Hearne contended, naming is a sacred and poetic act that integrates an animal into human kinship and moral life: "The grammar of the world we imagine when we call creatures by name is not the grammar of the world in which they have no names, is not the same form of life."[40] While people have commonly given names to domestic pets, that implied kinship is now being extended to wild animals as well.

In 1994, a black bear meandered out of the mountains near suburban Monrovia in Southern California and began lounging in one family's hot tub. The homeowner, Gary Potter, didn't know what to do; the soaking bear appeared content and not at all dangerous. Soon the bear was coming to the house often, and the Potters gave him a name, Samson. Still, sharing the tub with a bear, even if he did use it at different times, felt bizarre and uncomfortable. Potter finally called the California Department of Fish and Game, whose officers captured the bear. They were prepared to kill him, but a public outcry persuaded Governor Pete Wilson to stop the planned execution. Eventually Samson was taken to a nearby zoo, where stories of his former exploits in the hot tub brought media attention and a steady supply of visitors. Years later Potter told a *Los Angeles Times* reporter that he missed Samson and had learned to accept and welcome other bears who came to visit. "I fix cars for a living and deal with machines," he said. "Samson changed me. Makes you think different. Bears come to our pool all the time now, and destroy everything. I don't mind. The animals are part of me now." When Samson died in 2001, his passing was mourned in the *Los Angeles Times*: "Samson the Bear Dies a Celebrity's Death."[41]

In 1992, in a small town north of Boise, Idaho, a huge bull elk wandered into the yard of a house belonging to Larry Jones. When Jones approached the creature, it did not run away. In fact the elk stayed nearby all winter and through the spring. Jones and the elk, which he named Elvis, even took walks together, accompanied by Jones's dogs. Jones talked; Elvis bugled. The bull returned every fall and winter for the next three years, and then disappeared. Jones saw Elvis as a messenger from God. Grief-stricken, he was still looking for him in 1999.[42]

In Bear Valley Springs, a development in the Tehachapi Mountains east of Bakersfield, California, another bull elk took up residence near the seven-thousand-person community. Big Daddy, as he was soon called, did not seem to fear people. He freely led his harem of thirty females and a few young males around the twenty-five-thousand-acre project, where all hunting was prohibited. Everyone loved him and came to look forward to his mating calls in the fall. But in 2005, a poacher from outside the town shot the stately elk at point-blank range and crudely attempted to butcher his body. After a resident found Big Daddy's corpse in his neighborhood, hundreds of people signed a petition asking the court to prosecute the poacher to the full extent of the law. The petition organizer also began collecting funds for a memorial for Big Daddy. The other elk have stopped coming to the valley; the community mourns, hoping for their return.[43]

The quest for connection with wild animals can lead searchers into uncharted territory. Jacques Mayol's exploration of human-dolphin relationships began in 1957, when he met a female dolphin named Clown at the Miami Seaquarium. Until that day, Mayol had moved from job to job, country to country, without any deep commitments. He grew up in France during World War II, farmed wheat in Canada after the war, and then became the editor of a French-language newspaper in Miami in the 1950s. But he had always loved the ocean, and the encounter with Clown took him back to the sea in a new way. Her glance, he said, "communicated a 'message,' a look that in a flash went straight to my soul and touched my deepest being with true cosmic resonance."[44]

Mayol began to visit Clown every day. He also started to free dive in the ocean, returning to something he had done as a teenager in France when the sport was being invented. Over time, his "subconscious rapport with dolphins" grew.[45] By the early 1980s, when Mayol began to dive to depths of 230 feet, establishing new world records in free diving, wild dolphins would accompany him down to the bottom and back up again. His book, *Homo Delphinus: The Dolphin Within Man* (1999), shows photos of his dolphin friends Bimini and Stripe pulling him up to the surface after long descents and swimming with him just for the fun of it; the three radiate happiness. In the hope of finding an evolutionary basis for his feeling of kinship, Mayol began searching for a common ancestor shared by dolphins and humans. He discovered a potential relative in *The Aquatic Ape*, a 1982 book by British science writer Elaine Morgan.

According to the radical school of evolutionary theory at the heart of Morgan's work, roughly nine million years ago Earth's tectonic plates shifted, flooding parts of Northeast Africa near the Red Sea. One of our hominid ancestors, a creature speculated to be a manlike ape called *Ramapithecus*, consequently lost its forest habitat and was forced to hunt for food several hours each day in the water from which it had originated. (This theory about human evolution thus parallels the more scientifically established theory on the evolutionary origins of sea mammals such as whales, dolphins, sea lions, seals, and sea otters—namely, that they all evolved from land-based ancestors forced to return to the sea by climate and environmental changes.) After *Ramapithecus* spent some four million years in the aquatic environment, further tectonic plate shifts made the waters recede. A different hominid species, speculated to be the more humanlike *Australopithecus*, evolved from *Ramapithecus* and moved to the savannah, its body marked by traces of its life in the sea. These traces were passed down, in turn, to *Homo sapiens sapiens*.

As proof, the "aquatic ape" theory points to the fact that unlike other four-limbed land-dwelling animals, humans have spines that align with their legs, whether in a horizontal or vertical position. Aquatic mammals all share this spinal alignment, which allows them to take vertical positions in the water or to swim horizontally. Unlike other primates, but like water mammals, humans also have a layer of subcutaneous fat, and, to this day, some 7 percent of the population is born with webbing between the toes.[46] The evolutionary theorists informing Morgan's work contend that the fatty tissues that give women's breasts their shape first evolved to help them float, just as with the breasts of manatees. Cold water caused women's genitals to move inward, where the labia and thighs worked to preserve heat, while men's penises grew longer as a result. Like whales and dolphins, humans copulate face-to-face, belly to belly;

no other primates have sex this way. Most of all, the fact that humans can hold their breath easily, like dolphins and whales and other marine mammals, suggests a past common life in the sea. For Mayol, the theory of a lost aquatic ape provided a conceptual bridge to connect humans and dolphins. If humans had an aquatic ape ancestor, other aquatic mammals were surely some kind of kin.

Naturalist Roger Payne came to a similar conclusion. Payne pioneered the study of whale sounds, and became the first scientist to propose that the whales were actually singing to one another as they sent their low frequency bellows thousands of miles across the ocean. His recording *The Songs of Humpback Whales* (1970) became a bestseller. Impressed by the similar musical structures of whale and human music, Payne wondered whether whales and people were not biologically related. He noted that upon hearing whale songs, people often began to cry, "as though something unaccountably ancient was overmastering them. This commonality of aesthetic suggests to me that the traditions of singing may date back so far they were already present in some ancestor common to whales and us."[47] Interspecies empathy thus confirmed lost kinship.[48] Mayol's and Payne's ready embrace of theories far from mainstream science conveys a profound longing for intimate, familiar connection.[49]

BUT IF THE concept of human-animal families is still on the margins, it has lately received some support from surprising quarters. Contemporary evolutionary biology and related fields now stress the depth of human-animal kinship ties and encourage a revisionist view of Charles Darwin's work. Although Darwin sought to discredit theological doctrines that held that God created each species separately and to show the processes of evolution, his work was hardly an example of pure science. Instead, it was a hybrid discourse, with a strong spiritual and romantic strain. The famous last line of *The Origin of Species* (1859) celebrates the "grandeur in this view of life, with its several powers, having been originally breathed by the Creator into a few forms or into one; and that, whilst this planet has gone cycling on according to the fixed law of gravity, from so simple a beginning endless forms most beautiful and wonderful have been and are being evolved."[50]

Darwin always stressed the kinship and similarity between animals and people, even in terms of emotions and some kinds of thinking. In *The Descent of Man* (1871), he wrote: "The difference in mind between man and the higher animals, great as it is, certainly is one of degree and not of kind. We have seen that the senses and intuitions, the various emotions and faculties, such as love, memory, attention, curiosity, imitation, reason, of which man boasts, may be found in an incipient, or even sometimes in a well-developed condition, in the lower animals."[51] Darwin further developed this argument in *The Expression of the Emotions in Man and Animals* (1872) as a way to show the continuity among species and reject the religious argument that humans represented a separate creation.[52]

Although twentieth-century biologists accepted Darwin's work on evolution, his arguments about animal feelings and thought processes were mostly rejected as "the sin of anthropomorphism."[53] In reducing Darwin's work to a model of positivistic science and behaviorism, biologists severely distorted his approach. Darwin's emotional bonds with animals informed his scientific enterprise, and he considered his study of expressions and feelings in animals crucial to understanding that other animal species: humans.

These days, Darwin's love for creation and his sense of human-animal kinship have been taken up again by many scientists. While not all his arguments about specific animal species and their emotions are accepted, those who study animal cognition, emotion, and personality no longer treat other species as dumb beasts. Dolphins have now passed the mirror-test of self-recognition, the first mammal beyond primates to do so.[54] The famous chimpanzee researcher Jane Goodall says she observed a young male chimpanzee lose interest in life and slowly die of grief weeks after his mother passed away. Elephants are reported to shout in joy when a lost troop member returns, and mourn for days after the death of a comrade.[55] Video cameras in forests capture deer "kissing." Some whale species swim in embrace after sex. Desert tortoises show vast differences in how far they range and in their willingness to defend territories; females show considerable selectivity over mates.[56] And one philosopher-musician seeking to understand why birds sing plays his clarinet for songbirds, and studies how they change their melodies in relation to his.[57] Having rejected the modern view of animals as things, science and scholarship now spread the culture of enchantment, strengthening human feelings for other creatures and their habitats.

Beginning in the early 1980s, the concept of a human-animal family found additional allies among molecular biologists and geneticists. Scientists studying the mapping of human, plant, and animal DNA codes found more commonality among species than even Charles Darwin could have imagined. Chimpanzees' genes, for instance, are 99 percent identical to those of humans. Moreover, as the evolutionary biologist Edward O. Wilson summarized the findings, the greater genetic differences from humans to other primates, "and beyond them to other kinds of animals, are only a matter of degree."[58] As Wilson told his friend and colleague Canadian geneticist David Suzuki: "We have to discover our kin. We have to discover our relatives, the other plants and animals who are related to us through our DNA. Because to know our kin is to come to love and cherish them."[59] Even genetics has now become a double discourse, at once a science and a spiritual quest for totemic kinship.

IN THIS CONTEXT, the imminent extinction of an entire species or subpopulation carries a special charge. By World War II, the gray wolf—a creature some seven hundred thousand years old—was extinct in the United States except for Alaska and northern Minnesota.[60] Then, in 1979, a lone female (who had been tagged with a radio transmitting collar) traveled 150 miles from Banff National Park in Canada to Glacier National Park in northern Montana. In 1982, the footprints of a large male appeared beside hers; by 1985, an estimated fifteen to twenty wolves lived in Glacier and across the border in Canada.

Researchers came to study the wolves, but the more time they spent in the field, the more uncanny the experience became. In Glacier, the first returning wolves and their offspring were named the Magic Pack, because they appeared and disappeared from the park and adjacent Canadian territory in mysterious ways. Diane Boyd, one of the scientists studying the Magic Pack, says that she would often spend entire days searching for the wolves only to come home and find a pile of scat right outside her door. Boyd tried to trap the wolves to place radio transmitters on them. In her dreams, she would see captured wolves, and the next day, they would be in the traps. The wolves changed Boyd. She had begun her study as a traditional scientist, someone who never let her feelings inform her work. That changed, she says: Boyd became comfortable considering wolves subjectively, as intelligent creatures with their own emotions. She describes the wolf scat outside her door as a wolf way of laughing at her. On other occasions, she interpreted a wolf's barking and howling outside her cabin as an effort to "talk" or communicate. "Now I don't worry about that stigma [of subjectivity] anymore. Now I know it [the mysterious nature of wolves] with my heart and my brain."[61]

Renée Askins, another researcher, tells of flying over Minnesota in a small plane and spotting thirteen wolves on an ice-covered peninsula far out into a lake. The plane turned around for what should have been a second look. Askins says, "We came around to see them again and—*bump*—they were gone. The closest forest was a mile away—they couldn't have gotten there. They just disappeared."[62] Askins calls the wolves creatures of "dawn and dusk," animals that "offer a vehicle for us to talk metaphorically about the things in our lives that are not here or we wish were here."[63]

In 1982, Freeman House joined with his neighbors living along the Mattole River in northern California to form the Mattole River Watershed Salmon Support Group. A century earlier, the Mattole had been filled with tens of thousands of salmon in the fall and spring. By 1982, only a thousand at most made the journey. House felt the absence of the fish. He compared the sensations to an amputee's suffering from a phantom limb: "Salmon resides in the hearts of humans: for many, even the imminence of its absence creates an active ghost." House also "felt" the ghosts call out to him: "Tonight, by the side of the river, one of those ghosts, perhaps the ghost of the Bear Creek king salmon from just over the ridgeline, has found its way through my ears or through my eyes or my fingertips to lodge itself in the muscles at the base of my neck."[64] Helping the salmon to spawn became his obsession. Even during a New Year's Eve celebration, his thoughts were with them. Every few hours through the cold, rainy night, he checked the fish traps and milked the eggs from females in the hopes that more salmon fry would survive.

During the past twenty years, numerous small bands of dedicated naturalists have begun searches for species declared dead and vanished. For example, in 1952 the Colorado Division of Wildlife declared grizzly bears extinct in the state. Still, reports of sightings in the San Juan Mountains in southern Colorado continued to circulate. From 1980 to 1982 the division conducted a search using baited traps and snares. They caught many black bears, but no grizzlies. However, Tom Beck, the chief biologist leading the search, wryly commented that "failure to catch a grizzly bear does not mean a definite absence of bears." Years later, Beck reaffirmed the possibility that a few bears in the San Juans might well have eluded his searchers.[65]

In 1990, a grizzly bear expert and environmental activist named Doug Peacock gathered a group of friends and fellow bear lovers, including nature writers Rick Bass and David Petersen, for a mission. The 1980–82 searches hadn't been done right, Peacock insisted, because the grizzly bears knew they were being hunted: "Any creature that can ride a motorcycle in the circus and learn to dress itself is capable of learning other things, too."[66] Peacock believed that the San Juan bears had retreated to the most remote canyons and mountains, avoiding humans, foraging almost exclusively at night, existing on a mainly vegetarian diet. What was needed was a different kind of search.

The Round River Conservation Studies' San Juan Grizzly Project was indeed different. It began with hunters searching for the "grizzly within." As Rick Bass explained on the opening page of his book *The Lost Grizzlies*, "There is a place in our hearts for them, and so it is possible to believe they still exist, if only because that space of longing exists."[67] Bass and Peacock and the other members of the project all felt the bears to be out there, somewhere, living highly constrained existences. Bass even imagined a mother's instructions to her cub: "This is where you run when you hide. This is where you do not go. It is all right to eat berries from this bush. This stream, but only this stream, is all right to drink from. Beneath this tree is where we will nap, our family, for as long as we are on the earth. Only this tree, in this drainage."[68]

As the bear seekers journeyed deeper into the mountains, they began to ponder how these constraints affected not just the grizzlies—both living and ghost bears—but humans as well. What might happen if state and federal governments bought more land for the bears to roam and established greater protection for them in the South San Juan National Wilderness Area? "If only we could loosen the constricting bans around them, perhaps our own hidden wounds, our own limits to spontaneity, would begin to heal," wrote Bass. "We have lost these grizzlies and lost our relationship to them. We have lost a part of ourselves, of who we were and who we will be."[69]

For two summers the group wandered through the mountains looking for the bears. From time to time, they found signs of a bear's presence. Peacock once spotted a single nine-inch track, oddly positioned at ninety degrees from the rest of the smaller, black bear tracks; to him it was possible evidence that a grizzly, aware of being hunted, was trying to hide its trail. On another occasion the group found a huge rock overturned, to them an indicator that grizzlies had been digging for insects. Not far away they found a giant bear scat with fur attached. Back in the lab, scientists using DNA analysis confirmed that the hair came from a grizzly.[70] During the winter break, when Bass returned home to Montana, he dreamed of hibernating San Juan grizzlies. It was an intimate communication, "like sharing a secret with them, now that we believed they were still out there—and it was like holding a responsibility, too, believing that their future depended on how well we protected their country."[71]

Ultimately, Rick Bass saw a bear, species unknown, and the bear saw him. "And what I saw in those eyes, that brief wild meeting of eyes, was fright, looking so much like the frightened eyes of man that I was granted the beginning of a new perception."[72] Until that moment, Bass wrote, he had always celebrated "the importance of mystery," but was deeply afraid of it.[73] Now that fear finally gave way to acceptance. "The mysticism of the event is what leads me to believe it was a grizzly. The strangeness, the power of all that surrounded it."[74]

The ivory-billed woodpecker is another ghost species that has caught the public's imagination. The twenty-inch bird, known as the Lord God bird because it was so beautiful people would exclaim "Lord God!" when they saw it, had not been sighted for over fifty years.[75] The U.S. Fish and Wildlife Service declared it extinct in 1997, after logging had destroyed its southern swamp habitat.[76] Then, in 1999, a student at Louisiana State University reported spotting a pair of the woodpeckers at the Pearl River Wildlife Management Area. James Van Remsen, curator for birds at the university's Museum of Natural Science, found the claim credible. As word got out, a search team gathered. John W. Fitzpatrick of the Cornell University Lab of Ornithology supervised the installation of a dozen sophisticated listening devices and recorders, whose tapes would be analyzed by computers. Van Remsen recruited world-class birders, habitat biologists, woodpecker specialists, and computer software experts. Zeiss Sports Optics, the maker of binoculars favored by birders, funded the search.

When James Gorman, a *New York Times* reporter sent to cover the January 2002 search, walked through the Pearl River swamp, he felt the presence of something akin to Freeman House's ghosts: "These woods, a remnant of vast forests, inspired something of [a] sense of incalculable loss."[77] Then, one afternoon, days into the search, four team members heard a sequence of "double-raps," a tapping peculiar to the ivory-billed woodpecker. One searcher, habitat biologist Peter McBride, said that the sound "arrests you" and could "send a chill up your spine."[78]

After analyzing four thousand hours of recordings, especially those made on that particular afternoon, Fitzpatrick announced that the double-raps were gunshots. Still, just like the biologist Beck concluded of his grizzly bear hunt, Fitzpatrick felt that the absence of evidence did not decisively prove the absence of birds. He planned to keep looking elsewhere in Louisiana, as did Zeiss Optics' David Luneau, who told the *Times*, "I will definitely be searching, somehow, somewhere."[79] In the culture of enchantment, the search itself becomes a sacred ritual, what Emile Durkheim called an "imitative rite," meaning that the worshippers act in the hope that *"like produces like."*[80] The Lord God bird in the heart might lead to a manifestation, a Lord God bird in the swamp.

IN 2000, A TEAM of biologists from C. W. Post University headed by Matthew Draud began a study of diamondback terrapins on Long Island. These aquatic turtles faced numerous obstacles to reproduction, from boat propellers that killed them when they surfaced in the water, to beach-cleaning sweepers that crushed their nests, to habits like laying eggs below the high-tide mark that made them particularly vulnerable. For three years Draud and his team simply counted and recorded dead hatchlings. But by 2003 they had come to care too much for the creatures and began to move turtle eggs, sometimes to better locations on the beach, other times to incubators in the laboratory. Local residents began to rescue wounded terrapins. Nearby researchers in New Jersey even salvaged eggs for incubation from terrapins killed by cars, and released 150 to 200 one-year-olds back to the wild each year. Marc Bossert, the team member most responsible for the intervention, explained: "I started as a scientist. Then I evolved."[81]

In the Wind River Mountains of Wyoming, a formerly healthy twelve-hundred-animal herd of bighorn sheep had declined to eight hundred by 2001. Typically, only two of ten lambs survived, and even these suffered from failing immune systems. Scientists claimed that acid rain (caused by coal exhaust from power plants in Utah and Arizona, car exhaust from California, and fertilizer plants in the Pacific Northwest) had altered the Wind River ecosystem so that it could no longer support large herds. But the charismatic bighorns were not abandoned. The people of Wyoming put selenium mineral blocks out for the sheep to lick in the hope of restoring their immune systems. The director of the National Bighorn Sheep Interpretive Center confessed to the *Los Angeles Times*, "The town loves these sheep and we're proud of them."[82]

Similarly, in California people embraced an endangered bird species despite its unappealing looks and fondness for carrion. By 1982, only twenty-one California condors—birds with nine-foot wingspans and a history dating back over one hundred thousand years—remained alive.[83] Faced with the possibility that these last few birds might themselves perish from lead poisoning caused by bullets in their carrion diet, U.S. Fish and Wildlife officials captured the survivors. It was a sad and desperate effort. John Borneman, who worked for the National Audubon Society during the 1980s, recalls, "When he was captured in the wild—the last bird—I closed the door to my office and cried."[84] But in 1985 the captive condors began to breed, and in 1992 both adults and offspring were released in California and other southwestern states.

By then, the scientists and game managers were deeply attached to the birds. Biologist Bronwyn Davey says, "The condors become like friends. You get to know them individually, get to know their personalities."[85] Los Angeles zookeeper Michael Clark helped rear the birds by using hand puppets that looked like condors. "I don't think anyone who has ever seen such an animal up close would want to see it die out," he said.[86] By 2002, more than sixty California condors lived in the wild, with another hundred and one in captivity and nineteen in field pens waiting to be released.[87] In the Angeles National Forest, some of the wild birds began following hang gliders, who helped them find thermal wind currents.

In 2003, when a hunter killed a condor, the news media framed it as a murder. The dead bird, AC-8, was a female with a known history and personality. Just as at funerals, when the living tell stories about the dead, the friends of AC-8 bore witness to her passing, telling a reporter about her life. She was over thirty years old and could no longer have chicks, but she mentored others in the flock. Greg Austin, deputy director of the Hopper Mountain National Wildlife Refuge, recalled, "She was showing these other birds positive things; her foraging grounds, her roosting areas."[88]

Even the deaths of individual animals from species not approaching extinction now fill people with sorrow and compassion. No longer are majestic whales or endangered condors the only ones whose deaths make the morning paper or the evening news. In New York City a coyote somehow made his way to Central Park, where he romped around, swam in the lake, and killed a bird for dinner. He was captured and then released in a rural habitat.[89] When the coyote, named Hal by city workers, died a few days later, an obituary in the *New York Times* carefully detailed the causes of death: stress, heartworms, and rat poison.[90] In 2006, songwriter and singer Jonathan Meiburg from Austin's Shearwater band released "White Waves," a funeral dirge in honor of the largest hammerhead shark ever caught with rod and reel. Researchers found that she'd been pregnant with fifty-two nearly full-term pups. In the song, the shark appears to serenade her killer: "He took me out on the tide / To make pearls of my eyes / And uncover me."[91] And a woman in the Southern California foothill community of Monrovia found a deer impaled on a wrought-iron fence surrounding a neighbor's home and held its head in her arms as it died. "You think you're a mature person and can handle things, but I just stood there and cried," she told a reporter. "We could see three deer in the background watching, like they knew what was happening. It was just heartbreaking."[92]

Sometimes wild animals even have memorial statues. In Florida, speeding boats and increased water pollution have ravaged the manatee population, reducing it from around two thousand in 1988 to one thousand four hundred in 1993. After scuba diver Harvey Barnett found a wounded, dying manatee, he put up an underwater monument in Kings Bay to honor all manatees killed and injured. Its inscription reads: "Life must become more than the wants and needs of humans. We are not on this earth alone."[93]

This public, formal mourning is everywhere, testament to a growing hunger for connection with nature. When police in Palo Alto kill a mountain lion resting in a tree in a suburban neighborhood because it might hurt someone, the residents don't celebrate, they grieve. When a bear cub that has learned to beg for food in a national park one day grabs a backpack off a camper and is put to death for it, the park spokesman calls it "tragic and heartbreaking."[94] The deaths of "wild" animals at the hands of people, far from being "normal," unremarkable events, now more often lead to critical indictments: it was wrong to shoot Big Daddy, wrong to blast the mountain lion out of its tree, wrong to build a spiked fence where deer roamed, wrong not to close the campground where the bear cub first started begging so that it might be forced to return to the wild. Each death, each preventable accident, each case in which humans kill a creature out of fear is also a summons to extend the realm of enchantment, to recognize wildlife as sacred.

But the stories that recast ordinary animals as some form of kin aren't simply *about* consecration, they *are* consecration. Scientific findings, news reports, and popular films that present mystical, shared human-animal experiences form a new creation myth, one that promises an essentially religious redemption. They offer a new beginning, a return to the days before the Fall. As religious studies scholar Mircea Eliade wrote, "the *return to origins* gives the hope of rebirth."[95]

Richard Nelson once watched Koyukon elder Grandpa William speak and pray to a bird of a species that neither man had ever seen before. As he observed the exchange between man and bird, Nelson thought he could see back in time: "For how many thousand generations, I wondered, have people spoken and prayed to the natural beings around them, as a customary part of daily life? At any other time in human history, this event would be as ordinary as talking to another person. . . . More than anything else, I wished it had seemed quite unremarkable for me, wished my ancestors hadn't forgotten what Grandpa William still understood."[96]

In the modern era, where so many species have been so severely reduced, the mythic return to the time of origins offers a vision of plenty and harmony. Marine ecologist Carl Safina has written that we must "insist upon remembering the shape the world is supposed to have: round and whole. And may that vision of abundance someday gather power to levitate the dead."[97] The hope is that as animals return to abundance, filling up the skies, the seas, and the lands, humans will rediscover lost ways—or find new ways—of living with them.

Implicit in this vision is a new sense of man's place, a rejection of his position at the unquestioned apex of life on Earth. Philosophers, cognitive scientists, and other scholars are proposing a radical rethinking of the role of animals in shaping human evolution. Instead of portraying humans as the star species that progressed beyond all others, these thinkers stress human development through our relationships with other species. Philosopher David Abram argues that our very senses evolved through interactions with animals: "Our bodies have formed themselves in a delicate reciprocity with the manifold textures, sounds, and shapes of an animate earth—our eyes have evolved in subtle interaction with *other* eyes, as our ears attuned by their very structure to the howling of wolves and the honking of geese."[98]

Another philosopher, the late Paul Shepard, has argued that wild animals promoted psychological maturation and cognitive abilities in our ancestors. Only someone who could "establish lines of connectedness or relationship" (who could think and act according to totemic and animistic concepts) with the natural world could survive.[99] By repeatedly observing what animals did, and connecting animal behaviors with the stories told in their tribe's totemic myths—for example, stories describing and explaining what salmon or caribou did each year—hunter-gatherer peoples built up their knowledge of nature and refined their understanding of the human place in the larger order.[100]

Along the same lines, naturalist Peter Steinhart argues that human-animal interactions helped us develop symbolic, abstract concepts. "We don't only think *about* animals: we think *through* them. They become mental forms around which we wrap ideas, hopes, fears, and longings."[101] For example, if we describe someone as being "fierce as a bear," the concept of fierceness is made more vivid. And psychologist Anthony F. C. Wallace sees hunting and gathering peoples' efforts to categorize and understand animal behavior as the root of the human ability to categorize and create taxonomies. He points out that people now do not classify the world with more complicated categories or greater levels of abstraction than their forebears: "Psychologically speaking, it seems likely that the primitive hunter and the urban technician live in cognitive worlds of approximately equal complexity and crowdedness."[102]

Benjamin Kilham, too, posits the existence of evolving human-animal cooperation: "Black bears are a fully developed social species successfully occupying the same time and place as humans, evolving not behind us, but beside us."[103] Kilham's "mothering" of cubs, he is keen to point out, is matched by bears mothering humans, as when a small girl lost in the New England woods told rescuers that a black bear had found her and kept her warm through the night.[104] Similarly, a new social relationship is occurring in the encounters among people and whales in Baja California's San Ignacio Lagoon.

With these new relationships comes mutual dependence. Daniel Quinn's novel *Ishmael* (1993) tells the story of a captive gorilla who has learned to communicate with people and wants to teach them that they are only one part of the planet, with a role to play in ensuring that other animals have the space they need to survive. But more than that, Ishmael explains that humans are only the first creatures to become self-aware. Ishmael says, "Man's place is to figure out how it's *possible* to do that—and then to make some room for all the rest who are capable of becoming what he's become."[105] It is a vision of a future that reunites with a lost mythic past, a return to the time of origins, when humans and animals spoke the same language and their spirits and bodies mixed freely. But Ishmael's dream of coevolution ends with a warning. A poster in his cage faces outward with a message implying that gorilla survival is dependent upon human generosity, a message comfortable for people. But on the back, the side Ishmael sees, the message reads: WITH GORILLA GONE, WILL THERE BE HOPE FOR MAN?[106] In the culture of enchantment, forging a new totemic culture is not only a dream for interspecies companionship, health, and happiness; it is indispensable for human survival.

# 3

## Holy Lands

Until the rise of monotheism, nature was the site of what Mircea Eliade calls the "primary religious experience."[1] A group's notion of what was sacred could vary widely—springs, mountains, valleys, rain forests, prairie meadows, and coastal headlands were all possible sacred sites. These places shared one characteristic, however: They were experienced as sentient in some mysterious way, full of immanence. For example, Richard Nelson noted: "If I have understood Koyukon teachings, the forest is not merely an expression or representation of sacredness, nor a place to invoke the sacred; the forest is sacredness itself. Nature is not merely created by God; nature is God. Whoever moves within the forest can partake directly of sacredness, experience sacredness with his entire body, breathe sacredness and contain it within himself, drink the sacred water as a living communion, bury his feet in sacredness, touch the living branch and feel the sacredness, open his eyes and witness the burning beauty of sacredness."[2]

Holy lands, then, were much like totemic animals. While monotheism later limited sacralization to temples and churches, Eliade argues that for the majority of people, "nature still exhibits a charm, a mystery, and a majesty in which it is possible to decipher traces of ancient religious values. No modern man, however irreligious, is entirely insensitive to the charms of nature."[3] It seems that, much as they need animals, people need wilderness of some kind in order to flourish. The culture of enchantment seeks to tap this "memory of debased religious experience," to consecrate land much as it consecrates animals, transforming it from "profane" commodity to sacred site.

But this form of consecration is far more difficult to achieve, particularly in America. Since colonial times, land in the United States has been viewed almost exclusively as real estate, something to be bought and sold on the market. In Europe and Great Britain, the long history of feudalism that preceded the development of capitalism created legal frameworks and cultural traditions that sometimes restrained the prerogatives of a landowner. A feudal lord might own an estate, but custom granted peasants the right to farm part of it, as well as to gather wood from its forests and water from its streams. To be sure, such custom was hardly an ironclad guarantee. From the fifteenth through the late nineteenth centuries, for example, the English nobility increasingly "enclosed" their lands, often to raise sheep and sell their wool—first to small-scale commercial weavers, and later to the new industrial mills in Manchester.[4] Similar enclosures occurred in many European countries as village "commons" and grazing pastures were increasingly deemed private property. (In the 1830s, the young Karl Marx was fired from his job as a newspaper editor for protesting a law forbidding peasants from collecting firewood on private land.) Still, not all public rights were lost. In 1869 a lawsuit ended the practice of enclosure, and to this day the British retain "roaming rights" to walk on any farmer's land. United Kingdom law also places restrictions on "cropping public value," such as building a house that obstructs a view of the landscape.[5] Roughly one-third of Continental Europe was never privatized, and roaming and camping on private land are generally permitted.

But no such heritage existed in the United States. Indeed, the

Fifth Amendment to the Constitution stipulates that private property cannot be taken for public use without due process and payment at market value. As James Howard Kunstler notes in *The Geography of Nowhere*, "All subsequent land-use law in America has hinged on whether it might deprive somebody of the economic value of their land."[6] By the 1830s, the market approach so completely shaped ideas of land use that the entire continental United States was conceptualized by government, industry, developers, and pioneers as a set of grid squares, six miles on each side, subdivided into sections of one square mile (640 acres) each. All government and corporate land-use policy, such as the layout and construction of towns, followed this grid pattern. When the government gave publicly owned land to settlers for homesteading, or to the railroad companies as payment for constructing the transcontinental railways, it was deeded in square blocks.

Many key historical figures, the nation's founders among them, made their fortunes in real estate. Before the Revolutionary War, George Washington worked as a land surveyor and real estate speculator. Thomas Jefferson also bought and sold land, a background that prepared him well for negotiating the Louisiana Purchase agreement that secured for the United States the right to make first offers to Native Americans for land in the Mississippi River watershed. Popular frontier folk heroes such as Daniel Boone and Davy Crockett rode west hoping to stake out land claims and get rich selling property to settlers.

At the same time, the industrial revolution strengthened the urban real estate market. Factories needed to be near each other to facilitate the mass production of goods. Locating production in cities reduced transportation costs and created ready access to a pool of available labor. Consequently, the value of land that could be used for apartment buildings or factories increased dramatically. Urban "growth machines" ensured speedy approval of development projects by the local governments. These coalitions, encompassing local politicians seeking campaign donations, city governments wanting expanded tax bases, businesses needing properties to develop, and construction unions looking for jobs, usually favored growth at any price.[7] As urbanist David Harvey has remarked, capitalism's dynamics "are expressed through the restless formation and re-formation of geographical landscapes."[8]

It's worth recalling that Congress approved the creation of the nation's first national parks in Yosemite and Yellowstone only after backers gave assurances that the lands had little or no commercial value except as tourist destinations. And while Theodore Roosevelt and the early-twentieth-century Progressive movement saw preservation of wilderness parklands and national forests as central to the American national identity, their commitment had limits. They, too, focused on the preservation of land unsuited for commercial exploitation, what environmental leader David Brower came to call "ice and rocks" wilderness sites. Federal lands outside of parks, such as the national forests and the millions of acres controlled by the Bureau of Land Management, remained open to what Roosevelt's secretary of the interior Gifford Pinochet called "multiple use," such as timber harvesting, mining, and oil and gas drilling. As the extractive industries developed more sophisticated technologies in the twentieth and twenty-first centuries, publicly owned lands came under increasing pressure for economic exploitation.

When land is viewed predominantly in terms of its "exchange value," to use Marx's term, its characteristics as *land*—its climate, topography, and the kind of ecosystem it supports—disappear from consideration. For example, after the wars against the Native Americans removed them from the Great Plains, the region was opened to settlement: Prospective farmers could receive title to 160 to 320 acres apiece. Major John Wesley Powell, working for what later became the U.S. Department of the Interior, reported to the federal government in 1878 that land west of the 98th Meridian (which included most of the Great Plains) did not get nearly enough rainfall for farming, and that farmers on such homesteads could not survive.

He recommended instead that prospective farmers receive no more than eighty acres, and then only if the land could be irrigated by local rivers and streams.[9] For those intending to ranch, Powell recommended granting much more territory: 2,560 acres, or four square miles. But Powell's ecological critique was ignored, and public lands were allocated to homesteaders regardless of water supply. Many farms and ranches, their boundaries set by government surveyors following the abstract pattern of square 160-acre parcels, ended up with no access to local waterways, while other sites monopolized key watersheds. So began a century-long pattern of failed farming and ranching, leading to the devastation of the grasslands, and the eventual consolidation of landownership into much larger parcels—outcomes directly opposite of what the government's homestead policy intended.[10]

The view of land as a grid of private property also ignored the welfare and life cycles of animals. Species seasonally migrate hundreds and even thousands of miles. But what happens to antelope shifting between summer and winter ranges if the two territories are owned by different people? What happens if a railroad or a new town divides the ranges? What happens to ducks and geese if the marshes and ponds they need for their annual migrations from Canada to Mexico are drained for farmland? In this regard, too, America was different from other cultures. In medieval England, the nobility deliberately established forests as sanctuaries for wild animals, seeing the effort as analogous to the asylum the church granted fugitives and criminals. According to a 1592 treatise on the origins of forests, the very word comes from compounding *for* and *rest*, "the name being derived from the nature of the place that is privileged by the king for the rest and abode of wild beasts."[11]

In Germany the romantic folklorists Jacob and Wilhelm Grimm collected and published a vision of forests whose magic derived from their animal inhabitants. As literary scholar Robert Harrison says, "Animals are typically what animate the enchanted forests of the Grimms' fairy tales, bringing them alive with a strange but usually friendly presence. The forests in this sense represent the ancient unity of nature—the unity and kinship of the species."[12] An ancient Buddhist aphorism expresses the intimate tie between animals and their homelands: "Come back, O Tigers! To the woods again, and let it not be leveled with the plain. For without you, the axe will lay it low. You, without it, forever homeless go!"[13] The majesty and mystery of animals, the sense in which they remain outside human control and thus embody wildness, also give meaning to the land they inhabit.

But in the United States, except for the literary movement initiated by Emerson and Thoreau and followers like Aldo Leopold, few thought about the intimate connection between people, animals, and landscapes. Instead, the forests and other wild lands were deemed as valuable only for their timber, minerals, and other resources. Wild animals were killed to meet market demands, as when beavers and foxes were trapped for their fur, or were removed from their habitats—both literally, to become zoo exhibits, and metaphorically, being turned into advertising icons, inhabitants of a mythic past or remote wilderness far removed from contemporary society. This disconnected view of land and animals eventually spread to many other parts of the world.

THE CULTURE OF enchantment seeks to restore the connection. In most instances, it involves a basic strategy: tying a piece of land to a large, charismatic animal species—particularly animals nearing extinction. Biologist Sam LaBudde often gets credit for the tactic of emphasizing animals' life-and-death dramas in order to bring public attention to the need to save land. In the 1970s, LaBudde took videotapes of tigers in the wild, then filmed their capture and slaughter for body parts: penises to restore virility, bones to cure rheumatism, eyeballs to treat convulsions. LaBudde created enough public outrage and concern that some wilderness areas in Asia were preserved for tigers.[14] From his experiences LaBudde concluded that focus on animals was essential: "You can't promote habitat protection. It's not sexy enough. You've got to use a species as a charismatic symbol."[15] In 2002, LaBudde's video footage of a mother gorilla kissing and playing with her infant helped inspire Gabon president El Hadj Omar Bongo to preserve 11 percent of the country, some 11,294 square miles, as national parks.[16]

When Rick Bass, Doug Peacock, and their comrades in the Round River Conservation Studies' San Juan Grizzly Project took to the mountains each summer, they kept in mind nature writer John Murray's observation in *The Great Bear*: "Those who have packed far up into grizzly country know that the presence of even one grizzly on the land elevates the mountains, deepens the canyons, chills the wind, brightens the stars, darkens the forest, and quickens the pulse of all who enter it. They know that when a bear dies, something sacred in every living thing interconnected with that realm . . . also dies."[17] If the explorers from the San Juan Project could find grizzlies in the San Juans and prove it to Colorado wildlife officials and the broader public, the bears' presence would consecrate the mountains, rendering them an even wilder place. At the same time, such a discovery would also trigger the Endangered Species Act, and the bears' range in the San Juan Mountains would be declared by U.S. Fish and Wildlife officials as "critical habitat," protecting the land from further encroachment.

The return of wild mammals and predator birds to their historical habitat has the power to restore a landscape to its prelapsarian state—and not just metaphorically. When gray wolves were reintroduced in Yellowstone National Park in the 1980s, a powerful predator returned to its former range. It is estimated that in the early nineteenth century, some thirty-five thousand wolves roamed the Yellowstone region; by 1880, strychnine poisoning, hunting, and trapping had killed off all but a small remnant. Those survivors were relentlessly hunted down, until by 1923 no further documented wolf reproduction occurred in the region.[18] Bringing back the wolves took the national park back in time over a hundred years. With the return of the wolves, the whole Yellowstone ecosystem began to change through processes biologists call "trophic cascades." Although it's still too soon to see the full reach of these environmental changes, some are already clearly visible. With wolves back in significant numbers by the late 1990s, the elk began to avoid certain spots along the park's rivers where they were most vulnerable to attack. Once the elk left, willow trees grew back. When the willows spread, beavers returned and soon began building dams, recreating a riparian habitat that is home for dozens of species. Through their predation of elk and moose and other large game, wolves also created more food for the park's grizzly bears, who scavenge the wolves' kills whenever possible. Douglas Smith, a Yellowstone biologist deeply involved in the wolf reintroduction, says, "In a very real sense, with the return of wolves, we've gained the opportunity to glimpse the dynamic forces of nature that drove this region before the coming of the Europeans."[19]

A similar ambition motivates the work of Frank and Deborah Popper, professors of urban studies and geography at Rutgers University, who have reimagined the Great Plains as a restored prairie. Long-term population declines and failures of ranches and farms have confirmed that the original Native American inhabitants and Major John Wesley Powell were right about the Plains' unsuitability for conventional farming and cattle ranching. The Poppers have proposed that the federal government use the money currently being spent on farm subsidies to buy back part of the prairie, beginning with 139,000 square miles of wildlife preserves—fully a quarter of the area of the Great Plains, which stretch across ten states—to be called Buffalo Commons.[20] Once the cattle are gone and the farming ends, the prairie can begin to heal and grow its long grasses. With the return of the grasses, all the animals that had once roamed the plains could be restored as well: deer, elk, wolves, and, most of all, buffalo.

Although the federal government has not endorsed Buffalo Commons, the Poppers' vision has inspired both nonprofit conservation programs and private ranchers to bring back the tall-grass prairies.

When Dan O'Brien brought buffalo back to his two-thousand-acre Broken Heart ranch, for instance, he removed all the cattle fences and corrals, and suddenly the ranch seemed bigger, "the horizon more distant."[21] Once the buffalo returned, more profound changes occurred. Unlike cattle, the buffalo didn't foul ponds with their wastes, so water quality improved. Their wallowing created mud puddles for birds and other animals. Where cattle ate only the best prairie grasses, often eliminating them from a place, buffalo grazed a spot intensely, but not so much that its grasses were completely destroyed; they instead moved on to another patch. This grazing pattern, together with the way buffalo hooves broke up the ground, gave the prairie grasses exactly what they needed to thrive. The tall-grass ecosystem, with all its dozens of bird species and other wildlife, came back as well. Even suburban yards in the Great Plains are now being replanted with tall prairie grasses. New subdivisions such as Prairie Crossing, just north of Chicago, attract buyers by offering a common open space, a restored prairie. Every fall, just as the Plains Indians did for thousands of years, Prairie Crossing residents gather to set controlled fires, whose heat is necessary for prairie grass seeds to regenerate.[22]

LANDSCAPES TIED TO seasonal migration of animals are also candidates for enchantment. The expansion of wilderness areas and the use of wild corridors to reconnect lands that were formerly separated by agriculture and suburban sprawl can save species, allowing creatures to move when necessary to find food, water, habitat, and mates. In the mid-1990s, The Wildlands Conservancy began a decadelong project of buying nearly one thousand square miles of privately owned desert lands in California's Mojave Desert, then selling most of it to the federal government for ecological preserves. (They kept some of the land for their own conservation projects.) The new public lands connect the Mojave National Preserve to the Twentynine Palms Marine Corps Base and almost touch Joshua Tree National Monument, creating a massive territory in which desert animals and plants can thrive. The conservancy also bought nearly forty-one square miles of privately held land inside Joshua Tree National Park, turning the land over to the National Park Service and the Bureau of Land Management.

The Wildlands Conservancy is largely funded by former mathematician and hedge fund wizard David Gelbaum, whose deep interest in saving land grew out of his childhood camping trips to northern Minnesota and Yellowstone National Park and his reading of Aldo Leopold's *A Sand County Almanac*, a key work in the culture of enchantment.[23] Gelbaum's sentiments are echoed in the very words the conservancy uses to describe its mission: "To preserve the beauty and biodiversity of the earth, and to fund programs so that every child may know the wonder and joy of nature."[24] Executive Director Dave Myers explained how The Wildlands Conservancy was able to raise the tens of millions necessary for these land deals. "A big project takes on a life of its own. If you have a big vision, it really speaks to people's hopes and dreams."[25]

In that spirit, the Wildlands Project, a Tucson, Arizona–based group headed by conservation biologist Michael Soule, wants to create twenty-five massive wilderness preserves that would link together and span the entire North American continent. The project works on the tacit assumption that raising people's awareness of how both animals and plants need big, interconnected territories to survive and flourish will change the cultural status of the land and consecrate it. That, in turn, will generate the political will and the funds necessary to buy up the land. In the words of one participant, Professor Daniel Simberloff, "We have to act as if we can stop this horrible process of habitat degradation and extinction. If we act as if we can't do anything about it, then we're surely going to lose."[26]

MOST SUITABLE FOR consecration are those places where animals give birth. In the 1990s, when the Clinton administration negotiated an agreement with the timber industry to save a fraction of the Pacific Northwest's old growth forests, part of the impetus for the settlement was the fact that two endangered species, the northern spotted owl and the marbled murrelet, nest in the region. As television and newspaper stories showing adult birds with their young made the issue of saving the land more emotionally compelling, the debates moved beyond the timber industry's possible job losses or the correct application of the Endangered Species Act. The new question—whether to cut the forests at all—was evidence of an emerging cultural consensus that the place where nearly extinct animals give birth and raise their young must be respected. Even the report by the U.S. Fish and Wildlife Service, *Recovery Plan for the Marbled Murrelet*, combined scientific analysis with beautiful drawings of the birds. The report also featured quotes from Aldo Leopold, Rachel Carson, Alfred North Whitehead, and, astonishingly, *The Merchant of Venice:* "You take my life when you do take the means whereby I live."[27]

The idea that animal nurseries should be sanctified has been extended to include fish spawning grounds. In 2002, when the state of California and the National Park Service declared 175 square miles of the waters in the Channel Islands National Park to be marine preserves, off-limits to commercial and recreational fishers, they did so because the areas in question were birthing grounds for a number of decimated species. As one biologist explained, the larger the marine preserves, the larger the females can get, and "big, fat females in the system . . . produce an enormous amount of eggs."[28]

In recent years, the places where two charismatic mammal species—whales and caribou—give birth have been given legal protection even without a threat of imminent extinction. The San Ignacio Lagoon, where the California gray whales mate and calve, covers 9,840 square miles on the Pacific Coast of Baja California. In the 1970s, the lagoon was designated a Biosphere Reserve by the Mexican government, subject to restrictions designed to limit economic development; only activities with little environmental impact, like traditional small-scale fishing and the new whale-watching industry, were permitted. In 1993, UNESCO declared the lagoon one of 522 World Heritage sites, enhancing its recognition as an ecosystem that should be preserved. Nevertheless, the Mitsubishi Corporation and the Mexican government were not about to abandon long-standing plans to build the world's largest salt-refining operation in the lagoon. According to the environmental impact assessment released by the partners in 1995, the proposed operation was to be vast indeed, with a milelong pier jutting into the lagoon and 116 square miles of evaporating ponds, pipes, roads, and salt-processing machinery. The expected income was vast as well: eighty-five to one hundred million dollars per year in export revenues.

Despite projections that tremendous pollution would affect over 780 square miles, the government lifted all legal restrictions on development in the lagoon, giving economic development priority over environmental conservation.[29] But the Mexican environmental movement, led by intellectuals and artists known as the Group of 100, insisted that the whale nursery should be inviolable. Joining with the International Fund for Animal Welfare, the Animal Welfare Institute, and Greenpeace International, they set out to preserve it. In May 1995 the coalition took out a full page ad in the *New York Times* emphasizing the lagoon's sanctity: "There's more than one way to kill a whale. Gray whales rock their newborns to sleep in this warm Mexican lagoon. Their only enemy? Mitsubishi, a giant Japanese conglomerate with plans to suck it dry."[30]

As the coalition expanded, renaming itself the Campaign to Save San Ignacio Lagoon, its reach encompassed over fifty Mexican environmental groups. In the United States, the campaign was led by the Natural Resources Defense Council (NRDC) and Robert F. Kennedy Jr., founder of the Baykeeper and Riverkeeper organizations. In 1998, Kennedy traveled to Kyoto, Japan, to protest the development at a hearing of the UNESCO World Heritage Site committee. In language reminiscent of John Muir, Kennedy called the saltworks a sacrilege:

"I cannot conceive that Mitsubishi Corporation would ever propose to put an industrial plant amid the shrines and temples of Kyoto."[31] NRDC and the International Fund for Animal Welfare in turn orchestrated an extraordinary letter-writing campaign, motivating some 750,000 people to send protest letters to Mitsubishi. NRDC initiated a boycott of all Mitsubishi products in California. Protesters who owned mutual funds that held Mitsubishi stock were encouraged to lobby the funds to disinvest.

Homero Aridjis, the Mexican poet who founded the Group of 100 and led the campaign to save San Ignacio Lagoon, saw the group's mission in religious terms: "You must have local missionaries and you must convert people."[32] In 1999, Aridjis wrote a poem entitled "Genesis 1:21": "And God created the great whales / there in Laguna San Ignacio, / and each creature that moves / in the shadowy things of the water. . . . / And God saw that it was good, / that the whales made love / and played with their young / in the magical lagoon."[33] The next year, Mexican president Ernesto Zedillo paid a personal visit to San Ignacio and canceled the saltworks.

At roughly the same time, a similar struggle took place on Alaska's north coast over a Caribou nursery. The Arctic National Wildlife Refuge (ANWR) was first established in 1960 by President Dwight Eisenhower as a 13,900-square-mile wildlife "range," which gave it some protection; twenty years later President Jimmy Carter doubled the protected area, and designated nearly 1,400 square miles as wilderness, where no development of any kind could take place. But to appease the oil industry's supporters in Congress, Carter's 1980 legislation had an important loophole: Some 2,344 square miles of the refuge, on the coastal plain near the Beaufort Sea, were left open for oil exploration and development. Actual drilling, however, would require additional congressional legislation authorizing the Department of the Interior to sell oil leases.[34]

This coastal plain happens to be the spring and summer birthing grounds and nursery of the Porcupine caribou herd. Numbering from 120,000 to 160,000, the herd migrates annually to the coast from its winter range near the mountain headwaters of the Porcupine River. The caribou are of the utmost importance to the seven thousand members of the Gwich'in tribe, who live in the region: They require some dozen caribou per family to survive the long winter. In 1971 the Gwich'in refused to participate in the Alaska Native Claims Settlement Act, which distributed nearly one billion dollars and 68,750 square miles of land to Native American tribes in exchange for relinquishing all outstanding tribal land claims. The Gwich'in instead maintained their claims to some 2,800 square miles—including parts of the coastal plain—and insisted on living on the land to keep it healthy.[35]

In 1987 the Reagan administration, the Department of the Interior, and Congress announced plans to allow oil exploration in ANWR. Congressional committees began hearings on selling oil leases. These plans were postponed after the *Exxon Valdez* oil tanker ran aground in Prince William Sound on March 23, 1989, spilling eleven million gallons of oil and devastating one thousand miles of coastline. With the oil industry temporarily on the defensive, the Gwich'in elders decided that it was time to send out messengers in the hope of saving the coastal basin. Some of the Gwich'in messengers went to other tribes; others made contact with the news media and environmental organizations and lobbied in Washington, D.C.

To the Gwich'in, they explained, caribou meat is not simply sustenance, but sacred food. Tribal chief Evon Peter told nature writer Peter Matthiessen that the Gwich'in felt profound responsibilities to the creatures living on the land: "It is very difficult to speak of the animals, the rivers—we're essentially a voice for things that cannot talk. We don't see ourselves as separate from those things. If the things and animals are poisoned, the poisons will work their way into us, too." Trimble Gilbert, a Gwich'in elder, recounted one of his tribe's creation myths. At the beginning of time, he said, his people and the Porcupine caribou were joined at the heart. "Caribou has a piece of

Man's heart and Man has a piece of Caribou's heart in his heart, so that each will always know what the other is doing."[36] Because of this close relationship between Gwich'in and caribou, said one messenger, "Even in times of extreme starvation the Gwich'in never went over the mountains to hunt caribou there [on the coastal plain], because it was a time to leave them alone so they could bear the young. The area is very, very sacred."[37]

These extraordinary efforts by the Gwich'in resonated with a broader public increasingly sensitive to environmental issues. In 1995, when Congress passed legislation allowing the sale of drilling leases on the coastal plain, it was vetoed by President Bill Clinton. In early 2002, President George W. Bush and Republican senators and congressional representatives began another concentrated effort to authorize the sale of oil leases and actual drilling, claiming that it would lead to the creation of seven hundred thousand new jobs and that there would be no environmental risk because "modern technology allows us to bring oil to the surface cleanly and safely, while protecting our environment and wildlife."[38] But oil drilling had already been framed as a grave threat. In a 2000 *New York Times* op-ed, Jimmy Carter had compared ANWR to places many Americans already held to be consecrated. "The roar alone—of road-building, trucks, drilling and generators—would pollute the wild music of the Arctic and be as out of place there as it would be in the heart of Yellowstone or the Grand Canyon."[39] Across the top of the page ran a drawing of an Arctic Eden, filled with caribou, polar bears, geese, and fish. A July 2001 story in the *Los Angeles Times* about the controversy noted that very few calves had survived the previous winter, because unusually late spring snowfalls had kept the caribou from reaching the coastal plains before giving birth. The young calves, born in foothills full of predators, and faced with multiple river crossings, often died. "This is what happened when they're kept off the coastal plain by nature. The next thing is if they're kept off by industrial development. . . . It bodes really poorly," argued Dan Ritzman of the Alaska Coalition environmental group. Pictures of baby caribou feeding from their mothers accompanied the article.[40] Indeed, by the spring of 2002, newspaper and television pictures of caribou calves and their mothers were everywhere. Democratic senators successfully staged a filibuster against a bill allowing oil leases and drilling in ANWR.

The next year, after the 2002 elections had created a Republican majority in both the House and Senate, the Republicans tried again with another drilling bill. But right before the March 2003 vote, Democratic Senator Barbara Boxer received photographer Subhankar Banerjee's newly published collection of ANWR landscape and animal photographs, *Arctic National Wildlife Refuge: Seasons of Life and Land, A Photographic Journey.* In Congress, Boxer held up one of the photographs in Banerjee's book and said to her colleagues, "Cast your eyes on this. One cannot paint anything quite as magnificent as what God has created."[41] Democratic Senator Joseph Lieberman asked, "Do we value this land, and are we prepared to protect it, or are we going to desecrate it, diminish it, change it forever for a small amount of oil?"[42] Eight Republicans and an Independent voted with forty-three Democrats to defeat the bill.[43] That fall Congress removed the provision allowing drilling in ANWR from the proposed energy bill, an important indicator of the refuge's growing cultural importance. Although Banerjee's book did not lead Congress to pass a new law granting the author's deepest wish—"official, permanent wilderness designation for the coastal plain of the Arctic National Wildlife Refuge"—his photographs have clearly helped to consecrate it.[44] Though the threats are ongoing, the Gwich'in and their supporters have thus far succeeded in blocking oil development in ANWR.

WATER OFTEN PLAYS an important role in the quest for landscape consecration. In religious myths, Eliade argues, waters "disintegrate, abolish forms, 'wash away sins'; they are at once purifying and regenerating."[45] A prominent traditional healer from among the Diné

(Navajo) of the American Southwest says, "Where water is, there are living things. Where water is, life goes on. In a holy way it flows. It is alive in a holy way."[46] But even scientists have been known to feel this mysterious attraction to moving water. When biologist Harold Alexander started working on river fisheries for the Arkansas Fish and Game Department, he initially focused simply on increasing the fish population. But as he spent time on the rivers and streams, the water itself became alive and animate. "A stream is a living thing. It moves, dances and shimmers in the sun. It furnishes opportunities for enjoyment and its beauty moves men's souls."[47] In nearby Chattanooga, Tennessee, all that remained of the Ocoee River was a dry bed, because for decades the Tennessee Valley Authority had diverted the river for hydroelectric power. But when engineers shut down an aging flume for repair, the Ocoee sprang back to life. Overnight, whitewater rapids reappeared. Months later, when the Tennessee Valley Authority tried to reclaim the river and divert it again, they met with bitter resistance from scores of kayakers and rafters.[48]

By the late 1990s there was an active national movement to restore rivers. Several small dams in Maine and the Pacific Northwest were torn down to help endangered species.[49] In Washington State, the Save Our Wild Salmon coalition of environmentalists, scientists, and Native American tribes (who by treaty were granted perpetual salmon fishing rights) lobbied for the removal of four dams on the Snake River, a tributary of the Columbia. When Lewis and Clark first journeyed down the Snake in 1804, they reported that the river was "crowded with salmon," and scientists estimate that some two million adult salmon a year once made the trip from the ocean to the Snake to spawn. Although the seven dams on the Columbia and Snake rivers were not the sole cause of salmon decline, they delivered a mighty blow. The four dams on the Snake were thought to be especially deadly; the man-made solutions—building fish ladders and hauling salmon around the dams in trucks and barges—proved ineffective. Coho salmon have gone extinct on the Columbia and its tributaries. In the fall of 1999, the Idaho Department of Fish and Game reported that only 8,700 Chinook salmon and two sockeye made the upstream journey.[50] Both are now listed as endangered species on the Columbia and its tributaries.

Ed Bowles, the Idaho manager for salmon and steelhead trout, argued that the only way to avoid extinction was to "restore a natural river in the Snake."[51] In 2000, some 215 scientists concurred with Bowles that the dams were the primary cause for declining fish populations. In a letter to President Clinton they wrote that "the weight of scientific evidence clearly shows that wild Snake River salmon and steelhead runs cannot be recovered under existing river conditions."[52] And though the idea of breaching the dams has encountered opposition from the U.S. Army Corps of Engineers (who declared it was not cost-efficient) and from President George W. Bush, the dream of resurrecting the Snake River from its deep sleep at the bottom of man-made lakes still tantalizes.[53] One Sierra Club magazine article found the idea so inspiring that it called the removal of the dams "Salmon's Second Coming." If the water could flow again, mused nature writer David James Duncan, then the salmon—"transrational beings whose living bodies bring far-reaching, non-quantifiable blessings to a watershed"—would return and the entire natural life cycle of the Snake River could begin anew.[54]

Beyond the removal of dams, advocates for natural rivers and wetlands are exploring other means of achieving their goals. In the late 1990s scientists and water managers began to change the pattern of releasing water from Glen Canyon Dam, upstream from the Grand Canyon, to mimic the flood cycle of the Colorado River. They hoped that the restoration of something like natural floods would reintroduce sand into the river, building up beaches and creating habitat for native fish.[55] In 2002 the National Research Council came out in favor of a similar plan for changing the annual water flows on the

Missouri River, releasing more water from dams in the spring and less in the summer, to mimic the natural cycle and so create a richer food chain for fish and birds. While the restored river would no longer be navigable in all seasons—it would sometimes be shallower and have exposed rocks, sand bars, and erratic currents—its meandering flow would bring life-giving sediment.[56] Even the Mississippi, trapped behind a complex of locks and high levees, now has advocates who propose to breach the eighty miles of river levees south of New Orleans.[57] Allowing the waters to flow once again over southern Louisiana would replenish the region's fabled wetlands, regenerating fish, shrimp, oysters, and the bayou way of life. The proposal seemed radical when first offered in 2001, but after hurricane Katrina the Army Corps of Engineers and Louisiana state officials embarked on a serious study to reroute the Mississippi and restore the delta with 120 million tons of sediment a year.[58]

In 2002, California governor Gray Davis announced that the state would purchase nearly twenty-six square miles of polluted salt evaporation ponds and restore them to be the wetlands they were 150 years ago, when fish and birds abounded in San Francisco Bay.[59] In a similar vein, first the Clinton, then the Bush administrations put together plans for a $7.8 billion restoration of south Florida's Everglades. In 1850, the whole of south Florida below Lake Okeechobee was a vast wetlands fed by a broad sheet of water some fifty miles wide, ankle- to knee-deep, flowing from the lake.[60] It was known as "the river of grass." Then, in 1947, Congress approved a program to radically accelerate the draining of south Florida for suburban development, and the U.S. Army Corps of Engineers built canals and levees that dumped 1.7 billion gallons of freshwater a day into the ocean.[61] With the water drained, the Everglades began to die. Under the restoration plan the water would once again flow south from Lake Okeechobee over 156 square miles of newly purchased land. A new system of 333 wells would pump 1.6 billion gallons of water a day into underground aquifers and surface reservoirs, abolishing the former practice of releasing water into the drainage canals. The water stored in the aquifers and reservoirs would be returned to Lake Okeechobee, the river of grass, and other Everglades waterways when needed.[62] Although this massive effort would not return the south Florida Everglades to its original state, a substantial part of the wetlands and their wildlife would nevertheless come back.[63]

This belief in the healing powers of water, in its ability to restore long-lost natural places and the life once along its shores, now motivates conservation across the globe. In Chile, transnational lumber companies uprooted over seven thousand square miles of native rain forests from 1985 to 1995 to create commercial tree farms densely planted with Monterrey pine and eucalyptus to produce lumber for commercial markets. The nonnative trees sucked the water out of the ground, destroying streams and wells, threatening both the rain forest ecosystem and the indigenous Mapuche Indians. "We've entered into a period of darkness of water, and this is bringing us to the brink of extinction," warned Mapuche poet and playwright Rayen Kuyeh.[64] Medicine women prayed for the spirits of the water and the Earth to resist. Some of the tribe's activists burned logging trucks, while others reached out to the American environmental group ForestEthics to persuade Home Depot and other companies that used Chilean wood to support reform. In 2003, Home Depot helped the Mapuche negotiate agreements with the Chilean tree farms to limit their destruction of the rain forest and subsequent planting of trees for commercial export.[65]

THE ACT OF restoring degraded lands and waters changes people, embeds them deeply into places. In 1964, poet and essayist Wendell Berry bought twelve acres of Kentucky River valley land abused by decades of poor farming practices. He had grown up on a farm in the valley and had always dreamed of returning home. Berry understood what needed to be done to restore the land and ecosystem to health. But that knowledge came with a price. "A destructive history, once understood as such," Berry writes, "is a nearly insupportable burden. Understanding it [what people did to the land] is a disease of understanding, depleting the sense of efficacy and paralyzing effort, unless it finds healing work. For me that work has been partly of the mind, in what I have written, but that seems to have depended inescapably on work of the body and of the ground."[66] To really heal degraded lands and waters, Berry emphasized, requires intimate, detailed understanding of a place, what the anthropologist Clifford Geertz called "local knowledge."[67] Each generation that remains on the land inherits this local knowledge—the characteristics of each field and pasture, where water runs off when it rains, where erosion is likely—and adds to it for succeeding generations as restoration continues.

Such intimate understanding was characteristic of hunting and gathering peoples who developed detailed knowledge of their relatively confined territories, often no more than one hundred square miles or so.[68] (Interestingly, according to the geographer Yi-Fu Tuan, it is precisely the small, specific area—"a compact size scaled down to man's biological needs and sense-bound capabilities"— that stimulates topophilia, the love of place.[69]) These earlier peoples' cultures became inextricably connected to their homelands and most, if not all their most important myths or stories are dependent on location. For them, as anthropologist Christopher Tilley argues, "the landscape is the fundamental reference system in which individual consciousness of the world and social identities are anchored."[70]

Such close cultural connections to place have been mostly destroyed in the modern world. But more and more people are trying to reinvent them. The movement to eat only locally grown foods reconnects people to the land in a daily, visceral way.[71] Even participating in a sport can cause inner change. Writer Daniel Duane searched the coast of California's Santa Cruz County for the ideal surf spot, and he fell in love with a place where "waves will continue to break below these trees and over this reef and will continue to give whatever it is you imagine they give you."[72] Duane didn't simply surf the place he called the Point, he made it the center of his life. He studied its past, learning about the Ohlone Indians who had dwelled there, how they made seasonal journeys along the coast on foot and in reed boats. To Duane, the fact that both he and the Ohlone loved the same magical place deepened his attachment. History, the beauty of the ocean, and the excitement of surfing all lifted him into a rare state of consciousness. Sometimes, when surfing the Point, he "felt something rare in a life: the sense that I had been present and prepared for an instant of—what was the word I had used? Plenitude?"[73]

Plenitude, this sense of personal connection to a place and the place's connection to a larger, meaningful cosmos with a rich history— these are gifts of the culture of enchantment. When marine scientist Carl Safina looks out at the ocean, he simultaneously reminds us to look inward as well: "We are, in a sense, soft vessels of seawater. Seventy percent of our bodies is water, the same percentage that covers Earth's surface. We are wrapped around an ocean within."[74] And philosopher David Abram argues that the conventional Western way of thinking about human consciousness as something separate from nature should be replaced by an alternate paradigm: "We might as well say that we are organs of this world, flesh of its flesh, and the world is perceiving itself *through* us. . . . We may come to feel that we are part of this forest, consanguineous with it, and that our experience of the forest is nothing other than the forest experiencing itself."[75] (Nearly a century before, William James made a similar point in *A Pluralistic Universe* when he argued that "as we are ourselves a part of the earth, so our organs are her organs."[76]) In the culture of enchantment, consciousness and nature are one: The tree, the forest, the ocean are no longer just out there, separate from humans, but instead they are inside us, and we are inside them.

THE LAST, SADDEST way of consecrating land occurs after it has been destroyed. In Emile Durkheim's terms, what is sacred is sometimes only fully understood and appreciated after it has been "profaned" and the extent of the violation becomes known. The subsequent process of mourning creates a kind of consecration of what has been lost, and a prayer for its resurrection and return.

The Hetch Hetchy Valley, for example, continues to be a focus of the enchantment movement, despite—and, in some part, because of—the failure of John Muir's efforts to save it from being flooded by the O'Shaughnessy Dam. In 1987, after the valley had spent more than half a century submerged under three hundred feet of water, Donald P. Hodel, Secretary of the Interior for the Reagan administration, asked San Francisco officials to find another source for drinking water, tear down the dam, and restore the valley.[77] Although generally not known as a friend of the environment, Hodel had observed the successful removal of a damaged dam in Rocky Mountain National Park and the rebirth of a vibrant stream and valley there and became convinced that tearing down O'Shaughnessy was the right thing to do. When San Francisco officials rejected his suggestion, Hodel characterized their arguments as similar to those "made by slaveholders in opposition to abolition."[78] In 2002 a new group, Restore Hetch Hetchy, again called for bringing the valley back. In explaining the group's powerful attraction to the place, Executive Director Ron Good extended to Hetch Hetchy the culturally accepted status of Yosemite as an enchanted place: "Imagine the opportunity we have to allow nature to re-create another Yosemite Valley."[79] Even when, after several years of study, San Francisco's water agency reported that removing the dam and finding a new source of water for the city would cost up to ten billion dollars, Hodel—retired by then but still advocating destruction of the dam—was undeterred. "A dream of this type will hold people's attention," he explained. "Eventually there will be a critical mass who say, 'Phooey! We're going to do it no matter what the cost.' "[80]

The flooding of Hetch Hetchy is not the only act of destruction that has prompted second thoughts after the deed was done. In her work as a Miami newspaper columnist in the 1930s, Marjory Stoneman Douglas had supported dam-building and the draining of the Everglades as necessary for south Florida's development. But in the mid-1940s fires destroyed much of the dried-out swamp, and she had a change of heart: "The whole Everglades was burning. What had been a river of grass and sweet water that had given meaning and life and uniqueness to this whole enormous geography through centuries in which man had no place here was made, in one chaotic gesture of greed and ignorance and folly, a river of fire."[81] Douglas wrote *The Everglades: River of Grass* (1947) in an effort to change the meaning of the Everglades for people and make them see the value of the wetlands. It eventually became a key text for the Everglades restoration movement.

In the 1950s, when David Brower was executive director of the Sierra Club and the organization was still struggling to persuade its membership to focus on conservation rather than hiking trips, he promised the club's board of directors not to protest the building of Glen Canyon Dam on the Colorado River. At the time, Brower had never visited Glen Canyon. In the early 1960s, though, after the construction of the dam had begun, but before its gates were permanently shut, he took a series of float trips down the river. It was a devastating experience. Glen Canyon was immensely beautiful, and its 2,900 square miles—what he termed "the last large roadless area between Canada and Mexico"—would soon be drowned under Lake Powell.[82] In failing to fight to save Glen Canyon, Brower felt he had betrayed the Sierra Club's best traditions. It was as if John Muir had simply acquiesced to the flooding of Hetch Hetchy Valley without a fight. Indeed, Brower later paraphrased Muir's famous excoriation, saying that "putting water in the Cathedral in the Desert was like urinating in the Crypt of St. Peter's."[83] It was too late for him to do anything. But it was the last time he surrendered a place he'd never seen.

# 4

## Space Exploration, Gaia,
## and the Greening of Religion

In the late 1960s, when the Apollo astronauts orbited the planet and made several trips to the moon, they sent back the first photographs of the Earth. These pictures, with their startling colors—blue water, white clouds, green continents—had immense power. As Ansel Adams's images had sanctified the Western landscape, they consecrated the Earth itself.

The Sierra Club's executive director at the time, David Brower, was among the first to grasp their potential. He hired Jerry Mander, whose advertising firm had developed a successful campaign in the mid-1960s to save the Grand Canyon from being flooded by a dam, to design a new campaign aimed at saving the planet.[1] The result, a photograph titled EARTH NATIONAL PARK, became the heart of a 1969 Sierra Club advertising campaign calling for treatment of the Earth as a "conservation district in the universe."[2] Brower's thinking was too far ahead of a Sierra Club board of directors that wanted to appear moderate, pragmatic, and serious. Consequently, Brower later recalled, the concept of "Earth National Park helped get me fired."[3] But even after Brower had moved on to form Friends of the Earth and then Earth Island Institute, he frequently referred to the role of the space photographs in changing human perception of the Earth. In "The Sermon," a speech he gave hundreds of times to groups all over the country, Brower always admonished audiences to remember "the sudden insight from Apollo . . . how fragile our life is, how thin is the epithelium of the atmosphere."[4]

At the time of the Apollo moon missions in the late 1960s and early 1970s, astronauts did not typically express their feelings in public. But in 1983, when American astronauts and Soviet cosmonauts met in Paris to form the Association of Space Explorers, they spoke of their "enhanced reverence for the Earth as a result of their space flight experience."[5] A committee of the new organization began work on a massive collection of interviews with space explorers, presented together with an array of beautiful photographs. Three years later, it was published as *The Home Planet.*

In the preface, Soviet cosmonaut Oleg Makarov explained that in space "it is not the boring uniform blackness of the cosmic abyss that engages your attention, but the spectacle of our small planet haloed in blue. Suddenly, you get a feeling you've never had before, that you're an inhabitant of Earth."[6] Judging from the interviews, this consciousness affected all the space explorers. For Saudi astronaut Sultan Bin Salman al-Saud, each day in Earth orbit brought a deeper understanding of connection: "The first day we all pointed to our countries. The third or fourth day we were pointing to our continents. By the fifth day we were aware of only one Earth."[7] "It isn't important in which sea or lake you observe a slick of pollution, or in the forests of which country a fire breaks out, or on which continent a hurricane arises," said cosmonaut Yuri Artyukhin. "You are standing guard over the whole of our Earth."[8]

Many astronauts reported spiritual awakenings and conversion experiences. As cosmonaut Aleksandr Aleksandrov orbited Earth in late autumn, he saw the first snows in America, Europe, and Russia, and imagined that in each of them, people were getting ready for winter.

"And then it struck me that we are all children of the Earth. It does not matter what country you look at. We are all Earth's children, and we should treat her as our Mother."9 A Chinese-American astronaut, Taylor Wang, recalled an old Chinese story that "tells of some men sent to harm a young girl who, upon seeing her beauty, become her protectors rather than her violators. That's how I felt seeing the Earth for the first time. I could not help but love and cherish her."10

To Alexei Leonov from the Soviet Union, "the Earth was small, light blue, and so touchingly alone, our home that must be defended like a holy relic."11 James Irwin, an American on a journey to the moon, saw the Earth shrink and then fade away: "That beautiful, warm, living object looked so fragile, so delicate, that if you touched it with a finger it would crumble and fall apart. Seeing this has to change a man, has to make a man appreciate the creation of God and the love of God."12 Edgar Mitchell was stunned by the sight of the Earthrise as he stood on the moon. "There emerges a sparkling blue and white jewel, a light, delicate sky-blue sphere laced with slowly swirling veils of white, rising gradually like a small pearl in a thick sea of black mystery. . . . My view of our planet was a glimpse of divinity."13 On his way back to Earth, Mitchell's awareness deepened. "There was suddenly a very deep gut feeling that something was different . . . a nonrational way of understanding. . . . I suddenly experienced the universe as intelligent, loving, harmonious."14

These astronauts and cosmonauts considered themselves scientists, not spiritual mystics or aesthetes overcome by the beauties of light, land, and space. Most had spent their careers in military and civilian government bureaucracies. But their experiences in space fundamentally changed their relation to the Earth. As Edgar Mitchell said, "We went to the moon as technicians; we returned as humanitarians."15

While this intensity of feeling appears to have been particularly acute among the astronauts, others involved in the space program also began to feel differently about their world. Photographs of Earth helped create a growing sense that the planet was a global ecosystem, and this realization began to influence their work. By far the most famous expression of this new consciousness was James Lovelock's "Gaia hypothesis." In the 1950s, Lovelock, a British chemist, had become interested in Earth's biosphere—the part of the planet and its atmosphere that can support life. He developed sophisticated machinery that could measure chemical traces in the air, leading to the discovery of widespread toxic residues from agricultural pesticides. This scientific breakthrough inspired Rachel Carson's research that eventually led to *Silent Spring*.[16]

In the mid-1960s Lovelock began work for the National Aeronautics and Space Administration (NASA). At the Jet Propulsion Laboratory in Pasadena, California, he investigated ways an unmanned spacecraft in the Martian atmosphere could search for the chemical elements that form life. Thinking in planetary terms, Lovelock reported, led him and his colleagues to "formulate a new, or perhaps revive a very ancient, concept of the relationship between the Earth and its biosphere."[17] His thinking was further affected by the photos taken by the Gemini and Apollo crews. "To my mind the outstanding spin-off from space research is not new technology," he said years later, reflecting on changes in Earth science. "The real bonus has been that for the first time in human history we have had a chance to look at the Earth from space, and the information gained from seeing from the outside our azure-green planet in all its global beauty has given rise to a whole set of questions and answers."[18]

Lovelock developed a model to describe the dynamics of planetary life: The Earth is not just an inert stage upon which different kinds of life come and go, but itself a kind of complex entity "involving the Earth's biosphere, atmosphere, oceans, and soil; the totality constituting a feedback or cybernetic system which seeks an optimal physical and chemical environment for life on this planet."[19] All elements of life on the planet, as well as the rocks, the oceans, and the atmosphere, work together. As Lovelock's frequent collaborator Lynn Margulis said, "Each species to a greater or lesser degree modifies its environment to optimize its reproduction rate. . . . All species are connected, for the production of gases, food, and waste removal, however circuitously, to all others."[20]

Lovelock and Margulis used the term *homeostasis* to describe this concept of Earth as an entity actively seeking internal balance. It was Lovelock's neighbor, William Golding, who came up with the more poetic name: Gaia, the Greek earth goddess, or Mother Earth divinity. Lovelock liked the idea, later joking that his theory—which he called the Gaia hypothesis—was saved from "the creation of a barbarous acronym, such as 'Biocybernetic Universal System Tendency.'" More importantly, Lovelock loved the enchantment of Gaia, the name's connection to myth and ties to people's intuitive understanding and experience: "I find that country people still living close to the earth often seem puzzled that anyone should need to make a formal proposition of anything as obvious as the Gaia hypothesis. For them it is true and always has been."[21]

Lovelock's *Gaia: A New Look at Life on Earth* (1979) is a perfect example of a "double discourse." It expands the science of ecology, breaking the conventional disciplinary boundaries between physics, chemistry, biology, oceanography, and other earth sciences to show how Earth's climate and chemical conditions for life have always been optimal. At the same time, it suggests a more mystical explanation for the Earth's tendency toward balance: "For this to have happened by chance is as unlikely as to survive unscathed a drive blindfolded through rush-hour traffic."[22] Lovelock's next book, *The Ages of Gaia: A Biography of Our Living Earth* (1988), pushed the scientific argument even further. Earth, he emphasized, is best understood as a "superorganism" that encompasses both living and nonliving matter. Indeed, the long-held distinction between the two is misleading: "There is no clear distinction anywhere on the Earth's surface between living and nonliving matter. There is merely a hierarchy of intensity going from the 'material' environment of the rocks and the atmosphere to the living cells."[23] Again, Lovelock pointed to photos as a catalyst for his thinking: "It took the view of Earth from space, either directly through the eyes of an astronaut, or vicariously through the visual media, to let us sense a planet on which living things, the air, the ocean and the rocks all combine as Gaia."[24] And he was increasingly explicit about the spiritual side of his theory: "Gaia is a religious as well as a scientific concept, and in both spheres it is manageable."[25] Lovelock criticized monotheism because its idea of a transcendent almighty Father "seems to anaesthetize the sense of wonder, as if one were committed to a single line of thought by a cosmic legal contract."[26] In describing the Gaia hypothesis, he often writes as if Earth is alive, possessed of some kind of mysterious consciousness: "Her unconscious goal is a planet fit for life."[27]

In 1988 Lovelock still felt confident that his discourse about Gaia could be accepted by "both spheres," but by 1995 that confidence vanished. In a preface to a new edition of *Ages of Gaia*, he reported that his presentation at an academic conference on "The Self-Regulating Earth" had been poorly received because he said things such as "Gaia likes it cold" (in reference to enhanced biodiversity in glacial times). A colleague complained, "Jim, you can't say things like that. It takes us back to the days of Gaia as an Earth Goddess. The scientists sitting near me were shocked to hear you speak in such terms."[28] Lovelock consequently felt compelled to "disenchant" the revised edition, explaining that his previous references to Gaia were shorthand notations for the hypothesis or simple figures of speech, like calling a ship "she."[29] In 2000, in a new preface to his first book, Lovelock agreed that for the new Earth System Science, or Geophysiology, to be accepted, it "must be purged of all reference to mystical notions of Gaia, the Earth Mother."[30]

But even as Lovelock tempered his talk in order to achieve scientific respectability, "Gaia" (both as scientific theory and as a more amorphous cultural reenchantment of the Earth) had become wildly popular across diverse publics. She could not be vanquished by anyone's command.

INEVITABLY, RESPONSE TO Gaia varied by gender. A number of male intellectuals understood the resurrection of belief in Mother Earth, Gaia, as a return of the spiritual awareness and life force that Western society had repressed during modernization. Cultural historian and "ecopsychology" theorist Theodore Roszak saw acceptance of the idea of Gaia as new evidence proving the existence of what Carl Jung called the collective unconscious. "The survival of life and of our species would not have been possible without such a self-adjusting, system-building wisdom," said Roszak.[31] The fact that people were becoming aware of environmental degradation at the same time as the idea of Gaia entered the discussion meant that "the Earth hurts, and we hurt with it. If we could still accept the imagery of a Mother Earth, we might say that the planet's umbilical cord links to us at the root of the unconscious mind."[32] Environmental activism could thus be seen as an expression of people's new awareness of their connections to the planet, their nascent consciousness of being intrinsic parts of the Earth. In this context, people's efforts to change their lives, such as eating organic, locally grown food, riding bicycles instead of driving, installing solar panels on their roofs, or finding new careers in nonpolluting industries, are part of larger Gaian processes of self-regulation (homeostasis) that restore planetary health.[33]

Perhaps the most prestigious proponent of this idea of Gaia was Václav Havel, the noted Czech playwright and then-president of the Czech Republic. In 1994, accepting the Liberty Medal for his lifetime commitment to political freedom, Havel spoke on "The Need for Transcendence in the Post-Modern World." He decried the split between Western civilization's scientific advances and its culture: "The abyss between the rational and the spiritual, the external and the internal, the objective and the subjective, the technical and the moral, the universal and the unique grows deeper." Havel saw hope for the future, though, in what he termed "postmodern" science—"ideas that in a certain sense allow it [science] to transcend its own limits." Havel said that the idea of Gaia helped people in modern society recall forgotten myths and dormant archetypes, and recover the "awareness of our being anchored in the Earth and the universe, the awareness that we are not here alone nor for ourselves alone, but that we are an integral part of higher, mysterious entities against whom it is not advisable to blaspheme."[34]

Some women writers and intellectuals agreed that the return of the idea of Gaia to Western culture represented the recovery of a lost spiritual awareness. But to them it was more important that the concept of Mother Earth as a goddess was a call to specifically feminine spirituality. Lovelock and Margulis's work on the Gaia hypothesis in the late 1970s and the 1980s coincided with the widespread success of the women's movement. As part of that movement, a whole generation of women authors sought to rediscover, rethink, and reimagine the relationship between women and nature. In *The Death of Nature*, historian Carolyn Merchant analyzed the development of modern science in seventeenth-century Europe—when "two new ideas, those of mechanism and of the domination and mastery of nature, became core concepts of the modern world"—as the triumph of a masculine ethos: "The image of the earth as a living organism and nurturing mother had served as a cultural constraint restricting the actions of human beings. . . . As long as the earth was considered to be alive and sensitive, it could be considered a breach of human ethical behavior to carry out destructive acts against it."[35]

Others took a more direct spiritual approach. Susan Griffin's book-length prose poem, *Women and Nature: The Roaring Inside Her* (1978), argued that women and nature shared a common language, one most men could not hear: "He says that woman speaks with nature. That she hears voices from under the earth. That wind blows in her ears and trees whisper to her. That the dead sing through her mouth and the cries of infants are clear to her. But for him the dialogue is over. He says he is not part of this world, that he was set on this world as a stranger." Consequently, says Griffin, it should not be surprising to find that in many Western folktales, women, but not men, speak with the animal characters. "And so it is Goldilocks who goes to the home of the three bears, Little Red Riding Hood who converses with the wolf, Dorothy who befriends a lion, Snow White who talks to the birds, Cinderella with mice as her allies, the Mermaid who is half fish, Thumbelina courted by a mole."[36]

Renowned poet and science fiction writer Paula Gunn Allen similarly linked women and feminine Earth spirituality in her essay "The Woman I Love Is a Planet; the Planet I Love Is a Tree." For Allen, "believing that our mother, the Beloved Earth, is inert matter is destructive to yourself," since it cuts both women and men off from both their bodies and nature.[37] Gaia, on the other hand, offered a vision of oneness and communion:

> *I have grown tall as a cedar tree in Lebanon,*
> *as a cypress on Mount Hermon;*
> *as the rose bushes of Jericho;*
> *as a fine olive on the plain. . . .*
> *I am like a vine putting out graceful shoots,*
> *my blossoms bear the fruit of glory and wealth.*
> *Approach me, you who desire me,*
> *and take your fill of my fruits.*[38]

This feminist embrace of the idea of Gaia led to a search for other lost goddesses. Long-marginalized figures such as the twelfth-century abbess Hildegard of Bingen found new audiences. Hildegard's poems to honor the Earth resonated with the contemporary movement:

*Glance at the sun,*
*See the moon and stars,*
*Gaze at the beauty of Earth's greenings.*
*Now, think.*
*What Delight*
*God gives to humankind*
*With all these things . . .*
*The earth . . . is mother of all . . .*
*The earth should not be injured.*
*The earth should not be destroyed.*[39]

Marija Gimbutas and Riane Eisler found evidence of Neolithic Earth Goddess worship scattered across Europe and the Middle East. Gimbutas, in *The Language of the Goddess*, concluded that "The Goddess in all her manifestations was a symbol of the unity of all life in Nature."[40] Eisler, building on her work, claimed that societies where goddess worship prevailed had relatively egalitarian social structures, with families and clans headed by women. In these societies, power did not mean violent domination—men, for example, were not necessarily "perceived and treated as subservient."[41] Rather, it meant that the Earth Goddess (as a symbol of the unity of life) had been internalized as the "feminine power to nurture and give," what Eisler called "actualization power."[42]

The idea of Gaia as a kind of internalized spiritual force was central to the goddess movement that appeared in the early 1980s. Starhawk (Miriam Simos), an intellectual and activist who helped resurrect the ritual practice of witchcraft, or Wicca, giving it both a feminist and a radical political direction, called goddess worship a way to summon internal powers. As she writes: "Yet power-from-within *is* the power of the low, the dark, the earth; the power that arises from our blood, and our lives, and our passionate desire for each other's living flesh."[43] Summoning this power-from-within in turn created a connection to Earth—"Our personal energy field is never wholly separate from the earth's field. We are each a ripple in the earth's aura."[44]

Starhawk claimed that through Wiccan rituals she could tap the Earth's energy for political purposes. While protesting the construction of the Diablo Canyon nuclear reactor on the central California coast, she felt the "trees, the earth, come alive. They speak. They are angry, and we can let ourselves be pulled by the currents of their deep earth power."[45] Starhawk and her sister witches, concerned by the prospect that the sacred place would be "contaminated, off-limits, ruined forever," said that they channeled Earth energy "down to find the plant's weakest spots, the fault lines within its structure-of-being."[46] The power plant was eventually built, after many construction problems and long delays. Still, the mystical experiences reported by many at Diablo Canyon brought new adherents to the radical activist wing of the goddess movement.

On a more contemplative, individual level, Jungian psychoanalyst Clarissa Pinkola Estés founded a therapeutic approach for women based on the notion of resurrecting connections to a lost Earth Goddess archetype, which she calls the "Wild Woman." Estés argues that over the past thousands of years, Western societies have repressed women's "feminine instinctive nature. . . . The spiritual lands of Wild Woman have, throughout history, been plundered or burnt, dens bulldozed, and natural cycles forced into unnatural rhythms to please others."[47] For Estés, the repressed Wild Woman represents powerful animal energy or wildness that male-dominated societies seek to control. Thus, the historical destruction of wild lands, together with the campaigns to eradicate powerful animals, are intrinsically connected to the domination of women.

To change a world where "Wildlife and the Wild Woman are both endangered species," women need to recover their "shadow" selves, their repressed wildness.[48] "The remedies for repair or reclamation of any lost psychic drive are contained in stories," Estés argues. "Stories enable us to understand the need for and the ways to raise a submerged archetype."[49] Estés' most famous story, "Women Who Run with the Wolves," in her book of the same name, tells of *La Loba*, a witch or female shaman living in the deserts of Mexico or the Southwest. *La Loba* collects animal bones, but her specialty is wolf bones. After assembling a wolf skeleton on the floor of her cave, *La Loba* begins to sing. Slowly, as the singing continues, flesh appears on the wolf's bones, and finally the wolf is brought back to life. As it runs, "The wolf is suddenly transformed into a laughing woman who runs free toward the horizon."[50] Estés' message: Once a woman comes to acknowledge her internal goddess power—the Wild Woman within—and her connections to other animals and Mother Earth, she can break through the bonds of domination and laugh with joy. In telling this story, Estés herself becomes *La Loba:* her narrative takes the place of the witch's song and the wolf's resurrection symbolizes the reader's growing awareness. First published in 1992, *Women Who Run with the Wolves* sold over one million copies in five years.

The connection of women, wildness, and spirituality quickly made its way even into popular culture. In 1980, novelist Jean M. Auel published her historical romance *The Clan of the Cave Bear*, the first of a six-volume Earth's Children series that appeared over the next twenty-four years and sold over thirty-seven million copies. Earth's Children creates a fantasy world involving ancient hunter-gatherer tribes in Europe sometime during the late Pleistocene Epoch, roughly thirty-five thousand to twenty-five thousand years ago. Auel's central character, Ayla, a beautiful young woman, represents human creativity and responsibility. She is charged with protecting the Earth by a Neanderthal shaman. Aware that his people will soon die out, yielding the Earth to Ayla and her people (*Homo sapiens*), he says: "The earth we leave is beautiful and rich; it gave us all we needed for all the generations we have lived. How will you leave it when it is your turn? What can you do?"[51]

The answers to the shaman's questions emerge in subsequent volumes, as Ayla travels alone from the northern Black Sea westward across Europe in search of other *Homo sapiens*. Along the way she spears a horse for food, but adopts its foal and decides to raise it. She performs the "Neanderthal naming ceremony" reserved for humans on the foal—"This girl's . . . this female's name is Whinney."[52] Later she adopts a cave lion cub, naming it Baby. Whinney the horse adopts Baby, too. "She guided him, and guarded him, and if he responded in ways that were puzzling at times, it did not lessen her attentive care."[53] The cave lion, horse, and woman learn to hunt together after Ayla invents horseback riding: "They were her family, her clan, living creatures who shared her cave and her life."[54]

When a man appears in her life, Ayla's human-animal family is already well established and it is he, Jondular, who must adapt, accepting that for Ayla, "the horse could never be very far from her thoughts; their lives had become inextricably intertwined."[55] Ayla has Jondular name Whinney's colt as his own, to help consolidate the family bonds. Later, after the cave lion leaves, Ayla adopts a wolf cub. This mixed human-animal family—the first in history—finally arrives at Jondular's tribal home in what is now France.

Jondular's people are organized into matrilineal clans, with political power shared equally among men and women. Politics, however, is not their core organizing principle. Instead, their culture centers on the worship of Mother Earth, and is led by a group of shamans called the Zelandoni, "Those Who Serve the Mother."[56] These shamans, both male and female, heal the sick with herbal medicines and spiritual rites, have visions, and lead the people in rituals honoring Mother Earth. It is Mother Earth who brings fertility, who creates sexual energy in humans and gives the Gift of Pleasure. The Zelandoni are keepers of the people's traditions and myths, most of all their creation myth, Mother's Song. From the void, came Mother Earth. She created the sun, "her pale shining lover." From their unions all life is born. After the Earth's mountains and waters and animal life, Mother Earth gives birth to humans and gives them their home: "To Woman and Man the Mother gave birth, / And then for their home, She gave them the Earth, / The water, the land, and all Her creation. / To use them with care was their obligation. / It was their home to use. But not to abuse."⁵⁷

Auel's romantic epic borrows heavily from the Native American spirituality that helped give rise to the culture of enchantment in the 1970s. But it also incorporates the Gaian-inspired connection of women, nature, and spirituality. Essentially Auel managed to infuse a mainstream fictional genre, the historical romance, with a feminist culture of enchantment. It was not an isolated success story. In the late 1990s, for example, Nickelodeon's cartoon series *The Wild Thornberries* featured an adolescent girl who had become a shaman. She could speak with animals and dedicated her life to saving them and their habitats.

THE EXPLOSION OF Earth consciousness that began in the early 1970s mostly bypassed organized Christianity and Judaism. The conversion experiences of the astronauts, Lovelock's Gaia hypothesis, and all the creative interpretations of a consecrated Earth found little resonance in traditional Western religions. Indeed, for a number of scholars the refusal of Christianity and Judaism to consider the Earth as sacred was these faiths' special contribution to Western civilization. Thus Harvard professor Harvey Cox, in *The Secular City* (1965), argued that Judaism and Christianity, by their rejection of animism and insistence on a monotheistic God removed from the world, created the cultural ground from which natural science and technology developed. To Cox, the disenchantment of the world was a profound— and positive—accomplishment.⁵⁸

There were some dissenting voices. In 1967, historian Lynn White published "The Historical Roots of Our Ecological Crisis" in the journal *Science*, reiterating the concerns raised by Weber and Jung about disenchantment.⁵⁹ While both Weber and Jung emphasized disenchantment's cultural impoverishment, White also stressed its environmental consequences: "In antiquity every tree, every spring, every stream, every hill had its own *genius loci*, its guardian spirit," he wrote. "These spirits were accessible to men, but were very unlike men: centaurs, fauns, and mermaids show their ambivalence. Before one cut a tree, mined a mountain, or dammed a brook, it was important to placate the spirit in charge of that particular situation, and to keep it placated." With animism rejected and suppressed as demonic heresy, Christianity "made it possible to exploit nature in a mode of indifference to the feelings of natural objects."[60]

White's short essay provoked an intense, decadeslong controversy within the broad Jewish and Christian communities, particularly among religious scholars and theologians. It became a virtual template for discussing how organized religion had contributed to the environmental crisis and how religious/theological reform might contribute to solving it. Scholars who accepted White's general thesis began to search the Bible and the religious canon to detail the role of religion in the desacralization of nature.

Their reexamination logically began with Genesis, Western religion's creation myth. As religious studies scholar Norman Wirzba says, "The teaching of creation, besides being a teaching of how the world began, is about the characterization of human identity and vocation within the world. In it we see who we are and what we are to become."[61] From this perspective, it's readily apparent that Genesis codifies and legitimizes human domination over animals and land. In Genesis 1:28, God creates man and woman, then says, "Be fertile and multiply; fill the earth and subdue it. Have dominion over the fish of the sea, the birds of the air, and all the living things that move on the earth." According to Hebrew linguists, the operative Hebrew verbs, *kabash*, usually translated as "subdue," and *radah*, translated as "have dominion over," are used throughout the Old Testament to convey violent domination and the process of enslavement, such as in the rule of patriarchs over household servants, King Solomon's officers' control over his conscripted labor force, and the fate of Israel itself after foreign conquest.[62]

Similar examples are easy to find elsewhere in the Old Testament.

In Genesis 9:2, for instance, God promises Noah that humans after the flood will once again have dominion: "Dread fear of you shall come upon all the animals of the earth and all the birds of the air, upon all creatures that move on the ground and all the fishes of the sea, into your power they are delivered." Many scholars argue that such passages were in part motivated by Judaism's need to distinguish itself from pagan religions. The Old Testament repeatedly condemns the Canaan fertility god, Baal, who brought rain and whom the Canaanites honored with stone pillars, and the fertility goddess, Asherah, who was symbolized by the tree of life and honored with sacred groves, carved poles made from trees, and bread and clay idols.[63] In Exodus 34:13, the Lord tells Moses to drive out the inhabitants of Canaan (the promised land), and "tear down their altars; smash their sacred pillars, and cut down their sacred poles." In subsequent chapters Biblical narrators blame the victories of foreign armies against Israel and Judea on the wickedness of those Hebrew kings who allowed the Canaanite ways to flourish among the Jews, and ascribe the victories of other Hebrew kings to their smashing of pillars and poles. As Norman Wirzba concludes, "Interpretations of the Bible that spoke too much about nature ran the risk of suggesting that perhaps pagan religious ideas were not so bad after all."[64]

Christian theologians, the Neoplatonists in particular, made their own contributions to the radical separation between humans and nature. Thinkers from Plotinus (205–70 BCE) to Thomas Aquinas (1225–74) conceived of a Great Chain of Being, with God—pure reason and spirit—at the apex, animals and plants—pure matter—at the bottom, and humans—creatures of spirit and matter—occupying the middle ground. In this hierarchy, humans were clearly dominant over nature.[65] Whereas pagan animism saw totemic kinship relations between tribes and animal species, Christian theology informed by Neoplatonism refused all human-animal solidarity and commonality.[66] The central Christian doctrine of "the Fall" extended God's curse from Adam and Eve to all of nature. Martin Luther saw the "wrathful,

alien hand of God" everywhere, especially in species he thought repug-
nant: "What of thorns, thistles, water, fire, caterpillars, flies, fleas, and
bedbugs? Collectively and individually, are not all of them messengers
who preach to us concerning sin and God's wrath?"[67]

Christian orthodoxy completely rejected the idea of nature as the
sacred creation of God, a pathway to the recognition of "divine mystery."[68] Salvation or redemption could only come through God's intervention or his manifestation at the end of history: the coming of
the Messiah in the Jewish tradition and Christ's second coming for
Christianity. As the highly influential early-twentieth-century Biblical scholar Gerhard von Rad concluded, in neither case is "the creation of the world" considered "for its own sake, nor as of value in
itself. On the contrary . . . it performs only an ancillary function. It
provides a foundation for the message of redemption, in that it
stimulates faith. It is but a magnificent foil for the message of salvation."[69]

Christianity also developed the notion that if an individual led a
virtuous life and developed a relationship with Jesus, she or he would be
rewarded in heaven. Norman Wirzba calls it a "life preserver" approach. Just as the individual with a life preserver survives his ship's
sinking, the doctrine of personal salvation renders the fate of the planet
meaningless. Wirzba writes, "It is no accident that, having privatized
the idea of salvation, and then postponed its fulfillment to another time
and place, professedly religious individuals have no difficulty abusing
the earth and other people to achieve their own ends. This life, suppos-
edly, can be sacrificed for another."[70]

All of these intellectual developments, from Neoplatonism
through the doctrine of personal salvation, removed God from creation. As modern science emerged in seventeenth-century Europe, it
too became a subject for Christian concern. The Protestant doctrine
of "nominalism," working to reconcile religion and science, held that
God created the world according to natural laws and then withdrew
to a separate, supernatural realm. "This God has no intimate, abiding

relationship with the world, and the world can no longer be considered as a created realm daily sustained and directed by the divine creative spirit," concludes Wirzba. Following Weber, he argues that such beliefs contributed mightily to disenchantment, "the reduction of the world to the status of objects."[71] In this historical context, Francis Bacon, a nominalist and one of the founders of modern science, called for making nature subordinate to man: "Nature must be 'bound into service' and made a 'slave,' put 'in constraint' and 'molded' by the mechanical arts."[72]

EVEN AS SCHOLARS and theologians reaffirmed religion's insistence on a transcendent God removed from nature, others looked outside the canon to document the validity of a spiritual appreciation of animals and the land. For example, the Reverend James Parks Morton, dean of the Cathedral of Saint John the Divine in New York City, asked James Lovelock to address the congregation after the 1979 publication of his first book on Gaia. Morton became famous for emphasizing the spiritual dimensions of Gaia, what he called "Earth as God's Body," part of the "sacramental universe" theological movement in which God is conceived as both immanent within nature and transcendent beyond it.[73]

The space photographs of Earth reappeared in unexpected contexts. In his 1987 New Year's address, Pope John Paul II cited them as catalysts to spiritual awakening and renewal: "From the time that we were first able to see pictures of the world from space, a perceptible change has taken place in our understanding of the planet and its immense beauty and fragility."[74] The Evangelical Lutheran Church offered a similar reflection in the 1980s: "The Bible tells us of the goodness of creation. The first photographs of the earth relayed from space a quarter of a century ago gave us a portrait of a good planet. On a seemingly endless and void background, the earth appeared as a shimmering planet glowing in the light of the sun. An earth-bound audience now had a portrait of the planet God made: the blue oceans, the green and brown continents, the white clouds and ice caps."[75]

Starting in the 1970s, new schools of Jewish and Christian religious interpretation, collectively known as "creation theology," endeavored to reconcile traditional faith and a new covenant with nature. No longer was Genesis read simply as the story of God's unconditional grant of dominion over animals and plants. Religious scholars from different denominations pointed to passages such as Genesis 1:21–22 to show God's all-encompassing approval of his creation: "God created the great sea monsters and all kinds of swimming creatures with which the water teems, and all kinds of winged birds. God saw how good it was, and God blessed them, saying, 'Be fertile, multiply, and fill the water of the seas; and let the birds multiply on the earth.'" In Genesis 1:31, God's embrace of all creation is reiterated: "God looked at everything he had made, and he found it very good." At minimum, these scholars argued, God's repeated approval of creation meant that human dominion was limited; destroying creatures and the land would go against God's will. One group of Christian scholars interpreted such passages as a call for human "stewardship" of nature: While humans stood superior to the rest of creation, they were obligated to rule or manage animals and the land benevolently.

To other scholars, "stewardship" lacked sufficient critical power to challenge the core traditions. Over the years, creation theology has shifted its emphasis to a part of Genesis that had been virtually ignored, namely the Second Story of Creation. The First Story of Creation was written by an author known as the "Priestly Writer," who lived sometime in the sixth century BC, a time when Judaism was firmly established as a religion, with its priests clearly organized and affiliated with the upper class. Israel was occupied during this period and the Jews were forced into exile—realities that affirmed the importance of violence and domination to religious leaders. These historical and social circumstances influenced the Priestly Writer's view of the natural world.

Contrary to its name and placement in Genesis, the Second Story is thought to have historically preceded the Priestly narrative and to have been written sometime between 1000 and 800 BC. Biblical scholars call the author the Yahwist, because he preferred to use the divine name "Yahweh" in referring to God. The Yahwist's story of creation was placed second in the Bible by the Priestly Writer and his associates when they codified the Old Testament.[76] The Jews abiding in the hills of Canaan at the time of the Yahwist lived close to the land and to animals, and had no firmly established class and religious hierarchy. Consequently, the story of creation set down by the Yahwist and based on Jewish oral traditions and other Near Eastern religions offered a different cosmology than the story told by the Priestly Writer.

The Yahwist stressed an intimate relationship between the first people and the land. In Hebrew, arable land was called *adama*. Thus, the first man, *Adam*, was fashioned from the very soil he farmed—"the God [Yahweh] formed man out of the clay of the ground and blew into his nostrils the breath of life, and so man became a living being" (Genesis 2:7). Seeing that man was alone God then "formed out of the ground various wild animals and various birds of the air." As Old Testament scholar Theodore Hiebert notes, in Hebrew both humans and animals are called *nepes hayya*, meaning "animate creature." God blew the "breath of life," *nismat hayyi*, into both animals and humans. The breath of life includes both physical life and soul or spirit—the two are not separated in this account. Thus, in the Yahwist creation story, humans and animals are fundamentally alike. Hiebert concludes, "This point has been muddled for centuries in English translations by a succession of translators determined to draw a distinction between human beings and animals where none exists in the Hebrew text."[77]

The Yahwist text makes no references to human domination over nature. Nor does it mention God offering man a Covenant after the flood, in which "dread fear of you shall come upon all the animals of the earth and all the birds of the air" (Genesis 9:2). Instead, the Yahwist reports that God made an infinitely more benign promise: "Never again will I doom the earth because of man, since the desires of man are evil from the start; nor will I ever again strike down all living beings, as I have done. As long as the earth lasts, / seedtime and harvest, / cold and heat, / summer and winter, / day and night / shall not cease" (Genesis 8:21–22).

To the Yahwist, God is not really separate from nature. He manifests himself in thunderstorms, in the hail that plagued the Egyptians before the Jews' exodus, and in the canopy of a majestic oak tree.[78] He requires only the plainest of altars, one made of earth (*adama*) or uncut field stones, because "by putting a tool to it you desecrate it"[79] (Exodus 20:25). As Theodore Hiebert concludes, "Nature therefore cannot accurately be described as desacralized, inert, or profane in the Yahwist's epic. It is the realm through and within which God becomes present in the world."[80]

The Book of Job, too, provided a remarkable source for the reenchantment of nature. Written sometime between 700 and 500 BC, the narrative portrays Job as a wealthy and pious man who is tested by Satan and God in a series of painful misfortunes. Job loses his wife and children; his wealth vanishes; and he breaks out in severe boils "from the soles of his feet to the crown of his head" (Job 2:7). Job finds his punishments both unjust and mysterious; he begs God, his "accuser," to "write out his indictment" (Job 31:35). In response, God speaks to Job out of a desert thunderstorm, setting before him a vision of Earth in which humans are not the sole focus of creation. God asks Job question after question: "Have you entered into the sources of the sea, or walked about in the depths of the abyss?" (Job 38:16); "Do you hunt the prey for the lioness or appease the hunger of her cubs, / While they crouch in their dens, or lie in wait in the thicket?" (Job 38:39–40); "Who has given the wild ass his freedom, and who has loosed him from his bonds?" (Job 39:5–6); "Does the eagle fly up at your command to build his nest aloft?" (Job 39:27). As Norman Wirzba says, this is a "wild God who delights in wildness," taking pleasure and pride in every part of creation.[81] Each of God's rhetorical questions to Job is in essence a blessing, a consecration of nature and its creatures.

Scholars of the New Testament and Christian traditions also participated in the reevaluation. Focusing on elements of Christianity that rejected Neoplatonism and the "life preserver" approach to redemption, they looked, for example, to Saint Augustine (334–430), who affirmed the worth of all creation as testament to the glory of God. Criticizing those who regarded nature as a source of evil after the Fall, Augustine wrote: "They do not consider how admirable these things are in their own places, how excellent in their own natures, how beautifully adjusted to the rest of creation, and how they contribute grace to the universe, as to a commonwealth."[82] His essays celebrated Earth and its creator: "Shall I speak of the manifold and various loveliness of sky, and earth, and sea; of the plentiful supply and wonderful qualities of the light; of sun, moon, and stars; of the shade of trees; of the colors and perfume of flowers?"[83]

Saint Francis of Assisi (1182–1226) was another inspiration to the new theology. His "Canticle of the Sun" praises God by celebrating all his creation: Brother Sun, Sister Moon and the stars, Brother Wind, Sister Water, Brother Fire, and Mother Earth—"Who nourishes and governs us, / And produces various fruits with many-colored flowers and herbs."[84] In 1979 Pope Paul II named Francis the "heavenly Patron of those who promote ecology," and subsequently referred to him as an inspiration to maintain "fraternity with all those good and beautiful things which Almighty God has created."[85] Since the 1970s Francis of Assisi has become a widely honored religious figure even outside Catholicism. Many Protestant churches, especially Episcopal ones, mark the anniversary of his canonization with ceremonies blessing animals and emphasizing human-animal kinship ties as sacred bonds.

More obscure religious figures have also been rediscovered in the quest for reenchantment. Norman Wirzba called his 2003 critique of Christian denigration of nature *The Paradise of God*, in reference to

the works of the seventeenth-century English poet Thomas Traherne. Traherne wrote, "The world is a mirror of infinite beauty, yet
no man sees it. It is a Temple of Majesty, yet no man regards it. It is a
region of Light and Peace, did not men disquiet it. It is the Paradise
of God."[86] And in this paradise, man had an obligation to love, because "by Love our Souls are married and solder'd to the creatures
and it is our Duty like God to be united to them all."[87] Meanwhile,
well-known religious leaders such as John Wesley, the nineteenth-
century founder of Methodism, have sometimes been shown to have
ideas far different from the dominant Christian canon. Wesley rejected Martin Luther's belief that nature embodied the "wrath of
God" and instead thought all animals would be redeemed by God.
Thus all merited human respect, even those considered monsters,
predators, or hideous: "It may enlarge our hearts towards those poor
creatures to reflect that, as vile as they appear in our eyes, not one of
them is forgotten in the sight of our Father which is in Heaven."[88]

Having recovered lost traditions and forgotten leaders, this new
creation theology postulated what theologian John F. Haught calls in
*The Promise of Nature* (1993) a "sacramental universe," a vision of the
natural world as "the primary symbolic disclosure of God. Religious
texts and traditions are still important, but the cosmos itself is the
primary medium through which we come to know the sacred."[89] Many
different Christian denominations adopted variations of this teaching. The United States Conference of Catholic Bishops (in a pastoral
statement printed with a cover photo of the Earth) credited the environmental movement for reawakening "appreciation of the truth
that, through the gifts of nature, men and women encounter their
Creator."[90] Evangelical Lutherans declared that "the God who is
wholly other is very near. . . . The sacraments underscore the intimate relationship between God and a nature that is neither unclean
nor unspiritual. In a variety of ways nature imparts God's faithfulness
and loving kindness."[91] One influential report to the 1988 meeting of
the World Council of Churches called the universe God's "body."[92]

In creation theology's sacramental universe, redemption became something quite different from individual salvation in which a soul ascends to a distant heaven. Instead, Earth was what had to be saved. In the words of the American Baptist Churches, USA, "The Creator-Redeemer seeks the renewal of the creation and calls the people of God to participate in saving acts of renewal."[93] Thus environmental restoration is not purely a secular activity, but instead is a sacred act, a crucial form of redemption, what Norman Wirzba calls "the setting right of creation so that it can be what it was first intended to be."[94]

BY THE EARLY 1990s the ideas articulated by creation theology were spreading throughout religious circles and beyond, further extending the culture of enchantment. The notion of nature as sacred found support in unlikely places. In 1991, for example, thirty-two Nobel laureates and other eminent scientists wrote an "Open Letter to the American Religious Community," urging mainstream religious denominations to embrace environmental restoration as a spiritual obligation: "Many of us have had profound experiences of awe and reverence before the universe. We recognize that what is regarded as sacred is most likely to be treated with respect. Efforts to safeguard the planetary environment need to be infused with a vision of the sacred and as a universal moral priority."[95]

Such initiatives prompted the formation in 1993 of The National Religious Partnership for the Environment (NRPE), a joint program uniting the United States Conference of Catholic Bishops, the coordinating body embracing all policy agencies for the Catholic Church; the National Council of Churches of Christ, a federation of thirty-four Protestant, Eastern Orthodox, and African-American denominations; the Coalition on the Environment and Jewish Life, a group encompassing all four branches of Judaism; and the Evangelical Environmental Network, including twenty-three evangelical religious organizations and educational institutes.[96] All told, NRPE claims to encompass faith groups serving over one hundred million Americans. In the 1990s, NRPE sent out over four hundred thousand study guides to congregations, who in turn reproduced more of them for members. More recently, in 2002, the Evangelical Environmental Network launched its famous "What Would Jesus Drive?" campaign to foster awareness of the connections between auto exhaust and global warming, promoting fuel economy as a Christian obligation.

Public opinion surveys point to the widespread diffusion of creation theology. In the mid-1990s, when anthropologist Willett Kempton and his colleagues asked if people agreed that "because God created the universe, it is wrong to abuse it," 78 percent concurred. In extensive face-to-face interviews with a sample of survey respondents, the anthropologists found a variety of beliefs in the sacredness of nature. Religiosity, Kempton noted, seemed "not to be getting in the way of environmental support, but instead is reinforcing and justifying it."[97] A decade later, in 2004, political scientist John C. Green found that 55 percent of respondents agreed with the statement, "Stricter rules to protect the environment are necessary even if they cost jobs or result in higher prices." It was a negative way to pose a question about protecting the environment, and unsurprisingly, those especially attuned to the plight of the poor and working class—African-American and Latino Protestants and Catholics—were less likely to agree. However, in all the other religious groups, more than half of those surveyed were in favor of even costly environmental reforms: They received support from 52 percent of Evangelical Protestants, 60 percent of Catholics, 61 percent of mainline Protestants, and 67 percent of Jews.[98] There cannot be any doubt that beliefs in the sacredness of creation have radically increased since the culture of enchantment first emerged in the early 1970s.

CREATION THEOLOGIANS AND religious leaders have also reconceived the notion of environmental sin for the contemporary

era. Ecumenical Patriarch Bartholomew I, leader of the Greek Orthodox Church, sees the development of nuclear energy and weapons, toxic
chemicals, and biological weapons as destroying the world's "perfect
divine harmony." In a 1988 Encyclical Letter to church leaders,
Bartholomew warned that "Nature has rebelled against humanity,
which abuses it."[99] Similarly, the Evangelical Lutheran Church declared in 1993 that "scripture sees human sin as disrupting the rest of
creation. . . . Massive degradation, suffering by humanity and the rest
of creation—such are the signs of our failure to follow God's call."[100]
James Nash, one of the principal proponents of a sacramental universe,
reiterates the notion of sin as failure to follow God but also stresses the
ways in which environmental disruptions remind us of limits we must
respect or else perish: "Theologically interpreted, the natural order
sets boundaries to rebellion."[101]

Thinkers outside the Christian tradition have taken up the theme
of environmental disasters as nature's revolt against human arro-
gance. In *Turtle Island*, poet Gary Snyder warned that if animals and
landscapes are not taken into account, "they will revolt against us.
They will submit non-negotiable demands about our stay on the earth.
We are beginning to get non-negotiable demands right now from the
air, the water, the soil."[102] Theodore Roszak has reminded his readers
that premodern peoples often understood their environmental catas-
trophes as signs of the goddess's wrath: "Many of the oldest rituals
are acts of propitiation offered to a sometimes fierce and punishing
divinity, an Earth who can be an angry mother as well as a bountiful one."[103]

More recently, the notion of environmental disasters as forms of
mysterious demonic or divine retribution have made inroads into the
wider culture. Stories about nature's "revenge" created new types of
hybrid discourses. Take, for example, the mysterious illnesses that
emerged in North Carolina in 1995, after tremendous floods washed
massive amounts of wastes from industrial hog farms into coastal waters. Within months, fish started dying from compromised immune

systems and bleeding sores, and people who swam in the waters came down with strange illnesses, reporting odd symptoms like a sensation of electricity running through their bodies. North Carolina State biology professor JoAnn Burkholder eventually discovered the cause to be a rare species of dinoflagellate. Dinoflagellates are microscopic, single-cell organisms that cannot readily be classified as plants or animals, since some species use photosynthesis like plants while others eat microscopic animals. And some species resemble both plants and animals, such as the one Burkholder found, *Pfiesteria piscicida*—colloquially termed by some scientists "the cell from hell."[104] The microbe, which normally lived in coastal waters, acted like a benign plant when dormant, but could take on animal characteristics when activated by a massive nutrient influx, such as the wastes from hog farms. In its animal form, *Pfiesteria* released a virulent toxin that destroyed connective tissue.

Burkholder's research met with serious resistance from scientists and state agencies involved in environmental regulation. *Pfiesteria* is quite rare and it readily resumes its dormant plant phase when nutrients are not present—thus some scientists simply missed it in their studies. But Burkholder never gave up. She saw herself on a holy mission, wrote journalist Rodney Barker in *And the Waters Turned to Blood* (1997). "Though she didn't like to talk about it much, there was a religious drive behind a lot of what Burkholder did. It was her own brand of religion, and it had nothing to do with church but rather expressed a reverence for nature. She credited her father for its tenets, though they were also summed up nicely in the Book of Revelation: Honor the earth and its creatures. . . . If there was such a thing as a moral absolute, to her way of thinking it was that desecration of the natural environment, and the risk to animals and humans when land and water were fouled by others, was more than wrong. It was a sin."[105]

Journalistic accounts of other disasters show this same cultural conception. Jon Krakauer's bestselling *Into Thin Air: A Personal Account of the Mt. Everest Disaster* (1997) gives a first-person account of the deaths of nine climbers and Sherpa porters on Mt. Everest in May 1996. While in many ways Krakauer simply tells the story of an adventure gone wrong, he offers a cautionary morality tale as well. The climbers who died had all paid tens of thousands of dollars to join commercial expeditions that virtually guaranteed ascent to the Everest summit, the highest and one of the most dangerous treks in the world. What was once a calling for elite climbers had now become a form of tourism.

The process of commercial transformation had profaned both Mt. Everest and the whole region. The village of Khumba had formerly been "an earthly paradise, a real-life Shangri-La," writes Krakauer, but by 1996 "entire valleys have been denuded of trees to meet the increased demand for firewood."[106] Near the Khumba Glacier base camp, "the three or four stone toilets were literally overflowing with excrement. . . . Huge stinking piles of human feces lay everywhere."[107] The indigenous Sherpas practiced Buddhism with what Krakauer calls a "distinctly animistic flavor," venerating "a tangled mélange of deities and spirits who are said to inhabit the canyons, rivers, and peaks of the region."[108] Most tourists, on the other hand, showed no respect for the land. Some even disregarded local customs, such as the Sherpa taboo against unmarried people having sex near the mountain. "The goddess Chomolunga," Krakauer reports from his interviews with the Sherpas, "doesn't tolerate 'jiggy jiggy'—*anything* unclean—on her sacred mountain."[109]

Krakauer's account clearly lays the disaster at the feet of the trip leaders who violated important safety rules, leading to the group's exposure to a violent snowstorm. But he also suggests that the climbers died because they dishonored Mt. Everest, whom the Sherpas call Sagamathaji, "mother goddess of the earth." As for the Sherpa casualties, Krakauer ends his book with a quote from a Sherpa orphan explaining that his people had a moral obligation to protect Mother Earth, but instead "they helped outsiders find their way into the sanctuary and violate every limb of her body by standing on top of her, crowing in victory, and dirtying and polluting her bosom."[110]

Even pulp novels picked up the theme of nature's revolt. In James Polk's *Sea Change* (1999), scientists from the U.S. Army's Chemical Corps and the U.S. Navy's Biological Defense Program create a new species of *Pfiesteria* as a weapon. But the beast turns on its creators and escapes into the open ocean, where it becomes a mass organism with a primitive will, awareness, and ability to move on its own: "*Pfiesteria junkers* thirsted for warm blood. Marine mammals and humans were the most plentiful source of that."[111] *Sea Change* is virtually a popular fiction version of Ecumenical Patriarch Bartholomew I's warning about nature rebelling against humanity for abusing it.

IN LATE DECEMBER 2004, an earthquake on the floor of the Pacific Ocean gave rise to a tsunami that killed over two hundred thousand people in Thailand, Sri Lanka, Indonesia, and India. As the scale of the disaster became evident, the theme of nature's revolt permeated the major media. Carlos Fuentes, writing in the *Los Angeles Times*, argued that "when Nature punishes us, we should try to reflect on all our persistent, man-made tsunamis against Nature and Life. Global warming. The hole in the ozone layer. Acid rain."[112] Environmentalists noted that countries such as the Maldives, which preserved the coral reefs surrounding it, suffered far fewer casualties than countries such as Thailand, where reefs had been damaged and extensive mangrove forests removed for hotel development and shrimp farms.[113] Simon Winchester, a student of earthquakes and volcanic explosions, harked back to James Lovelock's Gaia theory as a way of coming to terms with the disaster. The deaths and destruction were horrible, he wrote, "but they may also serve some deeper planetary purpose, one quite hidden to our own beliefs." His op-ed in the *New York Times* was entitled "The Year the Earth Fought Back."[114]

At the same time, the media ran many stories about indigenous peoples whose premodern cultures had helped them predict the tsunami and find high ground. The chief of the Moken, an indigenous people living on South Surin Island off the west coast of Thailand, noted that the tide that day had receded farther than any in his memory—tribal elders had warned him this was a sign a "people-eating wave" was on its way. Chief Klathalay moved his tribe to high ground. Thai media and politicians subsequently declared the tribe to be heroes whose culture—based on animistic beliefs that the ocean, their island, and all objects have spirits—should be preserved. Tsunamis, the Moken believe, came because the sea was angry.[115]

The Jarawa and Onge tribes of India also escaped thanks to ancient cultural traditions that told them how to interpret nature's warnings. A Jarawa elder saw a boy become dizzy with a strange headache, an early sign of an offshore earthquake; the elder led his people to safety. The Onge noticed that water in the creek near their village had disappeared, something their elders had told them meant the sea was retreating to form a massive wave. They fled.[116]

These stories represent yet another strand in the cultural reenchantment of nature. Indigenous people survived because their cultures were still firmly tied to the land and sea, and they conceived of the land and sea as enchanted—as constantly communicating with them. Modern people, living at a remove from nature, could not understand the signs of impending catastrophe, even if some, like Sri Lanka fishermen, knew the ocean well. Cultural and emotional distance from the Earth left them vulnerable to an "angry" ocean.

Some have sought to close that distance through ritual. Surfers in Southern California held a memorial service for the tsunami victims, a Hawaiian "paddle-out." Organizer Mary Setterholm explained: "Surfers believe life comes from the sea, and the paddle-out brings it back to the beginning. It's closing the cycle of life." Surfers honored the dead in each country, and a Chumash Indian medicine man blew a conch shell and recited the Four Corners prayer to the spirits of the west, the south, the east, and the north. With the dead remembered and blessed, relationships with the ocean could be renewed. "We've been so afraid of the ocean, and it's so beautiful again. I was mad at it, and this allows me to forgive," said one participant.[117] Surfers in Santa Monica forgiving the ocean and the Moken on South Surin Island asking each year for the ocean to forgive them—both ceremonial rituals aim to renew communication and reestablish kinship with a living sea.

# 5

## Eco-Warriors and Blood Sacrifice

Within the culture of enchantment, the eco-warrior holds a special place. Born out of the tattered vestiges of the counterculture, the environmental militant combined a belief in the sacredness of nature with the conviction that the political and social system that should have guarded it was utterly corrupt—not only failing to protect the natural world but complicit in its destruction. Beginning in the early 1970s, the desire to stand in opposition drew together a disparate collection of former hippies, practitioners of Native American spiritualism, New Leftists, antiwar Vietnam veterans, and public lands activists enraged by the compromises of mainstream protest. They had no clearly defined ideology, but shared a willingness to break the law. Eco-warriors pulled surveyors' stakes on new roads and construction sites; blocked logging roads; "spiked" redwood trees in ancient, old-growth forests with metal rods or nails to shatter saw blades; sank "pirate" whaling vessels violating international laws; burned half-built ski resorts being constructed on undeveloped lands; and released animals scheduled for slaughter or medical experimentation from their cages. In actions ranging from civil disobedience to violent attacks, the culture's most extreme wing sought to stop business as usual and demonstrate that the destruction of nature was neither necessary nor inevitable.

These kinds of actions had a long history, of course. Billboard destruction was a popular pastime for early environmentalists in the late 1950s in New Mexico and northern Arizona, with some teams destroying as many as thirty a night.[1] Later, a group known as the Eco-Rangers staged similar attacks in southern Arizona. A far more serious campaign raged in the northeastern part of that state after the Hopi and Navajo tribal councils secretly voted in 1964 to allow Peabody Energy to take eight million tons of coal a year from reservation lands, an operation that would create a forty-one-square-mile strip mine.[2] The coal was to be shipped as a water-fed slurry two hundred miles from the mine on Black Mesa to Laughlin, Nevada, to fuel the region's massive Mojave electrical power plant. Water for the slurry would come from the aquifer underlying Black Mesa, which supplied drinking water for both the Hopi and Navajo and their livestock, as well as from two-thirds of the Navajo Colorado River allocation.[3] Five additional plants were slated for the Four Corners region of Utah, Arizona, Colorado, and New Mexico, a plan the National Academy of Sciences blasted as turning the entire region into "a national sacrifice area" for electrical power.[4]

In 1970, as the mining operation got under way and the full scope of the project became apparent, Jack Loeffler, a jazz musician and former army bugler radicalized by witnessing three nuclear explosions while stationed at the Nevada Proving Grounds, formed the Black Mesa Defense Fund. The group generated extraordinary publicity, ran newspaper ads comparing mining on the mesa to "ripping apart St. Peter's to get the marble," and filed numerous lawsuits.[5] When all else failed, some members tried to blow up the coal slurry. They did not succeed, and the group ultimately dissolved, but for years afterward a mysterious figure known as the Arizona Phantom persistently sabotaged Peabody Coal's train tracks and heavy equipment.[6]

Still, property destruction by environmentalists was scattered, and those behind it little known outside their regions. All that changed in 1975 with the publication of Edward Abbey's *The Monkey Wrench Gang*. At the simplest level, the book is a rollicking tale of four malcontents who emerge from the 1960s angry and ready to fight, this time against developers who are turning their beloved New Mexico into "open desert . . . scraped bare of all vegetation, all life, by giant D-9 bulldozers [like the] Rome plows leveling Vietnam."[7] The gang pulls down billboards, destroys construction equipment, and even blows up a bridge, leading to the crash of an unmanned Peabody Coal train crossing it. Their ultimate goal is to destroy Glen Canyon Dam, using three houseboats filled with ammonium nitrate fertilizer and diesel oil. The book is clearly meant as satire—the Monkey Wrench gang members are funny, sexy characters who never actually hurt anyone. At a deeper level, however, Abbey was dead serious. A committed environmentalist, he had participated in billboard destruction in the 1950s, had publicly declared his opposition to Glen Canyon Dam, and was close to Black Mesa activist Jack Loeffler. (A character much like the Arizona Phantom even makes an appearance late in the book.) Indeed, most of *The Monkey Wrench Gang* characters were based on real people (sometimes composites of several activists) who had fought real battles. The novel turned these previously unknown men and women into folk heroes and heralded the arrival of a new type on the American cultural landscape.

From the beginning of U.S. history, America's core mythology has involved a warrior, often a loner living on the margins, who defended society and defeated its enemies. Each of these victories—whether the lone gunfighter killing Indians in a nineteenth-century Western novel, or the determined G.I. holding off the Germans or the Japanese in a World War II movie—confirmed the basic technological and moral superiority of the United States; in the American myth, might and right went together. Each also reinvigorated the country's social and moral order through a process historian Richard

Slotkin calls "regeneration through violence," and affirmed the masculine warrior as the nation's iconic figure.[8] But the U.S. defeat in Vietnam left this core mythology in shreds. During the 1970s, many American men sought to reconstitute it with a right-wing fantasy culture of paramilitary heroes. Warriors like Rambo and Dirty Harry fought outside a military and police establishment controlled by cowardly liberals, defeating Communists, terrorists, and drug lords, and in doing so restored the lost pre-Vietnam social order.[9] Abbey, however, turned the mythology in a new direction, redefining patriotism and heroism in a world faced with severe, ongoing environmental degradation.

The hero of *The Monkey Wrench Gang*, George Washington Hayduke, was modeled on Abbey's friend Doug Peacock, who would later lead the search for "ghost" grizzlies described in chapter 2. Peacock had served as both combatant and medic for a U.S. Army Special Forces Unit in the Central Highlands of Vietnam. Deeply embittered by the killing of Vietnamese civilians and indigenous hill people he had witnessed, and by the lack of a viable American mission, he returned to the United States in 1968, determined to find solace and isolation in the American West.[10] Only his search for grizzlies, he said, kept his memories of the war from dominating his daily life: "Something big was out there. For the first time since returning to the world, my thoughts chose themselves without Vietnam intruding."[11] Peacock's quest to commune with the bears soon led him to study Native American spiritualism, where bears were seen as "gods sent down to earth to make men humble."[12]

Peacock, along with other Vietnam veterans who had fled mainstream society for the Rocky Mountains, became the prototypes for the eco-warrior. The former soldiers were already outsiders, renegades, with contempt for a system that had destroyed the country of Vietnam and the innocence that had led them to fight there, and now was destroying their postwar mountain refuge. Some of the more radical veterans began to actively sabotage development projects.

Peacock describes removing the cap of an oil well in southern Colorado, and dropping pipe and used drill bits down the hole. "It was a token gesture; just so the scumbags would know not everyone applauds."[13] Another time, while Peacock was living in Montana, an oil exploration helicopter was fire-bombed. While no one was caught, the veterans thought the arsonist was one of their own. Peacock reports the celebration among the vets at the local hangout, the Goliath Bar: "A small piece of the world had been corrected. Our unspoken solidarity grew out of an unfinished war that we still seemed to be fighting."[14]

Like many Vietnam veterans of that time, Peacock remained heavily armed, by his own account carrying three pistols, a rifle, and a shotgun in his jeep at one point.[15] (Hayduke has virtually the same arsenal and car.[16]) But unlike the frontiersman-gunfighter of traditional mythology or the paramilitary warrior of the 1970s, the eco-warrior possesses weapons to symbolize his strength and seriousness rather than to actually use them. Peacock reports that early on in his quest to be near grizzly bears, a big male charged him, coming within thirty feet. Peacock slowly drew his Western-style Magnum revolver and "peered down the gun barrel into the dull red eyes of the huge grizzly." But just like in the last days of his Vietnam service, "I knew once again that I was not going to pull the trigger. My shooting days were over."[17] In putting down his pistol, Peacock thus came to the same realization that Aldo Leopold did in the 1940s after he shot a wolf and watched her die: Big predators like wolves and bears had a right to live. And like Leopold, Peacock came to feel a compelling personal moral obligation to help them survive.

Edward Abbey understood quite well that he was subverting America's core cultural mythology: It's no accident that Hayduke's first and middle names are George Washington. His eco-warrior—unlike the old-fashioned gunfighter or the modern paramilitary warrior—does not kill to regenerate the world; he sabotages to *preserve* it. The eco-warrior who removes survey stakes or burns bulldozers to stop society's encroachment upon the land and its creatures does not fight a foreign "enemy" as much as the power structure of his own society. While neither the gunfighter nor the rage-filled paramilitary warrior is ever at home or at peace, the eco-warrior is well grounded—he draws strength from and loves the land he protects. Moreover, by making monkey-wrenching seem simultaneously important, full of wit, and part of the nation's fundamental cultural tradition, the book—Abbey's most popular, selling 750,000 paperback copies from 1975 to 2000— helped inspire thousands to join direct-action movements and even fostered some degree of public sympathy for eco-sabotage.

One of those inspired by Abbey was Paul Watson, who founded the Sea Shepherd Conservation Society in 1978. Watson, whose high-seas adventures in ramming whaling ships were discussed earlier, saw himself as a vigilante patrolling the ocean frontier: "I guess I plead guilty to being a vigilante, but I can tell you something. If there are no police, then vigilantes will appear, because there will always be somebody to see that crime is never given a free rein."[18] Abbey clearly approved: In his last novel, *Hayduke Lives!*, a sequel to *The Monkey Wrench Gang*, he portrays Watson and his command ship rescuing Hayduke from the Sea of Cortez.[19] In 1991, two years after Abbey's death, Watson named Sea Shepherd's newest vessel, a surplus U.S. coast guard patrol boat, the *Edward Abbey*.[20]

Earth First!, founded in 1980, became the land-based equivalent to Sea Shepherd, and grew from the same disappointment with mainstream environmental organizations. During the late 1970s, several of the largest environmental groups, including The Wilderness Society, the Sierra Club, and the Audubon Society, had joined together to lobby the U.S. Forest Service to grant wilderness designation to some roadless lands under their control and so permanently protect them from road-building or other development. But their lobbying strategy failed. In 1979, when the U.S. Forest Service released its comprehensive study of 125,000 square miles of roadless lands, the coalition got only 23,400 square miles saved as wilderness, a third of them in Alaska. And most of these lands were remote mountain ranges that were not under any real threat from development, rather than a broad range of ecosystems. By contrast, the Forest Service recommended that 56,250 square miles be open for development, and another 17,200 set aside for future consideration. Dave Foreman and Howie Wolkie, working for The Wilderness Society, noticed that the Forest Service study failed to even mention some 28,125 square miles of roadless lands in the West, meaning that these lands were never considered for protection as wilderness in the first place.[21] "We played the game," Wolkie told journalist Rick Scarce. "We were moderate, reasonable, and professional. We had data, statistics, maps, graphs. And we got fucked. That's when I started thinking, 'Something's missing, here. Something isn't working.'"[22]

Despite the coalition's failure to win more extensive wilderness designations, the mainstream environmental groups continued to pursue a strategy of compromise and negotiation. As The Wilderness Society became ever more technocratic, a number of core staff members, known as the Buckaroos for their blend of redneck and counterculture strains and aggressive advocacy for wilderness, found themselves out of favor.[23] In the fall of 1980, the Buckaroos, including Dave Foreman, Howie Wolkie, Bart Koehler, Ron Kezar, and Mike Roselle, journeyed to the famed Pinacate Desert of northern Mexico, a place noted for its austere beauty and mystery. During that trip, a series of long and intense conversations led to a vision of a new kind of environmental organization and strategy, informed by a shared love of Edward Abbey's *Monkey Wrench Gang*. Dave Foreman came up with the name for the new group, Earth First! Mike Roselle drew its logo, a clenched fist in a circle, and someone (no one remembers who) invented its slogan, "No Compromise in Defense of Mother Earth."[24]

From the beginning, Earth First! styled itself as a warrior society to dramatize what Dave Foreman called "visionary wilderness proposals."[25] As former Buckaroo Tim Mahoney explained, "We felt like we were descendents of the frontier ethic."[26] But in this case, "warrior" didn't mean carrying weapons—in fact, they were forbidden. Rather, as Foreman explained in his autobiography, *Confessions of an Eco-Warrior*, society membership required "absolute commitment to and love for this living planet. . . . A warrior recognizes that her life is not the most important thing in her life. A warrior recognizes that there is a greater reality outside her life that must be defended."[27] This new kind of warrior was creative rather than destructive. "If you think of monkeywrenching in the context of the Boston Tea Party instead of the October 1917 Revolution," Foreman says, "it comes off . . . as a very honorable American tradition."[28]

A closer source of inspiration than the Boston Tea Party was Native American spiritualism. Earth First! would become a tribe and develop what Foreman called its own "culture, myth and ritual." In 1967, after leaving the marine corps, Foreman had spent the summer teaching in a Head Start program on a Zuni Indian reservation. There he learned about the Zuni religion and visited many sacred sites. "The Zuni rituals probably had more effect on me than I realized," he later reflected. "Just coming into contact with that whole approach that was so different from the Church of Christ."[29] The Native American "trickster" figure exerted a particular pull on Foreman and his fellow activists. Tricksters like Coyote and Raven are half-human, half-supernatural animals that face foes far more powerful than themselves yet emerge victorious. For example, Raven steals the sun from monsters and so illuminates a dark world, while Coyote steals fire from supernatural beings, giving humans their first chance to keep warm and cook their food. But while tricksters dramatize what can be accomplished with bravery, their characters are also flawed, marred by egotism, greed, and lust. The tricksters' failures provide comic relief and a sense that humans need not be perfect before attempting heroic deeds.

For Earth First!, the trickster tradition became an inspiration for developing creative guerrilla theater. While on the road promoting the group, Foreman was known to tear off his shirt and mime a liminal figure from the wilderness: "I'm the old original half-grizzly, half-wolf, half-rattlesnake from the wilds of Wyoming. I'm the man they call Summer Thunder and Sudden Avalanche. *Hoo-ooo!!!* . . . I eat nineteen oil executives and a barrel of whiskey for breakfast when I'm in robust health and a dead bulldozer and a bushel of dirt-bikers when I'm ailin'."[30] As Foreman explained, "There have always been shamans in society."[31]

On March 21, 1981, the spring equinox, Earth First! convened for the first time, bringing "wilderness warriors, shamans, and chiefs from around the West" to Glen Canyon Dam.[32] There, standing on Glen Canyon Bridge, Edward Abbey told the crowd that the Colorado River had been desecrated by developers who "stole this treasure from us in order to pursue and promote their crackpot ideology of growth, profit, and power—growth for the sake of power, power for the sake of growth." He urged them to "oppose the destruction of our homeland by these alien forces from Houston, Tokyo, Manhattan, D.C., and the Pentagon. And if opposition is not enough, we must resist. And if resistance is not enough, then subvert."[33] As Abbey finished his speech, five Earth First! activists unraveled a three-hundred-foot-long strip of black plastic down Glen Canyon Dam, symbolically creating a fatal crack in it. By ritually dramatizing the destruction of the dam and the renewal of the Colorado River (acts first envisioned in *The Monkey Wrench Gang*), Earth First! created a media event that attracted more than a thousand new subscribers to the *Earth First! Journal*, the group's flagship publication.[34]

This romantic mix of direct action and the culture of enchantment made Earth First! extraordinarily appealing to people who had little or no previous involvement in environmental groups. In 1983, Earth First! planned a road blockade in southern Oregon to try to save the remote Siskiyou Mountains from logging. Steve Marsden, who had once been a logging road engineer, joined the blockade and found that he was not the only person out there who was pushing far beyond his previous commitments. "Most of the people in the blockades weren't environmentalists. They had a feeling for the land, the place. There was a spiritual connection. But they were mostly back-to-the-landers and liberal arts college majors who had moved to the boondocks. Environmental groups had never catalyzed that energy because these people weren't environmentalists."[35] Direct action at Siskiyou, in which people used their own bodies to block the logging trucks, deepened their spiritual connection to the land. As it had at Glen Canyon, direct action also attracted the media, which disseminated images of activists resisting the logging and made the public aware of the consequences of the planned timber harvest. The exposure also brought in even more new members. By the late 1980s over ten thousand people identified themselves as Earth First! supporters.[36]

During the same period other groups emerged to follow the lead of Earth First! and Sea Shepherd in staging events that connected active resistance to enchantment. Randall Hayes first got involved in the defense of Black Mesa in the 1970s. "I hung around the Southwest for ten years, basically as a secretary and chauffeur to the Hopi elders," he told a *Los Angeles Times Magazine* journalist.[37] In March 1981, when Earth First! held its rendezvous at Glen Canyon, Edward Abbey asked Hayes to be on hand with his camera to film the unrolling of the black plastic strip down the side of the dam.[38] Four years later Hayes founded Rainforest Action Network (RAN), which focused on saving both tropical and temperate rain forests from destruction. Central and South American ranchers were burning down forests to convert them to cattle pastures, with much of the meat being sold to fast food chains. In 1986 RAN launched a consumer boycott against Burger King for importing beef from cattle raised in these tropical pastures. Burger King's sales declined by 12 percent the following year, and it subsequently canceled thirty-five million dollars in beef contracts from Central America.

In the 1990s, RAN came to the aid of the U'Wa, an indigenous mountain people in Colombia. Occidental Petroleum and the

Colombian government had rejected many U'Wa territorial claims and wanted to build pipelines and drill for oil on land the people held sacred. Like the Hopi, the U'Wa saw it as their mission in life to keep the Earth in balance; they believed that by protecting their traditional mountain rain forest territory they helped maintain the seasonal and rainfall cycles of the whole planet. After a decade of consumer boycotts against Occidental Petroleum, numerous protests, and national tours featuring U'Wa spiritual and political leaders, the oil company and the Colombian government abandoned the drilling plans.

Next, RAN took on Home Depot for selling redwood from ancient forests in the Pacific Northwest. Demonstrators protested in front of stores, urging consumers to boycott and write letters to the company. Home Depot eventually stopped buying such lumber and switched to wood from commercially grown trees. Subsequent campaigns in the early 2000s took on Citibank, demanding that it stop financing projects such as mining, logging, and ranching that lead to the destruction of rain forests, and urging consumers to destroy their Citi credit cards. A full page ad in the *International Herald Tribune* featured a picture of Citibank's president and the headline, "Put a Face on Global Warming and Forest Destruction." In New York City, RAN eco-saboteurs released a banner across the Citibank corporate headquarters proclaiming "Citi Ethically Bankrupt."[39] Negotiators from RAN and Citibank reached a preliminary agreement in 2004.[40]

Although these campaigns focused specifically on not patronizing Burger King, Home Depot, or Citibank, they implicitly raised a larger issue: RAN was asking the public to affirm that the land and creatures were more important than consumerism. The group has also reached out to Hollywood, both to seek donations and to encourage movies about the world's rain forests and the indigenous people who live in them. Hayes has credited films like *The Emerald Forest* (1985), *At Play in the Fields of the Lord* (1991), *Medicine Man* (1992), and *FernGully: The*

*Last Rainforest* (1992) with helping to promote RAN's direct action campaigns. Viewers made the connection between boycotting companies and preserving the enchanted forests they saw in the films.[41]

GROUPS LIKE RAN advocated nonviolent civil disobedience and used boycotts as their primary forms of direct action. In its early days, Earth First! favored both symbolic protests (like the plastic crack on the Glen Canyon Dam) and acts of actual sabotage—although at first the sabotage, too, was primarily symbolic, and there was often a mischievous tone to their actions. In 1982, five miles of survey stakes marking the proposed path of Getty Oil's new exploration road in Bridger-Teton National Forest disappeared. Bart Koehler, one of the Earth First! founders, says, "We didn't do it. Hell, we were doing a big rally the next day. According to legend, it was a daring daylight raid. It was either beavers—beavers are real fond of survey stakes—or ravens. We have learned over the years that ravens really like survey tape. They like to wear it as headbands and they like to fill their nests with it."[42]

Sea Shepherd also took a multidimensional approach to environmental action. Captain Paul Watson sent out press releases protesting drift-net fishing and illegal whaling, and showed up at all kinds of conferences covering the fate of the oceans. He once had one of the group's ships outfitted with a cannon rigged to fire canned pudding at unwanted boarders or at sailors on another vessel. But Sea Shepherd ships also attacked and rammed illegal whalers on the high seas, and activists scuttled whaling vessels docked in Norway and Portugal.

As the 1980s progressed, however, it became more difficult for environmental groups to practice both the milder forms of direct action and the more serious eco-sabotage that threatened or actually destroyed property. Eco-sabotage was potentially dangerous; people might get hurt or killed. Because tree spikes could injure loggers whose saw blades hit them, Earth First! called for activists to mark the trees they spiked, but sometimes people acting in its name failed to do so. It didn't help that most of the direct-action groups were highly decentralized and did not obey any one authority.

The Reagan administration's crackdown on eco-sabotage further pushed the groups to move in one direction or the other. In 1985 Dave Foreman wrote a how-to manual, *Ecodefense: A Field Guide to Monkeywrenching*.[43] The book, combined with Foreman's many lecture tours as an Earth First! leader, made him a target for a massive Federal Bureau of Investigation campaign. FBI agents found an informer in Arizona's radical environmental circles, and that informer taped conversations among three activists who had previously destroyed electrical towers whose power lines led to uranium mines. The saboteurs were planning another attack in May 1989, targeting electrical towers whose lines powered pumps that took water from the Colorado River. The FBI stopped the attack, arriving just as the men were cutting through the towers. Meanwhile, back in Tucson, FBI agents arrested Foreman on charges of serving as a bagman or conduit for money given to the saboteurs. The bureau's own agents were caught on tape saying that Foreman "isn't the guy we need to pop, I mean, in terms of actual perpetrator. This is the guy we need to pop to send a message." But Foreman agreed to plead guilty to a felony conspiracy charge in exchange for a sentencing arrangement in which his prison term would be delayed for five years. If during that time he was not convicted of other crimes, his felony sentence would be reduced to a misdemeanor and the prison term dropped.[44]

Foreman also agreed to stop mentioning monkey wrenching in public. In 1990, he and his wife, Nancy Morton, published "Good Luck, Darlin'. It's Been Great" in the movement's journal. The two called for Earth First! to disband, adding, "We should then regroup under different names to continue the work to which we are individually best adapted and with those we are most closely related."[45] Foreman subsequently founded the Wildlands Project, a network of groups trying to save large ecosystems from development and connect them with wildlife corridors.

Foreman wasn't the only Earth First! leader to pull back. Judi Bari, an Earth First! leader in the late 1980s campaign to save ancient redwood forests in northern California, favored tactics like leaflets, protest marches, even outreach efforts to loggers, combined with mild civil disobedience like tree-sitting and blockading logging roads. But tree-spiking (at times unmarked) done by some activists made even Bari's milder efforts a target of intense anger from loggers. Although she and her colleague Darryl Cherney both renounced tree-spiking in April 1990, the following month their car was bombed, leaving Bari critically wounded. (No one was ever brought to trial for the attack.) In 1994, convinced the two movement tendencies had to be disconnected, Bari wrote in the *Earth First! Journal* that "it's time to leave the night work to the elves in the woods."

"ELF" WAS THE acronym for the Earth Liberation Front. Begun in England in 1992, it was a splinter group from Earth First! and favored large-scale property destruction. ELF followed the lead of an earlier movement, the Animal Liberation Front (ALF), which was organized into autonomous secret cells, and attacked facilities like animal research laboratories and mink farms. ELF cells likewise operated freely, picking their own targets. Both the ALF and ELF proclaimed their goal to be "anarchist primitivism"—a world in which people would live in leaderless tribes, subsisting on a bountiful, renewed Earth.[46]

ELF attacks in the United States began in October 1996, when activists, frustrated by the Clinton administration's "salvage logging" policy that opened many national forests to the timber industry, burned a U.S. Forest Service station and a truck in Willamette National Forest near Eugene, Oregon. The group's first public statement appeared on the Internet in 1997, dated "Beltane" after the Gaelic

May Day festival, and laid out the movement's manifesto. Through attacks and press communiqués, ELF would act to "speed up the collapse of industry, to scare the rich, and to undermine the foundations of the state. We embrace social and deep ecology as a practical resistance movement. We have to show the enemy we are serious about defending what is sacred."[47] Later that year, also in Oregon, ELF cells burned down a horse-rendering plant and a Bureau of Land Management corral for captured wild horses, while an ALF cell claimed credit for releasing twelve thousand captive mink from their cages.

In 1998, ELF started carrying out actions on a much larger scale, including burning a planned ski resort near Vail, Colorado. In 1999, after the demonstrations against the World Trade Organization in Seattle, activists began to target global capitalism and the consumer society. Research labs working on genetically modified organisms, like special grasses for golf courses, were destroyed. Sport-utility vehicle dealerships across the country went up in flames. By 2001 ELF and ALF attacks were estimated to have caused over forty million dollars in property damage. That year, FBI director Louis Freeh publicly declared that the Earth Liberation Front constituted the number one domestic terrorist threat in the United States.[48] In 2003, ELF saboteurs in San Diego set fires to large apartment complexes and houses under construction in what were once open spaces, causing over fifty million dollars in damages.[49]

As dramatic as they were, these attacks, like Earth First!'s direct actions and monkey wrenching, were mostly symbolic—that is, they followed the nineteenth-century anarchist tradition of "propaganda by the deed," in which violence was theoretically justified as the best way to communicate to a numbed, oppressed populace that radical social change was possible. ELF's actions were not intended to inspire the masses to pick up weapons for outright war against the state and industry, but rather to awaken the public to an increasingly urgent situation and to the fact that the environmental movement would no longer be

appeased by token reform. Activists also used the mythological significance of fire as both a punitive and a transformative force. Burning
down a horse-rendering plant or a ski resort in a previously undeveloped area simultaneously punished business owners and eradicated
stains of evil, preparing the ground for a new beginning where nature
could once again bloom.

But despite the shared symbolic charge, the ELF attacks marked
an important break from civil disobedience practiced by groups like
the Rainforest Action Network. The stakes were higher: Activists engaged in civil disobedience typically face arrest and prosecution for
relatively minor offenses such as trespassing and disturbing the peace,
but burning down fifty-million-dollar apartment complexes, research labs, and truck dealerships are all major felony offenses that
can result in decades in jail. Other risks are higher as well. Both the
Animal and Earth Liberation Fronts have declared that cells need to
plan actions to avoid hurting people, and so far, their attacks have
not led to any human deaths. But unlike more moderate groups,
which see avoiding bystander injury or deaths as absolutely necessary
to preserve their moral authority, these groups admit it could happen
and find the risk acceptable. In 2002, Craig Rosebraugh, a longtime
spokesperson for the Earth Liberation Front, was asked by a House
of Representatives subcommittee on ecoterrorism: "Are you personally concerned that one day an ELF- or ALF-perpetrated attack will
wind up killing or wounding someone?" Rosebraugh replied, "No, I
am more concerned with massive numbers of people dying at the
hands of greedy capitalists if such actions are not taken."[50]

Eventually, Rosebraugh resigned his spokesperson position, in part
because he no longer agreed that burning a few SUVs or a timber
yard could accomplish the movement's goals. In rejecting these symbolic politics he stopped being an eco-warrior and instead became a
revolutionary soldier. He wanted a Ford plant dynamited and outright violent revolution against the state. "Reformist measures, by

their very design," he said, "do not stand a chance against the privileged white male capitalist power structure."[51]

IF ECO-WARRIORS BY definition cannot kill people and maintain a superior moral position, they can still suffer and even die for their beliefs. Just as the sacrifice of dead and wounded soldiers in war culture is used to prompt others to join the battle, so, too, do the sacrifices of environmental activists spur other recruits.[52] After Craig Marshall (known as "Critter") and his comrade Jeffrey Leurs ("Free") were convicted and sentenced for firebombing an SUV dealership, another ELF cell attacked the same business, leaving a communiqué: "Romania Chevrolet is the same location that was targeted last June, for which two earth warriors, Free and Critter, are being persecuted. The fire that burns within Free and Critter burns within all of us and cannot be extinguished by locking them up."[53]

Most strikingly, the sacrifice and death of eco-warriors can lead to a consecration of the land and animals they tried to protect. When Brazilian activist Chico Mendez was murdered in 1987 because he tried to stop the Amazon rain forest from being clear-cut, burned, and turned into ranchland, his death received worldwide media attention and brought new attention to the destruction of the Amazon. The 2005 death of Sister Dorothy Stang, a longtime forest activist and advocate of sustainable development in the northern Brazilian state of Para, evoked a similar reaction. Stang, who helped organize the poor to save the forests from clear-cutting, was shot multiple times by hired gunmen believed to be working for a local rancher.[54] Within a week, more than sixty environmental and human rights groups from around the globe signed a letter to Brazilian president Luiz Inácio Lula da Silva demanding immediate action lest the president "risk making history as the champion of rural violence, illegal occupation of public lands, and illegal logging."[55] Da Silva immediately sent in military forces to hunt for Stang's killers, and signed decrees establishing a national park of nearly 1,720 square miles and a forest preserve of over 12,700 square miles.

In 1990, after Earth First! activist Judi Bari was nearly killed by a car bomb, the media suggested that she had made it herself and that it had gone off accidentally. But by the time Bari died of cancer in 1997, she was remembered as a hero, a gallant figure who played her fiddle in Earth First! demonstrations blocking logging roads. After part of Headwaters Forest became California parkland, activists built a shrine there dedicated to her.[56] The City of Oakland declared May 24, the date of the car bomb explosion, Judi Bari Day to commemorate her blood sacrifice for the land.[57] In 1998, another redwood forest defender, David "Gypsy" Chain, died after a Pacific Lumber Company logger felled a tree that struck him on the head (fellow activists who witnessed the event describe the logger's act as deliberate murder). Chain's death motivated a whole new generation of tree-sitters and forest activists whose trespassing and civil disobedience curtailed lumber harvests.[58] Their protests compounded Pacific Lumber's economic problems and in 2006 the company put ninety-four square miles of land—over a quarter of its total holdings—up for sale.[59] Two years later, the Fisher family (of Gap stores fame) bought the company through bankruptcy court, ended clear-cutting, and pledged to harvest no more wood than the forest could grow each year. The tree-sitters began coming down: They'd won.[60]

In 1977, Kenyan environmentalist Wangari Maathai formed the Green Belt Movement because she grew up believing in the "sacredness of nature and the environment." The movement planted over thirty million trees and successfully fought to save Uhuru Park, Nairobi's last open space, from development.[61] During her twenty-seven years of environmental struggle, Maathai was arrested many times, and was once beaten to unconsciousness by the police. In 2004 she was awarded the Nobel Peace Prize.

Not surprisingly, the figure of the martyred environmentalist has attracted the attention of the film industry. Dian Fossey, who was murdered in 1985 after working for many years to protect endangered mountain gorillas in Rwanda, was honored in the 1988 film *Gorillas in the Mist.*[62] Likewise, the 2003 Chinese film *Mountain Patrol* was based on a conflict that had raged in the mountains of Tibet during the 1990s. Tibetan poachers were shooting tens of thousands of antelope to sell their pelts for wool, while Chinese and Tibetan government officials did nothing to halt the slaughter. Faced with the impending extermination of a species sacred in traditional Tibetan culture, a few men formed a militia to hunt down the poachers and honor the slain animals—whose skinned carcasses had been left to rot—with burials and cremations. Most patrol members died on these missions, killed either by the poachers or brutal winter storms. After a Beijing newspaper publicized their fight, the Chinese government established a national park in the mountains and instituted military patrols that reduced the poaching. *Mountain Patrol* achieves mythic resonance by reframing classic Western and war movie traditions to show honorable men fighting and dying to protect animals and places.[63]

Around the world, blood sacrifice by eco-warriors is increasingly seen as reasonable, even noble. *Outside Magazine* journalist Peter Heller expressed this growing sensibility in his account of Sea Shepherd's 2006 efforts to stop the Japanese whaling fleet hunting in the Antarctic Sea: "The whales could not advocate for themselves. They had no allies on the entire planet who were willing to intervene at all costs, even their own death—except Watson and Sea Shepherd. What was insane about that? Human beings were willing to lay down their lives for territory, resources, national honor, religion. What was more insane about being willing to lay down your life for another species?"[64] Blood sacrifice adds depth to the culture of enchantment, and motivation for people and governments to honor fallen heroes by honoring their cause: forging a new covenant between society and nature.

# Part II

## TROUBLES
## IN PARADISE

# 6

---

## Loving It to Death

Radical changes to cultural traditions and social structures always occur unevenly: With every change, new problems and contradictions emerge. Often, the full implications of a new idea are not understood until change is well under way. In other instances, the very processes of change can provoke unintended consequences. This has certainly been true for the culture of enchantment. Enchantment may draw people close to nature, but these people frequently use the land and ocean in ways the creators of the culture never envisioned—indeed, in ways quite opposite from what they had in mind. The results can be disastrous.

The resacralization of land is a prime example. Nature writing, landscape photography, and the efforts of preservationists have made millions aware of magnificent, remote wilderness areas, but the very popularity of these formerly wild places has devastated them. In 1970, only four cruise ships were making regular journeys up the Alaskan coast to Glacier Bay National Park, where tourists could watch humpback whales and see a spectacular coastline of glaciers and mountain forests. A mere seven years later, as the culture of enchantment began to take hold, the number of these cruise ships surpassed one hundred. By the mid-1990s, there were 184 boats plying the route.[1] And every day at sea, each big cruise ship discharged an average of 17,000 gallons of human waste into the ocean, plus an additional 170,000 gallons of "gray water."[2] The gray water was hardly innocuous: Studies revealed that 70 percent of the discharges contained high fecal bacteria levels, as much as fifty thousand times the legal standard for treated sewage.[3] Federal laws, though, simply prohibited the dumping of sewage within three miles of the coast. They did not require any treatment of what was discharged farther out, and said nothing about gray waste water.

During the 1980s and 1990s, tropical paradises of the Caribbean and Pacific Ocean nations also began to draw millions of visitors—and drown in sludge. Cruise ships routinely dumped human waste and bilge water (water and oil collected at the bottom of a ship) along their coasts.[4] Major tourist destinations like Rio de Janeiro, Cancun, Acapulco, and Fiji routinely released untreated sewage into local waters. (A 2004 United Nations Environmental Program study found that 90 percent of the sewage from Caribbean nations is discharged untreated into the ocean, while Pacific island nations dispose 98 percent of their sewage untreated into local waters.[5]) These wastes cause algae blooms, which in turn cause coral reefs to die and fish populations to plummet. Sewage is not the only problem. When forests are cut down for lumber to build resorts, increased muddy runoff water further hurts the reefs. Tourist development also brings with it massive amounts of ordinary trash. As the beaches and reefs lose their beauty, tourism eventually declines, leaving behind stagnant resorts and degraded environments.[6]

Closer to home, the celebration of wilderness landscapes in America's national parks and forests brought millions of visitors—with similarly ruinous effects. Concern over what happens when large-scale tourism overruns public lands dates back to the nineteenth century, when increasing urbanization and the romantic writings of authors such as Emerson and Thoreau inspired widespread interest in nature. In 1849 Joel T. Headley published *The Adirondack: Or, Life in the Woods*, declaring that he had gone "from the haunts of men to seek mental repose and physical strength in the woods."[7] Thousands followed Headley's lead. Four years after the Civil War, W. H. H. Murray published a sequel to Headley's work, extolling the Adirondacks in *Adventures in the Wilderness*. The summer after the book appeared the region was inundated with campers, derisively called Murray's Fools. Thomas Bangs Thorpe, a nature writer, complained that the new visitors "profaned" the woods and had "neither skill as sportsmen, nor sentiment of piety enough in their composition, to understand Nature's solitudes."[8]

By 1929, the United States had twenty-three million automobiles on its roads, or one car for roughly every five people.[9] As more and more of the nation's original forests, prairies, deserts, and wetlands were transformed for commercial use and residential developments, people began to drive farther into the country's state and national parks and forests to put themselves in touch—however marginally—with the natural landscapes that modern society had destroyed. Ironically, this mass tourism often degraded the parks and forests, both through pollution and through the construction of gaudy roadside tourist motels and souvenir stands. Oftentimes those who came to experience the wilderness never even left their cars but observed the landscape through the windshield. Today, enormous crowds seeking "nature" routinely destroy any sense of the parkland as special or sacred space. By the mid-1980s, Yosemite National Park attracted fifty thousand visitors during July 4 weekends, creating what critics called a "camping slum" in a seven-mile-long section of Yosemite Valley. Drug and alcohol abuse, theft, and tensions from overcrowding meant that the park experience increasingly resembled life back in large cities.[10] While park officials eventually regulated camping at Yosemite, it is still highly congested in the summer. During the 1990s, finding a parking space during the peak summer season routinely took over an hour.[11]

By 2001, over fifty-eight million Americans were visiting national parks. In the words of Don Barger, a monitor from the National Parks Conservation Association, traveling to Great Smoky Mountains National Park in Tennessee is "mostly a windshield experience. You follow the tail lights of the guy ahead of you and by the end, you missed the entire reason you came."[12] Today, smog from the cars of all these visitors increasingly smothers and hides the very mountains, forests, and wide-open desert vistas that lured people from the cities in the first place. Visibility in the Eastern parks is about one-fifth of what it would be without air pollution, while in the Western parks, people can now see only one-half to two-thirds as far as they could in the 1950s, before coal-fired electrical plants and massive traffic exhausts became common.[13] In 2004, the U.S. Environmental Protection Agency listed eight of the nation's national parks as violating federal air-quality standards, with several having ozone levels high enough to pose health hazards. The list included Yosemite, Kings Canyon, Sequoia, and Joshua Tree in California, Rocky Mountain in Colorado, Great Smoky Mountains and Shenandoah in Virginia, and Acadia in Maine. (Many other parks suffered air-quality degradation just below the legal limit and thus were not listed.) Christine Shaver, chief of air quality for the National Park Service, lamented the situation: "It shakes me to think that we have to issue health alerts to visitors to tell them it's a bad day to go hiking because of air pollution."[14]

PERHAPS THE STARKEST example of the collision between enchantment ideals and their unintended consequences is the growth of what's been officially termed "outdoor motorized recreation." Through its insistence on the great beauty and desirability of the natural world, the culture of enchantment has undoubtedly contributed to the enormous popularity of these activities. Since 1976, the number of people using off-road vehicles such as dirt bikes, four-wheel-drive jeeps, and all-terrain vehicles has increased sevenfold, to nearly thirty-six million. By 2004, off-road industry sales totaled $4.8 billion per year. In California, 14 percent of all households reported possessing off-road vehicles.[15] And while off-road riders and off-road industry executives and political lobbyists demand access to undeveloped lands, they've shown no interest in protecting these lands or the animals that live on them. On the contrary, rider-industry coalitions vehemently oppose designating any federal lands as official "wilderness" areas, because motor vehicles are prohibited in such areas under the Wilderness Act. For the same reason, off-roaders have opposed efforts to stop construction of logging roads in national forests: Building roads for logging trucks opens an area for pickups and trailers carrying ATVs. Nor do the off-roaders support the Endangered Species Act. Whenever the U.S. Fish and Wildlife Service lists a species as endangered, its land becomes protected as "critical habitat" and is closed to off-road vehicles.

The community of off-road riders and the businesses catering to them have developed a wide range of rationales and strategies for opposing any such closure of public lands. Bill Dart, executive director of the Blue Ribbon Commission, an off-road lobbying group which claims six hundred thousand members, calls land closure undemocratic: "A tiny minority of people use wilderness, but there is a growing demand for outdoor recreation. This country is all about tolerance and diversity, but the wilderness advocates are promoting a lack of tolerance. We don't think setting aside vast landscapes for a tiny minority of the recreating public is a wise thing to do."[16]

When the Bush administration came into office in 2001, off-road lobbying groups and their allies in government sought to reverse earlier legal settlements that had protected endangered species. For instance, an agreement signed in 2000 by government agencies, environmental organizations, and off-road groups to prohibit vehicles in seventy-seven square miles of California's Imperial Sand Dunes in order to protect the endangered Pierson's milk vetch was cast aside. The Bureau of Land Management suddenly decided that the scientific studies by the U.S.

Fish and Wildlife Service which found the plant threatened were wrong, and should be replaced by new studies—commissioned by the American Sand Association, which wanted to mine the dunes—that found no problems in species health.[17] A spokesman from Republican congressman Duncan Hunter's office dismissed the first settlement as an absurdity, "all in purposes of saving a weed."[18]

But the off-road movement goes far beyond sponsoring political challenges to unfavorable administrative decisions, regulations, and legal settlements. Many off-roaders flatly disregard any legal prohibitions against their movement and deliberately destroy sensitive ecological zones. In Calaveras County, California, Sheriff Dennis Downum reported that on some weekends, up to eighty thousand ATV riders would converge on the Stanislaus National Forest. "They do what they want to do. I've seen signs that say 'This Area Closed' knocked down, with the tire tracks all over them. It's at the point where it's all out of control."[19] When nearby landowners tried to restore damaged areas—replanting wetlands destroyed by vehicle ruts, for example—the plants were pulled out within weeks, and the terrain gutted with tire tracks once again.

Some riders explicitly say that they reject any concept of maintaining the integrity of a landscape. Loren Shirk, who drives his four-wheel-drive SUV off-road in the sand dunes near Barstow, California, explained to a *New York Times* reporter, "I think my right to go where I want should not be hampered by the whims of somebody else that wants to leave the world looking like it was 40,000 years ago."[20] When the U.S. Forest Service enlisted companies like Ford and Toyota to fund a "Tread Lightly" environmental education program for off-roaders, one writer on an off-road Web site, calling himself "Davey the Endangered Desert Tortoise," countered, "I don't Tread Lightly. I trample. From tree-huggers to their totalitarian signage that follows, I trample all in the path of freedom's future."[21]

Some off-road activists even say they want to literally battle—whether with fists or guns is unclear—against environmentalists and

government officials. Enraged that Bureau of Land Management officials in California might protect a three-thousand-year-old Serrano
Indian burial ground and fertility ritual area from further motorcycle
encroachment, champion off-road cyclist Ty "Zipty" Davis prophe-
sied, "I can see this whole thing evolving into a ground war, which is
where it maybe needs to go. . . . If it was the old days, they [environ-
mentalists and government officials] wouldn't be so aggressive. In
those days, people fought for their stuff. They just duked it out."[22]

This attitude worries government officials responsible for public
lands. Barry Nelson, the chief ranger for the Barstow district in California's Mojave Desert, thought that some 15 to 20 percent of off-road
riders had a "total mindset and mentality of defiance."[23] Scores of
rangers have complained to the ten-thousand-member Public Employees for Environmental Responsibility (PEER), a watchdog group that
protests on behalf of federal and state government employees in natural resource agencies who cannot speak publicly against their agencies'
actions. They want to know how they are supposed to handle riders
who refuse to comply with regulations and actively abuse the land.
PEER's general counsel, Dan Meyer, summarized their feelings in 2002:
"There's a real sense of lawlessness out there. It's something out of *Mad
Max*."[24] Dale Bosworth, chief of the U.S. Forest Service, called "un-
managed recreation" one of the four greatest threats to the nation's
public forests, because of the tremendous amount of "erosion, water
degradation, and habitat destruction. We're seeing more and more conflicts between users. We're seeing more damage to cultural sites and
more violation of sites sacred to American Indians."[25]

Similar problems are caused by the growing popularity of snowmobiles and jet skis, or personal watercraft. There are about twelve
million registered snowmobiles in the United States.[26] While some of
these vehicles are used for transportation in remote rural areas, the primary appeal of snowmobiling is as an off-road sport. Snowmobiles
are allowed in forty-two national parks and monuments, and in the
early 2000s there were over sixty thousand of them in Yellowstone

and Grand Teton National parks each winter.[27] Although the cars in Yellowstone outnumber the snowmobiles sixteen to one, the snowmobiles, equipped with inefficient two-cycle engines that release up to one-third of their fuel unburned, are responsible for 68 percent of the carbon monoxide and 90 percent of the hydrocarbon pollutants released in the park each year.[28] (Environmental Protection Agency studies calculate that just one snowmobile can create as much pollution as one hundred cars.[29]) In the winter, a blue haze of exhaust runs from Yellowstone's west gate for dozens of miles along popular snowmobile trails.[30] Park workers are issued respirators because they are exposed to hydrocarbon emissions ten times higher than levels found on Los Angeles freeways.[31] Noise levels approach that of a large airport, overwhelming all natural sounds and forcing rangers to wear hearing protectors. As the Greater Yellowstone Coalition's Jon Catton puts it, snowmobiles are destroying "what makes the park magical in winter."[32]

Most jet skis also have two-cycle engines and pollute just as badly as snowmobiles, dumping 25 to 30 percent of their fuel unburned into the water. The U.S. Park Service at Lake Mead, Nevada, estimates that on a busy summer weekend jet skis pour 27,000 gallons of gas and oil into the lake. Nearly 100,000 jet skis are sold nationwide each year; over 1,500,000 are in use.[33] With their nearly flat bottoms and lack of propellers, jet skis can motor in close to shore, threatening wildfowl nesting areas and disrupting marine mammals such as dolphins and manatees, which often feed and rest in shallow waters. They're also just as noisy as snowmobiles. "Boaters, shoreline hikers, and wildlife enthusiasts complain that the noise from personal watercraft ruins their outdoor experience," reports the Bluewater Network environmental group.[34]

The highly aggressive culture of off-road vehicles, snowmobiles, and jet skis is a blend of several key traditions. The pioneer and Western theme of humans conquering nature has been reinvented: The off-roader is the new cowboy, complete with iron horse. Extreme sports

TV shows and television advertising sponsored by off-road manufacturers give the old Western contemporary packaging. As Daphne Greene, head of the California Off-Highway Motor Vehicle Recreation Commission, notes, "It is extremely difficult to educate the off-road community when you turn on the TV and you see a vehicle crashing through the air and slamming through meadows and rivers."[35]

To the militant off-roader, nature is also the mythic realm of what Mircea Eliade called "primeval chaos"—a place, like a battlefield, far from society's values and norms, where anything goes. Thus the libertarian wing of the off-road community, with its anarchistic air of defiance, bitterly resents any effort to regulate riders as totalitarian. In their judgment, government has authority only over society, not nature. They look to the primeval chaos of public lands as a place where they can escape society's encumbrances.

Last, the off-road community embraces the modern culture of speed as a peak aesthetic experience, a merger of man and machine. Speed, in turn, removes people from the land and its creatures, rendering them a distant blur. As Terry Weiner, botanist and coordinator for the Desert Protection Council, complained of the riders at the Imperial Sand Dunes in Southern California, "You cannot appreciate the dunes if you're raging across them at 40 miles an hour with smoke in your face and deafening noise."[36]

Motorized outdoor recreation poses a significant challenge for the culture of enchantment. Abusing public lands and waterways eventually disenchants them, creating places as dirty and charmless as derelict cities and suburbs. The fact that completely disenchanted public lands would no longer be compelling to visit or offer an attractive ride is a paradox that extreme off-road enthusiasts never address.

ANOTHER INADVERTENT CONSEQUENCE of the culture of enchantment has been the creation of a new kind of sprawl: "exurban" development. Of course, the idea of leaving the city behind and moving to the countryside, where nature could be experienced more directly, has always been a motive for suburban development. By the late nineteenth century, as the nation's railroads fanned out from Chicago, New York, and other big cities, the upper and middle classes began to move to more distant villages within commuting distance. Over time, those rural villages became the first suburbs.[37] In the decades following World War II, the federal government financed construction of the nation's interstate highway system, linking virtually all medium and large cities with freeways. This new highway system, augmented by an even larger spiderweb of feeder roads, gave rise to a vast suburban sprawl of residential developments and shopping malls that by the 1960s left most of America's downtown central cities reduced to hollowed-out "doughnuts." By the 1980s and 1990s, the sprawl also included "edge cities," which, *Washington Post* reporter Joel Garreau argued, were not bedroom suburbs but clusters of corporate office parks, shopping malls, entertainment centers, and residential developments built outside cities along major interstate highways and loops.[38] The culture of enchantment has had no real part in encouraging this transformation, since edge cities have little connection to the land and its creatures.

But the creation of exurbs—settlements far away from the city, in or adjoining formerly wild (particularly public) land—is a different story. Exurbs include upscale resort communities composed of vacation homes as well as small communities where corporations have decided to locate their new offices or high-tech manufacturing plants. The growth of Internet communications, the construction of new state and federal highways, and the spread of commuter airlines made it possible to hold a middle- or upper-middle-class job while living in a rural area, but it was the celebrated natural beauty of such places that made them attractive. Exurban migration boomed through the 1990s, in places as varied as the Rocky Mountain states, California's Sierra Nevada and Tehachapi Mountains, and the Arizona and Nevada deserts. All told, the Western states saw over eight million homes built since 1990 in what foresters call "the urban wild land."[39] To the east, the woods of Vermont, Maine, and Michigan's Upper Peninsula also saw rapid growth in home construction.

For various reasons, when the Department of the Interior buys land for national parks, monuments, forests, and wildlife refuges, it often cannot buy all the real estate within the park or refuge boundaries. Consequently, there are over 6,700 square miles of privately held property in the United States surrounded by public lands. In the past fifteen years, as demand for "wilderness living" grew, more and more builders have sought to develop these areas, reproducing many of the same problems that the huge increases in park visitations and off-road exploits have created, and on an even larger, more dramatic scale.

Near Palm Springs, California, for example, developers are constructing the luxurious Mirada residences (described by the *Los Angeles Times* as a "slice of Beverly Hills") inside the Santa Rosa and San Jacinto Mountains National Monument, intruding on the habitat of rare peninsular bighorn sheep. "This is the equivalent of living on the floor of Yosemite," says project director Chuck Strother.[40] Nearby, another developer is planning a fourteen-square-mile community sandwiched between the Joshua Tree National Park and the Coachella Valley Preserve. It will become the home of a new World Trade Center University, with 15,000 students, 7,000 homes, three hotels, two country clubs, twelve golf courses, and 15,000 employees. The golf courses alone will require six million gallons of water per day. The wildlife that currently passes freely between the two publicly owned areas will be constrained to using two narrow corridors surrounded by the massive project.[41]

Similar developments are in the planning stages across California's Sierra Nevada, either inside or adjacent to federal and state lands. In the Martis Valley north of Lake Tahoe, deer herds that formerly numbered at least 10,000 have fallen to 3,000 because of residential construction. "Is the Sierra Nevada going to be a high-altitude suburbia with a lot of golf courses, big developments and traffic congestion? Or is it going to be this majestic landscape?" asks Tom Mooers, executive director of the conservation group Sierra Watch. Meanwhile, these new exurban communities have created tremendous opportunities for the log home industry—in the 2000s, roughly 30,000 such homes were sold each year, compared to 15,000 a year in the mid-1980s. By now, over 550,000 log homes exist, mainly in rural environments.[42] One industry leader says that "there are more log homes today than ever in the history of the world." As a *New York Times* headline quipped, "A Return to Nature, Mostly by Cutting It Down."[43]

The nation's coasts are also under tremendous development pressure, as more people want to live near the water. Some fifty million people now live in coastal counties along the Atlantic and Gulf of Mexico.[44] Coastal counties in California, Oregon, and Washington contain the overwhelming majorities of those states' populations. Yet in order to accommodate these water-lovers, the natural geography of the coasts has often been destroyed. Saltwater wetlands, which many species of fish and shellfish need as nurseries, have been drained and replaced by homes. Storm-water runoff, filled with nitrates and phosphates from fertilizers and wastes, no longer gets filtered by the wetlands, but instead goes directly into the ocean, leading to toxic algae blooms. Seawalls, built to protect beachfront houses from ocean waves, lead to beach erosion, because waves bounce back from the walls with full force and take sand with them.[45]

In the 1980s and 1990s, as overfishing, polluted runoff, and other damages wrought by overdevelopment led to the decline of the commercial fishing industry, builders began to buy up many of the nation's docks and boatyards to transform them into residential projects, entertainment complexes, and marinas for high-end pleasure craft. In 2005, a *National Geographic* writer examining his beloved Chesapeake Bay found most of the bay's famous crab and oyster harvests gone, and its old fishing infrastructure virtually nonexistent. The new upscale restaurants built on the waterfront to serve tourists and exurban residents were offering "Chesapeake-style" crab dishes made with imported Asian crabmeat, and oysters from Louisiana and Texas.[46] The bay and its surrounding communities were no longer about living close to the water, but instead had become a coastal theme park, a fantasy setting for packaged amusement.

These exurban communities often have another dark side, as those drawn to "living with nature" encounter dangers they never expected. Since 1982, more than 8.2 million homes have been built in the West within thirty miles of a national forest, and they are at risk from fires like those that destroyed thousands of homes in the Rocky Mountains in the late 1990s and Southern California in the 2000s. "It's like a tsunami, this big wave of development that's rolling toward the public lands," says Volker C. Radeloff, a University of Wisconsin professor who has studied this migration. "And the number of fires keeps going up."[47] Mountain and canyon communities can also be devastated by mudslides: In the spring of 2005, mountains gave way in Southern California after heavy rains, destroying dozens of homes and killing several people. Along the Atlantic and Gulf coasts, 150 million people living within a hundred miles of the water are at significant risk from hurricane winds and flooding. In 2002, the director of the National Hurricane Center warned, "As you fly along the U.S. coastline and see the development, you can't help but be concerned that we're building for a hurricane disaster."[48] The devastation of the Mississippi, Louisiana, and Texas coasts by hurricanes Katrina, Rita, and Ike of course proved these fears correct. And some meteorologists argue that global warming, which increases the ocean's temperature, will lead to increasingly frequent and severe hurricanes in the future.

The building of exurban communities also often destroys the very natural beauty that attracted development in the first place. Air and water pollution increase. Animal life is decimated, with creatures driven from their homes and left to forage in fragmented habitats, moving across roads or around developments in desperate efforts to find mates, shelter, food, and water (this last frequently saturated with fertilizers from golf courses). At times, builders literally drain the water from under animals' feet. In Nevada, for example, developers are asking government officials to sell federal land for housing projects and give permission for drilling into an aquifer that feeds springs supporting both Death Valley National Park and Desert National Wildlife Refuge.[49]

Both grizzly bears and bald eagles, two endangered, highly charismatic species, face new threats from exurban development. The grizzly bear population at Yellowstone National Park has recovered to the point where some bears are now moving outside park boundaries and trying to reclaim their old range, a move many scientists think is necessary to ensure that they have an adequate food supply. But the counties surrounding Yellowstone have experienced a 30 percent population growth since 1975, when the bears were first listed as endangered. As the *Los Angeles Times* noted, "Today, when a grizzly fords a stream to forage, it can find itself confronted with swing sets and patio furniture."[50] It also may be confronted by gun-toting homeowners and police. In 2004, bear mortality at Yellowstone was two and a half times higher than the fifteen-year average.

The leading threat to the nation's bald eagles in the 1970s was DDT contamination: The dioxin disrupts reproduction by making eggs more fragile. For twenty years biologist Peter E. Nye has been in charge of an eagle reintroduction plan in New York. But in 2004, when he revisited what was once prime eagle habitat along the Delaware River, the woodlands along the river were gone, the hillsides "totally denuded" in preparation for residential building. Everywhere he drove, Nye saw signs advertising Eagle Valley Realty, Eagle's Nest Estates, and other eagle-branded projects. Fifty years from now, he wondered, would the open lands and riverfront that the eagles need "still . . . be here to support them or will we keep whittling it so that the habitat disappears?"[51]

When the shrinkage of animal habitat forces people and wild animals to come into contact with one another, the outcome is often tragic for both sides. In Southern California, solitary joggers, mountain bikers, and families with small children have increasingly intruded on mountain lion turf, and the cats have begun to regard humans as prey. Whenever a mountain lion attacks someone, state wildlife officials hunt and kill it. Black bears have learned to associate humans with food, and those that take to panhandling in the nation's parks are also killed by rangers, because the animals eventually lose their fear of humans and become aggressive. Bears living near cities and exurban communities, meanwhile, now routinely visit garbage Dumpsters. Male "city" bears can reach weights of four hundred to six hundred pounds, roughly twice what male "country" bears weigh. They also live much shorter lives. Many are shot because they approach homes looking for food; others are hit by cars. Dr. Jon P. Beckmann of the Wildlife Conservation Society warns that among these city bears, "mortality rates are much higher than reproductive rates."[52] Whole populations could die out.

In regions transformed by exurban sprawl, human introduction of new food sources like gardens and garbage dumps, combined with elimination of predators like mountain lions and coyotes, may combine to create animal populations that are wildly out of balance with the land. When that happens, even innocuous animals become a problem. White-tail deer are now so numerous that about 150 people a year die in automobile collisions with them.[53] Suburban and exurban residents complain that their gardens are devoured by hungry deer; the Audubon Society says that they denude forests of plants needed by birds.[54] North of San Francisco, wild turkeys, first introduced to the area in the late 1980s, now thrive in the thousands and threaten vineyards in Sonoma, Napa, and Mendocino counties.[55] In Santa Clara County, home of sprawling San Jose, thousands of wild pigs— descendants of escaped farm animals, now with long hair and tusks— come down from the hills in dry years to feed on suburban lawns. Some adult pigs weigh more than people, and although harmless, "have been known to chase the occasional unsuspecting resident."[56] Pigs gone wild: It's not at all what exurban paradise was supposed to be. Nor was this what adherents of the culture of enchantment had in mind.

EVEN AS ENCHANTMENT'S celebration of nature has led wilderness to be loved to death, a corollary problem is that its aesthetic—favoring magnificent landscapes and large animals—has hindered efforts to save creatures and lands that are equally worthy but far less beautiful. Ansel Adams, Eliot Porter, and their students deliberately offered the public images of stunning wilderness landscapes and photogenic animals, hoping that their beauty would pull people into a spiritual connection with nature and that this connection would then motivate them to protect it. It's a strategy that has worked: Photographs of large, charismatic "megafauna" and "monumental landscapes," the stock in trade of magazines such as *National Geographic*, have helped people imagine a resacralized world.

But this emphasis on beauty also inadvertently devalues and leaves vulnerable all that is smaller and plainer. Although the 1973 Endangered Species Act (ESA) protects all creatures threatened by extinction, enforcement of the act's many provisions requires political support from the public. Once a species has been listed as "endangered," the U.S. Fish and Wildlife Service is compelled to designate the animal's or plant's home as "critical habitat," protecting "all areas essential to the conservation of the species." But the bureau is reluctant to mark land as critical habitat unless there is political support for doing so. Moreover, the ESA also has a provision saying that the economic costs of designating land as critical habitat can be taken into account by government officials in deciding whether to protect an endangered animal or plant: A federal panel called the "god squad" can declare that the economic costs of critical habitat are too high and thus condemn a species to extinction. Landowners, loggers, and builders almost always ridicule any efforts to save small, plain-looking creatures as a giant waste, a ludicrous impediment to progress. And because the culture of enchantment has failed to celebrate these species, this ridicule often becomes the deciding factor in these debates.

The pattern began in 1977, when environmentalists protested the building of a proposed dam on the Little Tennessee River because it was home to the endangered snail darter. They were mocked on the national news for wanting to protect a three-inch "useless minnow." With the darter effectively stigmatized, dam supporters soon persuaded Congress to pass an amendment authorizing the Tennessee Valley Authority to complete the Tellico Dam "notwithstanding the Endangered Species Act or any other law."[57]

In the early 1990s, the mayor of Mammoth, California, called a decision by the U.S. Fish and Wildlife Service to stop new hotel and golf course development in order to protect the Owens tui chub, a small fish living in local wells, "mind-boggling."[58] In 2002, city and state officials from both parties in Albuquerque, New Mexico, lobbied the Department of the Interior to convene the "god squad" and declare that the city had no legal obligation to protect the endangered silvery minnow that lives in a sixty-mile stretch downstream from a city-owned dam on the Rio Grande. In effect, they were arguing that all the water collected behind the dam was for people, and people alone.[59]

That same year a federal judge in Los Angeles, acting on a Bush administration request, overturned a U.S. Fish and Wildlife Service ruling that had designated over 780 square miles in Southern California as critical habitat for the endangered coastal California gnatcatcher and the San Diego fairy shrimp.[60] California's fairy shrimp, small crustaceans no more than one and a half inches long, live in seasonal freshwater wetlands. They have few allies; even Carl Safina, whose 1997 *Song for the Blue Ocean* called for the reenchantment of the ocean and its creatures, said that "it would be hard to find a less compelling endangered species."[61] It is thus perhaps not surprising that over 95 percent of California's wetlands have now been drained for development.

Contempt for small fish is so pervasive that even species with proven value get overlooked. Scientists studying sardines, for example, have discovered that the small fish help reduce global warming because they eat phytoplankton, tiny plants that appear in huge numbers from upwelling of deep ocean water. If phytoplankton is not eaten by sardines, the plants die and decompose, creating "dead zones" that release methane gas. Sardine populations have been decimated by overfishing in recent years, but as one scientist involved in the study explained, "The problem with sardines is that the federal government is not that interested in them."[62]

Efforts to save other small or plain-looking creatures have evoked similar reactions. In the mid-1990s, when the U.S. Fish and Wildlife Service banned logging from sections of the Northwest's national forests to protect the endangered Northwest spotted owl, small-town cafés and hotels in the West started posting signs offering "roast spotted owl" on their menus. The Mexican spotted owl was similarly disdained in Southwestern states after timber harvests were curtailed to protect it.[63] When the pygmy owl population near Tucson collapsed to just eighteen birds in 2002, leading the U.S. Fish and Wildlife Service to set aside 875 square miles as critical habitat, the housing industry screamed in protest. According to a spokesperson for Tucson developers, "the pygmy owl probably represents the pre-eminent problem that they're finding not only in building new houses, but in keeping housing construction affordable."[64] His implicit complaint is quite straightforward: How could it be fair to stop a popular city from expanding merely for the sake of a seven-inch-tall bird? Three years later the U.S. Fish and Wildlife Service caved in to these homebuilder protests, and proposed delisting the pygmy owls after a one-year waiting period.[65] Although the most committed environmental groups stood up for the pygmies, the wider public didn't seem to care.

The same attitudes get in the way of preserving unspectacular-appearing landscapes. As Cornell ornithologist Tim Gallagher concluded, "Back when people were saving Yellowstone, Yosemite, and the giant redwoods, they didn't even think about the Southern forests. . . . What happened to the vast bottomland forests of the South during the past 150 years is one of the greatest environmental tragedies in the history of the United States, and few people know about it."[66] For example, although the ivory-billed woodpecker was already nearly extinct as early as the 1930s because its native habitat was mostly logged-out, there was no public demand to save its last known home, the 125-square-mile Singer Tract in Louisiana. The dense, lowland forest was not considered beautiful enough for national park status.

The plain, humble tall-grass prairies of the Great Plains, which once covered over four hundred thousand square miles from central Canada through north Texas, were similarly ignored. Even as the country's first great national parks were founded in the aftermath of the Civil War, the Great Plains were being put to the plow. Although explorers like Lewis and Clark loved the plains, with their herds of buffalo and other animals, the settlers who followed the new transcontinental railroads saw them only as sites for farms and ranches. Today, less than 4 percent of the original grasslands remain intact as prairie.[67]

Swamps and wetlands, which have been viewed as outright ugly and even a dangerous source of illness, also have fared badly. Over the past two hundred years, more than half of the wetlands in the continental United States have been drained and filled. Some states, including California, Missouri, Iowa, Illinois, Indiana, and Ohio, have lost over 80 percent of their wetlands to agriculture and development.[68]

Undeveloped, degraded, or reclaimed lands near cities have been rendered particularly vulnerable by the culture of enchantment's emphasis on preserving remote wilderness areas. Simply put, landscapes near cities cannot, and do not, look like national forests and parks. Instead, they resemble checkerboards: Suburban housing tracts, roadside stores, and billboards mix with farms or ranches, and are interspersed with various kinds of open spaces—creek beds, scattered woods, grassy hills, and meadows. This aesthetic isn't what the culture of enchantment defines as wild or beautiful. Consequently, only rarely is there concerted public pressure on states and cities to buy these remaining open spaces for parks, even though many plant and animal species would be helped if open lands near cities were preserved. Instead, sprawl expands, filling in the checkerboard until a region becomes fully developed.

Open spaces within urban regions are even less likely to be saved or protected, for they are often downright ugly, polluted, and filled with trash and detritus from failed businesses. These degraded places instead become prime targets for new development, since building anything is seen as an improvement. More development, more density—and less open land, fewer trees and animals—becomes the definition of progress.

Southern California provides several prime examples of this process. Virtually the entire coast is built out, but in 2002 developers succeeded in obtaining permits—and hundreds of millions of dollars in federal, state, and local subsidies—to build several thousand homes on the last large parcel of open space in Los Angeles, the eleven thousand-acre Ballona Wetlands. Located a few miles north of Los Angeles International Airport near Marina del Rey, Ballona was a classic degraded urban landscape. The construction of a huge marina in the early 1960s had radically reduced the wetlands' connections to Santa Monica Bay, leaving them parched, weed-choked, and ugly. Nearby Ballona Creek, which once fed into the wetlands, had been paved and straightened in the 1930s by the U.S. Army Corps of Engineers, turning it into a giant storm drain that dumped polluted water into the bay.

For nearly ten years environmental activists fought to reenchant the Ballona Wetlands in order to defeat development and restore the area. Demonstrators repeatedly stressed that this was the last open space in the city. Animal-costumed actors from a guerrilla theater troupe, FrogWorks, performed at local malls and schools. Documentary filmmakers captured images of the great blue herons, pelicans, ducks, snakes, fish, and foxes that still lived at Ballona, and their films tried to help people visualize what an ecologically restored landscape of that size might mean to both people and animals.[69] But it was too big a leap of imagination for most people to make. Even if Ballona was restored, it would never be "gorgeous."

Consequently, the struggle to save the wetlands never became a powerful mass movement enlisting activists across Los Angeles for political support. Even after contractors digging a storm water drainage ditch for the developer, Playa Capital, unearthed the bodies of 1,200 to 1,400 Gabrielino-Tongva Indians—L.A.'s first inhabitants—from an ancient burial site on Ballona, there was no mass public outcry. Calls to return the dead to their graves and simply move the ditch one hundred feet went unheeded.[70] Ultimately, the state of California did buy part of Ballona (though not the grave sites) for preservation, paying developers the astronomical price of roughly a million dollars an acre. And Playa Capital built its city—thousands of homes, condominiums, office buildings, restaurants, and retail stores. Contrary to its name, there is no beach view from Playa Vista; instead, the project and the traffic it generates make the beach and ocean even more remote. The wetlands that did get saved exist in the shadow of its pollution, noise, lights, and congestion.

In inland Los Angeles County, a few miles away from where environmental activist John Quigley made his stand to try to save the majestic Old Glory oak tree, plans for building thousands of homes in the Santa Clarita Valley north of Los Angeles are moving forward. The area, which has an "oak savannah" ecology, is lovely in its way, but too close to the city to have the mystique of a place like California's redwood forests. "We're eliminating trees," says a state forester. "We're letting them become trivialized; without really paying attention, we're letting them disappear."[71]

One of the last free-flowing rivers in Southern California, the Santa Clarita, runs through the region and will undoubtedly also be affected by the massive development. Meanwhile, efforts to restore other Southern California rivers have struggled because these waterways are urbanized and degraded. Environmental groups spent the 1990s and early 2000s in court trying to force municipal governments in Los Angeles to comply with the federal Clean Water Act—for example, to rebuild leaking sewers to keep sewage from entering rivers and creeks. Every environmental victory was met with delaying tactics and appeals to higher courts; governments spent millions in legal costs to maintain their right to dump partially treated sewage into waterways. Attempts to reduce the amounts of trash and toxic waste in storm-water runoff have met with similar resistance.

In 2003, a ruling by one of the California Regional Water Quality Control boards ordering all the cities and towns in Los Angeles County to reduce toxic runoff and keep trash out of the county's creeks and rivers provoked bitter resistance. Roughly half the municipalities formed a coalition to file lawsuits against the new rule on the basis that such changes would cost too much.[72] But fears about expenditures are only part of the explanation. Equally important is the lack of vision. Hundreds of politicians and government bureaucrats simply could not imagine the waterways of Los Angeles County being anything more than dead gray concrete storm drains taking trash, polluted runoff, and partially treated sewage to the region's beaches and the ocean. The problem isn't that no restoration is possible. Even drainage channels can be reconfigured to work with adjacent wetlands and parklands, making the rivers and creeks much more attractive and accessible to people, and capable of sustaining far more plant and animal life. But refurbished flood-control channels can't be made to look like the headwaters of the Colorado River in the Rocky Mountains—and even if beautifully landscaped, they still would remain surrounded by development. Unfortunately, without a promise of great, virtually transcendent beauty, spending millions of dollars to reduce trash and pollutants seemed not just expensive but meaningless. This failure of imagination among officials and the public—like the tragedy of wild places succumbing to their own popularity, and ordinary creatures being sacrificed for lack of charisma—points to limitations in the culture of enchantment.

# Imitation Wildness
# and the Sacred Casino

The ways in which the culture of enchantment interacts with the mainstream culture it hopes to change have created problems that its adherents never foresaw. In addition, contradictions within the culture have weakened the movement. One of the primary conflicts involves human relationships with animals. While all factions seem to agree that totemism implies the *symbolic* recognition and integration of animals into the human community, differences arise when people are faced with the question of how to live near real animals.

One prominent faction argues that people and animals can achieve an intimate coexistence—that with some adjustments and limitations, they can live side by side like small-town neighbors. For example, the Defenders of Wildlife, who advocate reintroducing wolves to the Rockies, handle situations when wolves kill cattle or sheep by paying compensation to the ranchers. Grizzly bear researchers Doug Peacock and Charlie Russell have both experimented with setting up encampments near grizzly bear habitats to test the hypothesis that humans and grizzlies were not destined to be mortal enemies but could share a territory. They hoped to demonstrate that as long as certain boundaries are maintained, grizzly bears could be reintroduced to what had once been their traditional territories in the Rocky Mountains.

Neither Peacock nor Russell tried to literally live among the bears, to camp with them, but instead kept some distance—Russell even used an electric fence around his cabin compound.[1] But among a certain segment in the culture of enchantment, the notion of forming a human-animal family was taken to mean that humans and wild animals should literally live together, without borders. By far the most famous of these advocates was Timothy Treadwell. Born in New York, Treadwell descended into alcoholism and heavy drug use as a teenager. His effort to start over in Long Beach, California, failed, leading only to more substance abuse. In a last-ditch attempt to remake himself, Treadwell journeyed to Alaska in the summer of 1989, hoping to fulfill a childhood dream—to see a grizzly bear. He got his wish, and when he saw his first bear, he was overcome with emotion. "For me, the encounter was like looking into a mirror. I gazed into the face of a kindred soul, a being that was potentially lethal, but in reality was just as frightened as I was."[2] This transcendent experience inspired him to create a new life.

Treadwell vowed to return to Alaska the following summer to become a bear guardian, protecting grizzlies from poachers by living among them. He got through that summer clean and sober, and bonded with some of the bears in Kodiak Island's Grizzly Sanctuary. But Treadwell feared that he would backslide in California. In his 1997 memoir, *Among Grizzlies*, Treadwell recalls the confession he made to a bear he named Booble. "I'll never really be your defender because I can't stop drinking," he told the bear. "I'm such a loser." Treadwell then had a mystical experience. "Booble trusted me with her life and I trusted her with mine. I begged forgiveness from a higher power, then made my pledge. 'I will stop drinking for you and all bears. I will stop and devote my life to you.'"[3] Fusing enchantment with the lessons he had learned from attending Alcoholics Anonymous meetings, Treadwell dedicated himself to the grizzlies. During the winter months, he showed videos to schoolchildren to promote understanding and love for the bears.

Returning to Grizzly Sanctuary each summer, Treadwell worked to develop personal relationships with the animals. Some would occasionally sleep close to his tent. Treadwell felt "contented by the sense of having a family," and spoke to the bears: "You sleep tight, children, I love you."[4] Treadwell also concluded that the largest alpha males in a region, creatures who had "splendid physiques and calm temperaments," were the safest for humans, because they felt less threatened by them.[5] But Treadwell wanted more than intimacy with the grizzlies—he wanted to become one himself. Following a bear into a freezing cold river, he chanted, "I am Grizzly. I am Grizzly."[6] In his videotapes, replayed in Werner Herzog's 2005 documentary *Grizzly Man*, Treadwell says, "I will be one of them; I will be a master samurai—a kind warrior." He explained his quest in a letter to his friends: "I want to naturally mutate into a wild animal."

In October 2003, Treadwell and his companion, Amie Hugenard, were killed and eaten by a bear in the "Grizzly Maze" section of Katmai National Park and Preserve on Alaska's Gulf coast. Park officials subsequently shot and killed the bear. At the time of the attack Treadwell had spent thirty-six thousand hours over the course of fourteen years with the Katmai bears.[7] Just the previous month, he had written to his supporters: "My transformation is complete—a fully accepted wild animal—brother to these bears. I run free among them—with absolute love and respect for all the animals."[8]

Treadwell's effort to live among the grizzly bears clearly represents an effort to overcome the modern separation between humans and nature. His language, too, showed the influence of enchantment. But he overreached. Not even the indigenous Native American cultures imagined the lifting of all boundaries. Although many tribes show bears tremendous respect and treat the animals as totemic kin, only in myths do people and bears cohabit. As one Kodiak Island Indian told Werner Herzog, "For us on the island, you don't invade their territory. . . . For him to act like a bear, it was the utmost in disrespecting the bear."

Both Doug Peacock and Charlie Russell insisted in their eulogies for Treadwell that he made important contributions by challenging the image of all grizzly bears as man-eaters and so demonstrating that bears could be reintroduced into some of their former habitats.[9] But Treadwell's fantasies led to his and Hugenard's deaths, thus reinforcing the very stereotype of the grizzly bear he had dedicated his life to refuting. And while Treadwell represented only the extreme edge in the culture of enchantment, his excesses have cast a dark shadow on all of it.

ANOTHER IMPORTANT DEBATE dividing the culture of enchantment concerns hunting. If wild animals are no longer regarded as property that people can take and kill at will, when is it morally permissible to hunt them for food and the use of their skins? Nature writers such as Richard Nelson, Freeman House, and Carl Safina follow Native American traditions and maintain that carefully controlled hunting and fishing (and eating) of wild game reconnects people with the land and sea and helps people recognize themselves as fellow animals. Conversely, animal rights advocates and vegetarians often view all forms of hunting and fishing as sacrilegious practices that should be abolished.

One particular conflict readily illustrates this problem—the highly publicized effort by the Makah Indians in the 1990s to resume their historic gray whale hunts. Like other Native American tribes, the Makah lost most of their land during the nineteenth century. The Treaty of Neah Bay, signed in 1855, allowed them to retain only small reservations on the Olympic Peninsula, the western tip of Washington State. But the treaty did guarantee their right to continue whale hunts, which were central to their culture. In the 1920s, though, after decades of industrial-style whaling in the birthing grounds along

Baja California's Pacific coast nearly drove the gray whale to extinction, the Makah abandoned their hunts, which had been conducted with hand-thrown harpoons and lances. They abandoned, as well, their centuries-old practice of building canoes for whaling and fishing; even the knowledge of how to build such canoes disappeared. But when the tribe tried to replace whaling with increased fishing for salmon and halibut, whites resisted.[10] The Makah became dependent on the Bureau of Indian Affairs for their subsistence, and many left their reservations for urban employment. Traditional culture weakened, and the tribe suffered from high rates of unemployment, poverty, and alcoholism.

Then came the Native American revival movements of the 1950s and 1960s. For the Makah, the revival began in 1965–66, after an archaeologist hired to dig in the ancient village of Ozette—near their reservation at Neah Bay—found thousands of bones from fish, sea lions, and whales, along with enough artifacts to prove that Makah had lived there 2,500 to 3,000 years ago. In 1970, an old cedar-plank longhouse was unearthed. Roughly fifty feet long and thirty feet wide, it had been preserved by a clay landslide dating back to the years before Columbus. Over the next decade, workers recovered some sixty-five thousand artifacts that became the foundation for a new museum of Makah history and a powerful wellspring for cultural renewal. In the new museum, one decorative object stood out from the ancient fish hooks, harpoon points, and other tools of daily life: a huge wooden carving of a whale's dorsal fin, covered with over seven hundred sea otter teeth. The longhouse had belonged to a whaler.[11]

During the 1970s the Makah (together with other Pacific Northwest Indian tribes) successfully filed lawsuits in federal courts to reaffirm their treaty rights to fish. In 1979 the U.S. Supreme Court upheld lower court decisions stating that Native Americans could take up to half the region's commercial catch of many fish, including salmon. During the early 1980s the Haida, another Northwest tribe, renewed their canoe-building tradition. The return of seagoing canoes intensified the Makah's longing for a lost past. In 1994, the U.S. Environmental Protection Agency declared that the population of gray whales had recovered sufficiently for them to no longer be considered an endangered species. The Makah petitioned the International Whaling Commission for permits to hunt gray whales, and in 1997, after complex negotiations, they received permission to take five gray whales a year for four years.[12]

Makah attorneys described their proposed whale hunt as justified by "cultural subsistence." This low-key, anthropological-sounding term, perfect for legal documents such as environmental impact statements, vastly understated just how much was at stake—both for the Makah, and for whales.[13] Elsewhere, though, members of the tribe spoke passionately about what whale-hunting meant to them. Marcy Parker, a member of the Makah Tribal Council, saw the resumption of hunting as a way of finding a long-lost "piece of the puzzle that's been out of place. . . . Doing this will help push that piece back into the puzzle to make a complete picture."[14] Keith Johnson of the Makah Whaling Commission thought that renewed whaling would return the tribe to its central identity. "No one can say we don't have the right to whale, or that we are not a whaling people. . . . It's who we are."[15] Whaling advocates also argued that although everyone in the tribe stood to benefit, the return of whaling would be particularly important in helping men restore a lost warrior tradition. As Joddie Johnson, a Makah restaurant owner, explained to a *New York Times* reporter, "This brings meaning and purpose back to the Makah men. For 70 years, they had what they did best taken away from them."[16]

By the late 1990s, the whole process of resuming whaling opened for the Makah a pathway to what Mircea Eliade calls a "cosmogonic" or "creation" myth, a story about their place in the world, their source of divine energy, the very essence of who they were as a people: "The return to origins gives hope of a rebirth . . . the prodigious outpouring of energy, life, and fecundity that occurred at the Creation of the World."[17] According to Emile Durkheim's *Elementary Forms of the Religious Life*, many premodern peoples hunted their sacred, totemic animal kin. The fact that men and animals were related was thought to confer "a special aptitude for hunting the animal with success."[18]

Not only hunting, but eating this sacred game is central to what Durkheim calls a "sacrificial banquet" in which "the worshipper and his god communicate in the same flesh, in order to form a bond of kinship between them."[19] While an individual animal must die for this banquet, the sacred game's vital essence or spirit continues to live, because those that eat the animals now "feel them living in their own hearts."[20] Hunting and eating sacred game are also particularly important as a rite of passage from childhood into adulthood, enabling a new generation to affirm its kinship with the totemic species. Last, while it's clear that some peoples needed to eat their sacred totems for sustenance, Durkheim noted that in their cultural myths, the gods or sacred animals "would die if their cult were not rendered."[21] Honoring a sacred animal species by hunting and eating it was thus thought essential to keeping the species alive.

At one level, the hope of many Makah that the resumption of whaling would restore their people clearly fit with what Eliade and Durkheim concluded from their studies of premodern tribes. But the Makah in the 1990s were not a homogeneous, premodern society; their culture mixed indigenous beliefs with contemporary American practices. The spiritual tradition they were trying to recapture or reinvent existed only in fragments, pieced together from snatches of old stories and newly discovered artifacts. So it's not surprising that although everyone in the tribe saw the gray whales as immensely important sacred animals, no consensus existed on how to treat them.

Even among the Makah who believed the tribe should hunt and eat the gray whale, there was no consensus on how the hunt should be conducted. Some tribal elders believed that the crew members preparing for the hunt were not adequate to the task. "Basically, they're fuckups," complained John McCarty, a member of the Makah Whaling Commission.[22] McCarty was particularly distraught to learn that several of the crew members tested positive for alcohol and drug use, findings that kept the Makah Whaling Commission from issuing a whaling permit. Wayne Johnson, captain of the Makah whaling crew, repeatedly told his friends (including a few journalists) that he wasn't "too good with the spiritual stuff." At one point Johnson contemplated abandoning the attempt to strike a whale with a traditional harpoon, instead arguing that "we can just go out there and shoot one."[23] In the end, the crew passed the required alcohol and drug tests, a permit was issued, and they used traditional harpoons and lances to spear a gray whale. But the actual killing of the whale was accomplished by a shooter in a motorboat, with a rifle firing a .50 caliber machine-gun shell.

Some Makah rejected flat-out the whole idea of a whale hunt. Alberta Thompson, a seventy-four-year-old elder, spoke before the International Whaling Commission in 1996, advocating denial of the tribe's request because the Makah Tribal Council had never asked the entire tribe to vote on whether to resume whaling. The next year, Jean-Michael Cousteau (son of the late Jacques Cousteau, the famous French underwater documentary filmmaker) and the International Fund for Animal Welfare offered to take the Makah to San Ignacio Lagoon in Baja to meet gray whales up close.[24] Only Thompson accepted the offer. She returned home to the Olympic Peninsula transformed: "I met what I was fighting for, face-to-face. . . . The mother brought her baby over to our little boat. I talked to them and petted them. I felt that their spirit of trust was somehow being conveyed to me. I laughed and I cried all the way back to shore, and all that night. I've never been the same since."[25] Thompson subsequently argued that the Makah should recognize "that this whale gave up its life for us a hundred years ago so that we could eat," and that now to honor its sacrifice, the tribe was morally obligated to "protect the whale until the end of time."[26]

Thompson's call for a new covenant between Makah and gray whales put her at odds with much of the tribe's leadership—she was fired from her job as a clerk in the Makah Senior Center—and allied her with white antiwhaling activists, most notably Paul Watson and the Sea Shepherd Conservation Society. A host of other white protesters joined them. One proclaimed that her soul was connected to the souls of gray whales. Another explained that while kayaking he once saw a gray whale pass underneath his boat, an event so profound that he knew that his life would "never be the same."[27] A third activist described the struggle between the antiwhaling protesters and the Makah who wanted to hunt whales as a "fight of good versus evil."[28]

Paul Watson understood that the Makah, by themselves, were not a serious threat to the survival of gray whales. "Sea Shepherd is not investing this time and expense, committing our entire fleet, to oppose a tribal whale hunt of four or five whales," he wrote in the *Seattle Times*. It was clear that the environmentalists and Makah whalers regarded each other with contempt: After the tribe's rifle-assisted kill in the spring of 1999, Watson called them "rednecks." But both sides belonged to the same culture of enchantment. Both agreed that the gray whale represented a sacred animal with which they were trying to establish or reestablish kinship ties. Both wanted gray whale populations to thrive in the wild. Both thought that honoring the whale had the potential to renew society. Neither group, however, was prepared to accept what the other was doing or to recognize that there were different ways of respecting the sacredness of whales.

As Durkheim pointed out, some premodern cultures believed in hunting and eating their totemic kin, while others adamantly refused to do so. Moreover, this second group of cultures promoted many other kinds of ritual abstentions (no drinking, no sex, no swearing, etc.) as a way for members to purify themselves. Through these rites of abstention, Durkheim notes, the premodern person became entitled to approach sacred beings: "The man who has submitted himself to this prescribed interdiction is not the same afterwards as he was before. Before, he was an ordinary being, who, for this reason, had to keep at a distance from the religious forces. Afterwards, he is on a more equal footing with them; he has approached the sacred by the very act of leaving the profane."[29] No doubt many of the antiwhaling protesters not only abhorred eating whales, but avoided all meat. Vegetarian and vegan practices are one version of modern-day purifying rituals, granting privileged access to the enchanted creatures.

For Durkheim, the difference between the tribes who hunted and ate sacred game and those who saw the sacred animals as "taboo" was an interesting feature of the sociology of religion, but one without practical significance. After all, by the early twentieth century virtually all the religions of indigenous peoples, with their emphasis on land and animals as spiritual forces, had been repressed and marginalized. In contemporary times, though, this division is of distinct importance. Failure to resolve these differences—or at least come to grips with them—distracts the emerging culture of enchantment from a more significant problem.

Both the pro-hunting Makah and their anti-hunting opponents believe that whales are sacred beings that should not be killed simply to make a profit. Their common enemy is the commercial whaling industry, which sees the whale as a type of desirable wild meat superior to domesticated cattle or chicken. During the Makah's long preparations for the hunt, several members of the World Council of Whalers came uninvited to a tribal party. A whaler from Iceland listened intently to the Makah descriptions of the religious and cultural significance of whaling. Afterward he told journalist Robert Sullivan: "Everyone in the business is interested in this. In Iceland, we do the whaling, well, like we are running a paper mill. Not in this religious way."[30] And Paul Watson reported a question raised by the leader of the Japanese delegation at a meeting of the International Whaling Commission: "What is the difference between cultural necessity for the Makah and cultural necessity for the Japanese?"[31]

There is, in fact, a vast difference between the Makah and the Japanese concept of wild whales. The Makah and groups such as Sea Shepherd share a belief in the deepest values of the cultural enchantment of nature, what might be called "full" enchantment. They recognize that an animal's special magic cannot be completely separated from the land or water where it lives. Wild creatures and their natural habitats must both be preserved, creating a realm somewhat removed from human control—an "outside" natural world distinct from "inside" society. (As Durkheim argued, "Sacred beings are separated beings. . . . There is a break in continuity between them and the profane beings."[32]) By contrast, the Japanese and Icelandic whaling industries focus only on the profitable potential of the newly charismatic animals themselves. It is this "partial" enchantment, not the conflict between the ritual hunters and the animal rights advocates, that poses the real threat.

THE DESTRUCTIVENESS OF the partial enchantment of animals extends beyond whaling. One clear example is provided by the zoo and animal theme park industries. These businesses use much of the rhetoric and images from the culture of enchantment, glorifying the majesty and wonder of wild animals. At the same time, they treat their animals very differently than reenchantment proposes. The zoo and animal theme park industries have grown enormously in the past fifty years and now include a wide range of animal brokers, wild animal importers, breeders, "safari" ranches selling hunts of exotic game, and covert slaughterhouses that sell wild animal meats, organs, and limbs for use as medicines and aphrodisiacs. All of these businesses seek to capture wild animals in forests, deserts, or oceans and bring them "inside" society, typically in cages and pens, where they can be commercially exploited. What these industries call "wildness" is implicitly presented by them as something that permanently belongs to the creatures, an independent property, rather than a relationship between animals and their homelands.

Animal "wildness" is thus radically reduced to easily purchased fantasy experiences that obscure the true condition of animals and their habitats. The lion in his cage at the zoo or on the field at a theme park serves as an imaginary substitute for an ecologically intact Africa. The small tanks at aquariums contain so much concentrated marine life that it is easy to conclude that the ocean is healthy and fecund beyond belief. Scripted theatrical performances at animal theme parks give the impression that animals are always happy to interact with humans, while they actually appear on demand because they have no place to hide and have been trained to perform in exchange for food. The various enclosures for land animals, and the holding tanks for fish and sea mammals, are decorated like movie sets to conjure up appealing images of the savannah, the jungle, the forest, or the coral reef.

Wild animals thus became commodities bought and sold on the market. Indeed, what's striking is just how large and sophisticated the wild animal industry has become. Each year the members of the Association of Zoos and Aquariums (AZA), which includes more than 180 institutions, make decisions on how to dispose of "surplus" animals: babies of a species that the zoo or theme park does not need more of, or creatures thought to be too old to interest visitors. Sometimes the animals are advertised in the *AZA Animal Exchange* journal. On other occasions, member organizations sell their surplus wild animals to what are known as AZA Related Organizations or Commercial Members, who are required to abide by regulations designed to protect the animals. But researcher Alan Green has found that many of the AZA institutions are just "the front end of an elaborate shell game" in which AZA members eventually sell their animals to a vast array of auctioneers and dealers, who in turn sell them to virtually anyone.[33]

Surplus game animals such as Nubian ibex, African addax, and Persian gazelle often end up in hunting ranches where hunters pay a fixed price to hunt (an addax at Forest Ranch in Texas costs $2,250) and are virtually guaranteed a kill, because the animals cannot escape. Safari Club International, a hunting organization, encourages members to seek out a range of game from throughout the world to collect points and move up in the club's status hierarchy—but the club does not set criteria for how a hunt must be conducted. In the fall of 2006, one trophy-hunting magazine in Texas featured a cover photograph of a big buck deer facing the camera, his massive rack beckoning to the viewer. The fact that the deer was standing right behind a high wire-mesh fence to keep him from running was not mentioned, clearly just a taken-for-granted part of trophy hunting. All that counts is the collection of points. There is even a black market for mounted heads of big deer and other game: Men buy the heads from poachers and then tell their friends that they killed the trophy bucks. As Jim Kropp, Montana's chief law enforcement officer for crimes against wildlife, told the *New York Times*, "There is almost a fixation on possessing or obtaining trophy-class animals. People will go to any length to have these things in their possession. It's big antlers and big egos."[34]

Or take the cute baby animals found in petting zoos and roadside parks each summer. Sometimes they are surplus animals originally belonging to the nation's prestigious AZA members; other times they come from animal breeders. But either way, the fate of the young is often tragic. At the end of the summer season they're sold to breeders or dealers, who in turn often sell them to hunting ranches or to slaughterhouses. There is a huge market for adolescent bear parts and organs. Their skins become rugs, their claws jewelry; their paws are exported to Asia, where they are considered delicacies. Most valuable of all are the bear gallbladders, which are used in many Asian medicines and aphrodisiacs. Sometimes the bears are kept alive so that shunts can be placed into their gallbladders and the bile milked every day.[35] Buying a bear's paw or bile offers the fantasy of absorbing the "wild" power and virility of the animal without entering into any kind of relationship with either it or its lands.

Some particularly charismatic animals, such as wolves and big cats—tigers, lions, cougars—are now bred in so-called sanctuaries for sale to private individuals to use in commercial exhibits (ten dollars for a photo op) or to own as pets. By the late 1990s Americans owned an estimated fifteen thousand big cats; mountain lion cubs cost $800 or less in wild animal auctions, while tiger cubs could be had for $350.[36] Apex predators, among the wildest and most enchanted of all creatures, were thus reduced to playthings. However, neither big cats nor wolves can ever really be domesticated. The cats remain potentially dangerous, while the wolves, although they do not attack people, cannot accept captivity. In an effort to make wolves more tractable, breeders began to sell wolf-dog "hybrids." The business was enormously successful and by the mid-1990s an estimated 100,000 to 300,000 wolf hybrids lived in suburban backyards and rural compounds. But the animals still remained uncontrollable, at once highly aggressive—unlike wolves, they will attack and kill people—and at the same time highly dependent upon their owners.

Randall Lockwood, a vice president of The Humane Society of the United States, likened wolf-dog hybrid owners to a cult group. "A lot of people mistakenly feel they're being put in touch with nature, closer to the wolf's spirit," he explained. "They see themselves as part of the environmental movement by owning this little piece of wild nature. For a lot of people it is a religion. . . . They have their own circle of friends, and often their other friends get pushed aside, and it becomes almost a substitute family for them."[37] In failing to see the animal's connection to the land as part of the wildness of the wolf, wolf-dog hybrid owners have created dysfunctional human-animal relationships in which both parties become captive to each other.

ANOTHER FORM OF manufacturing "wildness" is practiced by the mariculture industry. Many species of what used to be wild fish are now raised in pens: Trout, catfish, and prawns are all farmed. But it is salmon that best illustrates the pathologies of conceiving of the "wildness" of a creature as separate from its home lands or waters. Wild salmon spend their lives migrating thousands of miles. They begin life in clear, cold creeks and rivers; wash downstream to the sea during spring rainy seasons; spend years maturing in the ocean; and then return to the river of their birth to procreate and die. Freeman House was by no means alone in his assessment that fishing for salmon and eating their flesh brought people in intimate contact with elemental forces of nature. With their great power and speed, and stunning reddish orange muscled flesh, wild salmon have been regarded as among the most sacred of creatures by virtually every traditional society that knew them, from the Native Americans of the Pacific Northwest to the medieval English.

Maintaining wild salmon populations requires that rivers be clear, cold, and flowing (that is, unimpeded by dams); that the land remain forested to avoid muddy runoff; and that the ocean stays relatively unpolluted. Damming, deforestation, pollution, and overfishing have caused wild salmon populations to plummet. Obviously, restoring them would require major changes. Mariculture offers society an easier option: farmed salmon. The captive fish are raised in tightly packed pens along temperate coasts, fed pellets made from dried baitfish, and given antibiotics to reduce the infections that inevitably result from so much fish excreta in a small space. Raised under these conditions, salmon flesh lacks its famous red orange color, which wild fish gain from crustaceans in their diet. It's a highly symbolic flaw in farmed salmon: The reddish orange color signifies all that is magical about the fish. Consequently, the mariculture industry feeds its farmed fish red food dye to artificially color them. Every farmed salmon is thus part of an elaborate animal theme park, a theater creating the illusion of wildness for a creature that has been stripped of its connections to the sea and land.

All of these forms of partial enchantment, in which the wildness of creatures is reduced to a theatrical image, also represent a kind of *green-washing*. From the most prestigious zoos to the safari ranches and roadside petting attractions, from the tiger cub breeders to the managers of the salmon farming industry, all the businesses and organizations involved in packaging and marketing partial enchantment have the same message: The present relationship between society and nature is optimal and everything is in harmonious balance. They offer access to the world's "wild" animals in convenient, cost-effective ways, readily purchasable as packaged fantasy experiences and animal products. There's no need for massive social change or for a new covenant between society and nature.

NOT ALL OF the internal threats to enchantment involve interactions with animals. One of the least expected difficulties has come from the transformation of Native Americans. Once the iconic representatives of a lost connection with nature, they have recently instead become emblems of crass entrepreneurship. As we have seen, Native American spirituality underpins virtually the entire culture of enchantment. The Hopi outreach to other tribes in the 1950s and 1960s led to the resurrection of tribal histories, biographies, folklore, and religious practices. Their outreach to the emerging hippie counterculture, meanwhile, helped make Native American spirituality—with its enchanted cosmos of Earth and animal spirits—accessible and attractive to the broader society. This in turn helped give rise both to the feminist goddess movement and to powerful trends in mainstream Judaism and Christianity that focused on Earth as God's sacred creation. And within popular culture, Native Americans became liminal figures who guided whites from profane society to sacred communion with nature.

There have always been some challenges to the notion that Native Americans enjoyed a spiritual relation with nature. For example, religious studies scholar Sam D. Gill argues that Native American religions did not really have a concept of Mother Earth, and that the popular associations of Native Americans with an Earth Goddess is based on one line spoken by Chief Tecumseh in 1809 negotiations over Indian lands: "The earth is my mother—and on her bosom I will repose."[38] Likewise, anthropologist Shepard Krech contends that whites romanticized Indian relationships with nature; he shows that when Plains Indians stampeded herds over cliffs, they wasted buffalo meat, killing more animals than they could use. However, Krech himself does not disagree with Sioux leader Red Cloud, who said that "where the Indian killed one buffalo, the hide and tongue hunters killed fifty."[39] And Gill's argument has proved wrong: Indian scholar Vine Deloria Jr. has shown that minutes of tribal councils and treaty negotiations contain "numerous references to Mother Earth."[40]

But while these external criticisms have been blunted, new threats have emerged from within the Indian community itself. The American Indian Movement activists and others who led the 1970s struggle to restore tribal sovereignty envisioned recovering as much lost tribal land as possible, protecting it from abusive resource extraction authorized by the Bureau of Indian Affairs, and resurrecting Native American spiritual traditions. They dreamed of restoring Indian guardianship over consecrated lands. But in the 1980s more "modern," business-oriented Indian leaders took over many tribes. Their goal was not to recapture the old myths but to utilize the land for profit, and take advantage of the lack of government restrictions on land use that came with sovereignty. These new leaders took sovereignty in a very different direction—the development of casino gambling.

By 2005, Native American tribes in twenty-eight states ran 411 casinos generating $18.5 billion a year.[41] Today, dozens of additional tribes are negotiating to open more casinos, and hundreds of groups around the country have applied to the Bureau of Indian Affairs for federal recognition so that they, too, can open gaming resorts. Stories now proliferate about the development of Indian casinos—their impact on communities, the massive campaign contributions that tribes now make to secure political support for gambling, and the intense conflicts within tribes over who qualifies as an official member and is therefore entitled to a share of casino profits.

Ironically, the Indian casino movement started as an offshoot from the effort to recover Indian lands. In the 1970s, a handful of lawyers financed by the Native American Rights Fund (NARF) began to file lawsuits against state governments over allegedly illegal sales of former Indian properties. These suits claimed that the states had ignored a 1790 law called the Nonintercourse Act, which said that Indians could not sell their lands to white people without approval of the federal government. Apparently many states at the time bought Indian lands for resale to whites without this approval. These lawsuits filed by the NARF made existing land titles problematic, posing a serious threat to landowners, the real estate industry, and state governments. The value of property under litigation declined and often it could not be put on the market.

In order to end the threat caused by the litigation, politicians passed legislation at both state and federal levels. The state bills offered the Indian plaintiffs land somewhere in the state where the suit originated (though not necessarily the land whose title was being challenged), in exchange for requiring the litigants to abandon all existing land claims and future lawsuits questioning land titles. The federal bills provided money for the states to buy land for the Indian litigants. In 1980, after a decade of fighting a Penobscot tribe lawsuit challenging land titles, the Maine legislature passed an act requesting federal money to buy nearly 470 square miles of land for two tribes, and Congress allocated $81.5 million to buy the land. Part of that congressional bill, though, was addressed to a nonland issue. In the late 1970s, the Penobscots, like many other tribes across the country, had started holding high-stakes bingo games, and Maine—which had a public policy against all gambling except for low-stakes charity events—wanted to shut these down. In accordance with the state's wishes, the federal money came with a provision that specifically prohibited Indian gaming.

The Penobscot tribal council supported the sacrifice of gaming to secure the land purchase, but some Indians were furious. When the Pequot tribe in Connecticut was seeking similar state and federal legislation for a much smaller land purchase (less than three square miles), they were warned by a disgruntled Maine Indian to protect their right to legalized gaming, and succeeded in retaining such rights during negotiations with officials. In 1983, Congress passed laws ending the Pequot lawsuits and authorizing the land purchase. It was a notable victory, culminating years of litigation. It was also a definitive moment of cultural transition. The Pequot had only recently won federal recognition as a tribe; until then, none of its members had even considered themselves to be Indians. As journalist Jeff Benedict aptly described the process, the family members who filed the lawsuits underwent "a sort of cultural assimilation through civil litigation," changing from white to Indian.[42] When the Pequot bingo parlor opened in 1986, it grossed over twenty million dollars. The tribe soon began plans for a massive resort hotel and casino, Foxwoods, halfway between Boston and New York City.

In 1987, the United States Supreme Court provided crucial support for Indian gambling in *California v. Cabazon Band of Mission Indians*. The Cabazon and Morongo bands of Mission Indians ran bingo parlors in Riverside County during the 1980s, and both the county and the state of California sought to regulate the games. The Supreme Court ruled that while states do have the power to enforce criminal laws on Indian reservations, they cannot impose civil regulations there—and gambling is a purely regulatory issue, because most states do allow certain forms of it, even if only charity bingo games or state lotteries. The ruling was widely interpreted to mean that Indians could offer any form of gaming that a state permitted to occur off reservation land.[43]

In response to the surging movement by tribes to open casinos, Congress passed the Indian Gaming Regulatory Act in 1988. The bill presented gambling as a way to promote tribal self-sufficiency but tried to contain it by restricting it to reservation lands or lands contiguous to the reservation. Although these regulations seemed fairly stringent, attorneys and lobbyists saw loopholes that made it possible to build an Indian casino just about anywhere. Riders attached to congressional bills routinely permitted tribes to take off-reservation lands into trust to develop casinos. (Lands in "trust" were under federal ownership but tribal control.) Some tribes began to practice "reservation shopping," filing extensive land claims challenging property titles and then settling the claims in exchange for permission to develop off-reservation casinos. In 2004, for example, the Native American Land Group, a corporation composed of Alaskan Eskimo tribal associations and venture capitalist firms, filed lawsuits on behalf of the Cheyenne and Arapaho tribes of Oklahoma, making claims to over forty-two thousand square miles in Colorado. In a letter sent to 150 land-title companies, the group offered to settle its claims in exchange for eight-tenths of a square mile near Denver International Airport, where they could build a $150 million casino.[44]

The Cayuga in upstate New York, a tribe without a reservation, accepted a thirty-acre former horse-racing track in the Catskills in exchange for abandoning its hundred-square-mile land claim at the northern tip of Cayuga Lake. Although the Cayuga never lived in the Catskills, they wanted to build a five-hundred-million-dollar gambling resort there; analysts estimated that the resort could bring in one billion dollars per year.[45] So much money was at stake that non-Indian real estate developers and other businessmen began financing groups who were trying to obtain federal recognition from the Bureau of Indian Affairs to then get off-reservation lands for gambling. By 2004, some 291 groups had applied for federal recognition as tribes, and one investigator estimated that two-thirds of them had already made development agreements with private investors. Donald Trump and three partners have spent five million dollars in Connecticut alone financing would-be tribes.[46]

Tribes and their backers also engaged in political lobbying on a grand scale. The 1988 Indian Gaming Regulatory Act's stipulation

that states enter into "good faith" negotiations with tribes to determine the framework for casino gambling did not anticipate just how
political the negotiations would become. In California alone, from
1998 through mid-2003, tribes spent over $120 million in lobbying
and campaign contributions to win politicians' support for laws enhancing tribal sovereignty and voter approval for the right to develop
Las Vegas–style casino gambling.[47] Their contributions and campaign-
ing worked. By 2004 almost half of California's 107 federally recognized tribes ran casinos, bringing in five billion dollars per year.[48]

When tribes open casinos, bitter struggles frequently develop
over just who qualifies as a tribal member entitled to a share of gaming profits. Tribes, legally established at the state level as corporations
and regarded at the federal level as sovereign but "dependent" nations, can set their own membership requirements. The Pequot at
one time required applicants to prove that at least one great-great-
grandparent was listed in a 1910 tribal census (which included
sixty-six people, only three of whom were full-blooded Pequot).[49]
But in 1995, when new leaders took over the tribe, that requirement
was abolished. At the time, Foxwoods was already the world's largest
casino with over three hundred million dollars per year in revenue.
The tribe became swamped with applicants who had DNA tests
showing some Indian ancestry but no proven connection to known
tribal members. "People say, 'I just found out I'm Indian and I want
to know how I can start receiving my profits,'" reported enrollment
clerk Joyce Walker.[50] In 2005, the Pequot reinstated a stringent ad-
mission rule, requiring applicants to validate that they are the offspring of a tribal member.

When the San Pasqual tribe near San Diego reconstituted itself in
the 1960s, it required those seeking to claim membership to have
one-eighth Pasqual blood, but also accepted the children of tribal
members (called "lineals") as equals on the reservation even if they
had a smaller proportion than that. After the tribe opened a casino in
2001, members excluded lineals from casino profits and even attacked

them when they tried to attend tribal meetings. As UCLA anthropologist Russell Thornton has noted, "Maybe somebody has only one-sixteenth of a tribe's blood, but speaks the language or lives on the reservation, and someone else is a quarter . . . but has never been to the reservation. Who is more Indian?"[51]

Other tribes have also expelled members after casinos started to bring in millions. In the late 1970s and early 1980s, the Pechanga tribe in San Diego County accepted dozens of applicants who traced their Indian ancestry to Manuela Miranda, the half-blood granddaughter of a nineteenth-century tribal headman. The tribe's casino opened in 2001 and soon generated more than $184 million in annual revenue, with each member receiving over $120,000 every year. In 2004, the tribal council voted to expel all of the 130 descendants of Manuela Miranda—10 percent of the Pechanga—from the tribe on the grounds that the original decision to admit them had been a mistake. "The Pechanga Band has fought long and hard to preserve its sovereign rights and rights to self-determination," argues the tribe's attorney. "The right to determine its membership is the most basic of those rights."[52]

Apparently the Native Americans most attuned to nature have been among those expelled. As tribes expanded casino gambling and built resort hotels, they frequently ignored state environmental laws, and often showed indifference to the fate of the land and animals. The sheer scale of the larger casino-hotel-golf resorts, with up to several million visitors a year, inevitably creates environmental strains. In desert regions, the demand for water to support these resorts stresses aquifers; nearby springs go dry, threatening both neighboring residents and wildlife. Massive sewage systems must be built, and wastewater from treatment plants is discharged into local waterways. One tribe, the Agua Caliente band of Cahuilla Indians near Palm Springs, historically had a totemic kinship relation with Peninsular bighorn sheep. The sheep, declared an endangered species in 1998, were given some protection in 2001 after the U.S. Fish and Wildlife Service

designated 1,381 square miles of the Mojave Desert as "critical habitat," requiring any proposed development to undergo federal review
for its potential impact upon sheep. But in 2005, the Agua Caliente began to worry about their ability to develop seven square miles of their
reservation that fell within the habitat regulations. Consequently, they
sued the federal government, wanting to remove the "critical habitat"
designation from the entire 1,381 square miles on the grounds that the
tribe could lose "hundreds of millions of dollars" in development
profits. In return, the tribe offered a three-square-mile reserve, which
the Center for Biological Diversity calls a "tiny amount of land," inad-
equate to support the animals.[53]

Some tribal leaders insist that there is no conflict between Native
American culture and Indian casino theme parks. In 2004, Anthony
Miranda, the Pechanga head of the California Nations Indian Gaming Association, told a reporter that months before the Pechanga
opened their first Las Vegas–style casino in 1995, "A golden eagle
had swooped just inches above my head. It was a message from the
tribal spirits. I knew we couldn't fail." Miranda encouraged other
tribes to combine modern profits with traditional culture. "We've
shown that we can develop and run big businesses. But let us not for-
get our ancestors and elders, who are saying, 'Hang onto your sovereignty, land, and Indian ways. Those things are not up for barter.' "[54]

Indeed, the Pechanga have opened negotiations with Los Angeles's
financially strapped Southwest Museum of the American Indian; the
tribe wants to lease part of the Southwest Museum's collection to stock
a Pechanga museum, to be built next to a new $270 million hotel and
casino.[55] Foxwoods, for its part, has had a museum located at the resort
since 1998; constructed at a cost of $193 million, it is billed as the
largest Native American research facility in America.[56] But the museum is at most a secondary attraction. Foxwoods instead emphasizes its
multiple hotels, thirty restaurants, four-thousand-seat theater, golf
courses, seven thousand slot machines, and scores of shopping opportunities. The Pequot want the resort to become for Connecticut "what

Disney World means to the state of Florida."[57] By 2007, the casino operations took in over one billion dollars a year.[58]

While the casinos undoubtedly have allowed people faced with poverty on reservations unfit for ranching or agriculture to live more affluent lives, this newfound wealth often comes with its own bitter costs. Giving up land claims to traditional territories in exchange for casino sites is a completely different strategy for political sovereignty and economic well-being than the American Indian Movement's original program, which aspired to restore both traditional cultures and sovereignty over tribal lands. Once tribal membership is made contingent upon DNA, Native American culture and spirituality become essentially superfluous. Similarly, transforming Indian cultures into superficial theme park motifs and casino sideshows diminishes both the seriousness of these cultures and their connections to the environment. Not all Native Americans have embraced this change, and many continue to press for the renewal of traditional cultures and protection of their lands. But today, the image of the liminal Indian guiding whites back to Mother Earth competes with another image: the casino-gambling entrepreneur and real estate developer, flush with money for political lobbying, new investment opportunities, and luxury consumption. Native Americans are no longer pure icons of enchantment.

# 8

---

# The Right-Wing War on the Land

Most of the problems that plague the culture of enchantment can be understood as "growing pains"—dilemmas and contradictions that do not signify failure but rather stem from the culture's fragmentary development and increasing popularity. But not all of its difficulties fit this pattern. As the twenty-first century began, the enchantment culture and the environmental movement came under deliberate, organized attack from the Christian right, the Bush administration, and much of the business establishment. These simultaneous salvos—a fundamentalist Christian critique of enchantment spirituality and a corporate-driven effort to dismantle environmental protection—proved highly effective. It was not until the later years of Bush's second term that (as we shall see in the next chapter) the right's religious, political, and economic coalition lost momentum and began to disintegrate and fail.

In the early 1970s, the people serving as what Max Weber would call enchantment's "characteristic bearers" had been dissident, marginal groups: Native American activists, hippies, and environmentalists.[1] But over the next twenty-five years, the culture of enchantment won converts from many sectors of the population. Indeed, by the 1990s, its core themes—the Gaia theory, the spiritual importance of wild animals and places, Earth as God's sacred creation—were being echoed by political elites. Al Gore's book *Earth in the Balance: Ecology and the Human Spirit*, published during the 1992 campaign, became a national bestseller, selling over half a million copies in just a few years.[2] Like many admirers of Lovelock's Gaia hypothesis, Gore saw it not just as a vitally important scientific advance but as cause for spiritual reflection. Quoting from the hymn "Amazing Grace," the vice president emphasized that "by experiencing nature in its fullest—our own and that of all creation—with our sense and with our spiritual imagination, we can glimpse, 'bright shining as the sun,' the infinite image of God."[3] And he noted that many other spiritual and religious traditions offered similar versions of Earth as sacred creation.[4] Pointing to the speeches of Chief Seattle, for instance, Gore praised the Native American reverence for land. He acknowledged the goddess movement, citing Marija Gimbutas and Riane Eisler's argument that in neolithic Europe there was once a single Earth Goddess who was "assumed to be the font of all life and who radiated harmony among all living things." He also quoted Islam's Prophet Mohammed: "The world is green and beautiful and God has appointed you His stewards over it."[5] *Earth in the Balance* likewise found mentions of Mother Earth in both Hinduism and Sikhism, and additional references to water and sky as spiritual forces in many traditions.

These expressions of enchantment were at the heart of Gore's proposed world environmental policy, what he called "a global Marshall plan." Its goals included stabilizing world population; developing environmentally sensitive alternative technologies; changing the way economic indicators (such as gross national product) are measured to include the costs of depleting natural resources and the damages caused by pollution; negotiating international treaties to conserve animal habitats; educating the public about how human activities impact the global environment; and creating environmentally sustainable societies through promoting human rights, political freedom, and adequate living standards.[6] It was an extraordinary vision, offering new direction to the Democratic Party and the United States.

It was never put into effect. During their eight years in office, neither President Bill Clinton nor Vice President Gore ever sought to mobilize public support for this ambitious plan. Even though Gore went to Kyoto in 1997 to help negotiate the famous treaty requiring nations to reduce their carbon dioxide emissions, the Clinton-Gore administration did not push the U.S. Senate to ratify the protocols. Instead, the administration tried to reduce pollution by working out compromises with various industries. For example, their political appointees leading the Environmental Protection Agency spent years negotiating with electrical power companies about the 1977 "New Source Rules" of the Clean Air Act, which require coal-fired plants to install pollution-control equipment whenever the plants undergo major overhauls. Not until late 1999 did the EPA file lawsuits to enforce the regulations.[7]

When *Earth in the Balance* was released, the book's popularity both stoked and confirmed the fears of the nation's business establishment. An editorial in the *Wall Street Journal* decried beliefs that "the earth is sanctified," noting with disdain that the idea originated with the "Religious Left" and was a product of "a secular, or even pagan, fanaticism that now worships such gods as nature and gender with a reverence formerly accorded real religions."[8] Limiting development, as environmentalists proposed, would threaten profits; reducing toxic wastes would increase expenses. A widespread acceptance of the culture of enchantment might even reduce consumption. But strikingly, the backlash from the business world was dwarfed by the negative reaction from the nation's evangelical and fundamentalist Protestant leadership: figures such as Jerry Falwell, Pat Robertson, Tim LaHaye, and James Dobson. Along with many other conservative Christian theologians, scholars, and preachers, they saw the enchantment of nature as a dangerous threat both to their faith and to political and economic doctrines they derived from fundamentalist theology.

Attacking the culture of enchantment and the environmental movement was by no means the principal goal of the Christian right, nor did the various evangelicals preach exactly the same theology. Nevertheless, all of their theological positions concerning God's relationship to nature are similar, and their hatred of the culture of enchantment is based on several overlapping themes. Environmentalism, they argue, goes against God's laws of dominion as laid out in the Bible; worshipping nature is idolatry and therefore a form of Satanism. Moreover, according to some readings of the Book of Revelation, all true Christians, both dead and alive, will physically ascend into heaven during the Rapture; the fallen Christians who are left behind will fight the Antichrist. Then, after seven years of Tribulations, Christ will battle the Antichrist and eventually defeat him, destroying the planet and creating a new Earth. Various interpretations of the prophecy differ in their details, but the point is clear: If the Lord is going to destroy the old Earth and replace it with a new one, then there is no need for an environmental movement. On the contrary, it's a deadly distraction from the urgent need to accept Jesus Christ as one's personal savior and convert to Christianity before the Rapture.

Such beliefs are by no means new. In the mid-nineteenth century, Irishman John Nelson argued that a "common sense" reading of the Bible divides all of history into seven eras or dispensations, with the last era beginning with the Rapture.[9] Historically, popular interest in this theology, called "dispensational millenarianism," peaked whenever people threatened by societal changes sought refuge in promises of salvation and escape from worldly corruption.[10] After the upheavals of the 1960s, for example, the evangelical writer Hal Lindsey sold over two million copies of *The Late Great Planet Earth* (1973), which denounced the counterculture's paganism and drug use. Lindsey also attacked mainstream Protestant denominations for responding to the changes of the 1960s with new ecumenical thinking, charging them with the sin of apostasy. Both the hippies' and the liberal Christians' days were numbered: Soon the Rapture would begin.[11]

In the late 1980s and the 1990s, another wave of dispensational thinkers gained prominence and popularity. The social changes that caused anxiety for conservatives this time around included increasing globalization, high divorce rates, the increased visibility of gays and lesbians, and new technologies such as the Internet. The approach of the millennium in 2000 also heightened the sense of imminent apocalypse. At the same time, the growing popularity of the culture of enchantment within mainstream America struck many conservative religious thinkers as clear evidence of Satan's growing power.

Evangelical writer Frank Peretti made the bestseller lists with his 1989 novel *Piercing the Darkness,* in which a host of demons invade a small town to wreak havoc and capture unsuspecting souls. When not doing the devil's work, the demons relax at the Summit Institute for Humanistic Studies, where they take pleasure in attending seminars such as "Ecology: The Merging of Earth and Spirit." One of the presenters (modeled on the folk singer John Denver) plays a guitar before reading his paper; the celebrity-filled audience sings along. Peretti describes the scene: "The demons among them were enjoying it as well. Such worship and attention as they were now receiving was like getting a good back rub, and they even twitched and squirmed with delight at every bar of the song's carefully shaded double meanings."[12]

That same year Samantha Smith, another evangelical author, attended a Los Angeles conference on the "New U.S. Agenda for Environment and Development in the 1990s." The conference attendees included John Denver, CNN magnate Ted Turner, former president Jimmy Carter, former astronaut John Glenn, and U.S. senators Al Gore, Tim Wirth, and Mark Hatfield. To her dismay, a Native American spiritual leader named Little Crow made prayers to Mother Earth, Grandfather Spirit, and the Four Directions, declaring the conference a "sacred place."[13] Smith decried the attendees who "gave reverence to the demonic spirit called Mother Earth," and later wrote a book to expose the environmental movement's pagan agenda. According to Smith, it was God alone who was sacred; and "like it or not, when the earth has served His purpose, He will destroy it (2 Peter 3:10) and will create a new Heaven and a new earth."[14]

These ideas reached an enormous audience. In the 1990s, polls showed that around a third of adult Americans—some forty-five to fifty million people—considered themselves to be "born again," meaning they had reconfirmed their belief in Jesus Christ as their personal savior. About as many agreed with the statement that "the Bible is the actual Word of God and is to be taken literally, word for word."[15] The leadership of the Christian right had long ago concluded that this populace could be politically mobilized—in 1970, Jerry Falwell proclaimed that "we could turn this nation upside down for God"—and built a vast network of television and radio stations, newsletters, Web sites, and publishing houses to help achieve this goal.[16]

Pat Robertson, the famous evangelical television talk-show host, wrote three bestselling books in the early 1990s—*The New Millennium* (1990), *The New World Order* (1991), and *The Secret Kingdom* (1992)— which articulated many fundamentalist ideas about the environment.[17] In the first, he explains that it was President Ronald Reagan's secretary of the interior, Donald Hodel, who first alerted him to the religious dangers of the environmental movement: "Hodel told me that I would never understand the wilderness movement until I recognized that to these people, these activists, the wilderness is an object of worship. It is something they worship as an ideal."[18] In his more compassionate moments, Robertson saw the activists as "people desperately searching for something to fill the void in their own souls . . . and they are reaching out to nature as God."[19] But he made it clear that he thought they were wrong. "What happens in the wilderness may be important to nature and the natural processes of the earth, but it certainly is not holy."[20]

Indeed, wrote Robertson, in treating parts of the Earth as sacred, environmentalists committed the sin of idolatry, violating several important Biblical injunctions.[21] In *The Secret Kingdom* Robertson says that while he was thinking about these very issues, God spoke to him in a conversational voice, telling him to open his Bible: "Look at Genesis and you will see." Robertson reports that his eyes fell upon this passage in Genesis 1:26–27 (his emphasis): "And God said, Let us make man in our image, after our likeness, and *let them have dominion* over the fish of the sea, and all the earth, and over every creeping thing that creepeth upon the earth. So God created man."[22] Robertson believes that God had instructed him to stress man's authority over the Earth—"He wants him to rule the way he was created to rule. . . . God gave man a sweeping and total mandate of dominion over this planet and everything in it."[23]

To Robertson and many other evangelical thinkers, the notion that humans are made in God's image means that any doctrine stressing equality and kinship between humans and animals is a sin. Charles Darwin's theory of evolution is denounced both because it is "godless" and because it teaches that humans are biologically related to other mammals. Enchantment's goal of creating and affirming totemic relationships with animals similarly violates evangelicals' strict boundaries. Robertson argues that such "naturalistic and animist" tendencies are linked to older pagan worship, and that "in each of these pagan religions there was always a seed of Satanic root."[24]

In *The New World Order* Robertson offered a dramatic response to the ideas of international cooperation for preserving the environment, laying out a scenario in which something similar to Gore's "global Marshall plan" for the planet came to pass. There would be an internationally ratified "Law of the Sea" to regulate maritime commerce, preventing ships from dumping waste into oceans and controlling fishing to stop species depletion; and a "Law of the Land and Forest" to stop deforestation, especially in the tropics. A "Law of the Skies" would control ozone-depleting chemicals and other air pollution: "No one would be allowed to pollute the air that the people of the world, its plants, and its animal life must breathe." A "Law of Energy Conservation," meanwhile, would regulate automobile fuel mileage, and "develop electric automobiles, alternate power sources, and safe, cheap nuclear power."[25] And a "Law of Industry and Agriculture" would establish worldwide standards for guaranteed minimum wages, health benefits, and product safety.

Would this environmental New World Order be a utopia? In Robertson's view, just the opposite. To him, the quest to restore ecological balance and sustainable development is merely a ruse, a distraction for the masses, masking a sinister plot. The creation of world treaties would require a single world currency, administered by a world bank. A huge bureaucracy would inevitably develop to apply all the new regulations. The new international government would require a worldwide Internal Revenue Service, along with a United Nations army authorized to shoot American citizens for tax crimes—or for other violations, such as possession of firearms.[26] (In Robertson's assessment, "With the government as god, the major crimes in society involve breaking government regulations."[27]) These nefarious developments are all part of a Satanic plan: "Satan knows that world government must soon be prepared for the man whom he is preparing to receive his particular empowerment and authority."[28] The New World Order, ostensibly focused on saving the Earth, is actually a stage for the coming of the Antichrist.

ROBERTSON'S VIVID PORTRAYAL of a demonic, omnipotent world government certainly helped influence evangelicals' opinions about environmental treaties. But it was theologian Tim LaHaye who was responsible for the Christian right's most widely read and influential assault on the culture of enchantment. LaHaye, who served on Jerry Falwell's Moral Majority board of directors and was quite well known in evangelical circles, promulgated beliefs about the connection between environmentalism and the devil that were even more

extreme than those of Pat Robertson. In one book, LaHaye argues
that the entire surface of the planet and its atmosphere is the "abode
of Satan."[29] In another, he approvingly quotes a fellow dispensation-
alist scholar, Joseph Lam, who asserts that "the Himalayan Mountains of Tibet and Nepal gave Lucifer the high ground he adores
(Isaiah 14:13–14)."[30] In a 1999 work called *Are We Living in the End
Times?*, LaHaye and fellow evangelist Jerry Jenkins pointed to dangerous warning signs: "These days paganism is widespread not only in
backward countries but also in America. Have you noticed the increasing worship of the mother goddess Gaia? . . . It is quite possible that
we are on the verge of seeing a merging of the feminist movement, liberal Christianity (with its penchant for feminizing the scriptures), and
mother goddess worship."[31] To LaHaye and Jenkins, any movement
that saw the Earth as a whole, or particular landscapes, as sacred was
guilty of spreading Satan's influence. As Dr. Henry Morris, a right-
wing theologian cited by LaHaye, declared, worship of "the spirits of
trees and other natural objects . . . is in reality worship of demons."[32]

Starting in 1995, LaHaye paired up with Jenkins to produce a
twelve-volume series of novels called Left Behind, which used fundamentalist theological ideas to create a terrifying fictional world. The series is the story of a group of people who find Jesus Christ only after the
Rapture has occurred and the Antichrist is rising to take control of a
United Nations–dominated new world order. The heroes form a paramilitary commando group to fight the Antichrist and his many minions,
and ultimately to challenge Satan. The paramilitary novel was already a
familiar vehicle for conservative authors; since the late 1960s dozens of
such fictional series had featured heroes fighting outside the system to
defeat drug dealers, terrorists, and communists.[33] LaHaye and Jenkins
reframed the genre using evangelical doctrines. Left Behind made its
way not only into Christian retail outlets, but also into mainstream
bookstores such as Barnes & Noble and even into big-box stores like
Wal-Mart and Target. By 2003, sales of books from the series had exceeded fifty million copies.[34]

The Left Behind books attack the culture of enchantment on a number of levels. The Antichrist's official religion, called Great Enigma Mystery Babylon One-World Faith, is a reenchantment-like ecumenical mix. The head of this church addresses his audience with a benediction: "I confer upon this gathering the blessing of the universal father and mother and animal deities who lovingly guide us on our path to true spirituality."[35] The post-Rapture Earth is a hell, a place where "fallen," imperfect Christians suffer endless and hideous torments. Early in the Tribulations, massive earthquakes turn the sky black with volcanic ash, "burning up a third of all the earth's trees and all its grasses." Something like a giant meteorite crashes into the ocean, turning one-third of all ocean life into blood. Another poisonous meteorite contaminates one-third of the Earth's rivers and springs, making them toxic. Millions of locustlike creatures strike with venom so strong that people's bodies burn for "five long months." Midway through the Tribulations, half of the world's population has died terrible deaths.[36]

"And then," LaHaye and Jenkins write, "it gets worse." During the second half of the Tribulations, God's wrath "is poured out in full strength." A plague of "foul and loathsome" sores torments those who worship the Antichrist. God kills every animal in the oceans, and "dead sea creatures rise to the surface, spreading their corruption to the four winds." Angry that the Antichrist has killed many of those who have converted to Christianity after the Rapture, God turns the world's springs, rivers, and lakes into blood. Afterward, He increases the sun's power, to bake and torture the survivors.[37]

The message of the Left Behind series echoes that of Pat Robertson and other evangelicals. Humans cannot save the Earth—"Jesus Christ is the only one who has been given the authority to bring such a kingdom into being," writes LaHaye.[38] The Earth is Satan's home, and all animals and plants are connected to his demons. It makes sense, then, that true Christians should long for personal salvation and hope to be swept away in the Rapture, lifted to heaven where God resides.

After that, according to LaHaye, God "will destroy this earth that is so marred and cursed by Satan's evil. He will include the atmospheric heaven to guarantee that all semblance of evil has been cleared away."[39]

No one knows just how many of the millions who read the Left Behind series or belonged to extremely conservative Christian churches actually believed that Earth was the abode of Satan and the culture of enchantment the devil's handmaiden. Scholars who study dispensational premillennialism stress that tales of forthcoming apocalyptic horror shouldn't be taken literally. In the words of cultural and religious studies professor Amy Johnson Frykholm, "As an account of the end of time and the meaning of human history, rapture is rhetoric. It is used to persuade people of their need for faith and to persuade others of the superiority and rightness of that faith."[40]

But rhetoric can have real political consequences. Evangelical encouragement of the idea that the Rapture is coming (even if no one can say precisely when) teaches followers that working for conservation is not only unnecessary but an affront to the infinite power of God. Pat Robertson stressed this point in *The Secret Kingdom*, noting that God "is above the laws of nature and any restrictions that those laws might try to impose."[41] God can therefore restore nature if he so chooses. In turn, many conservative thinkers, even those not known for their religious devotion, began to spout theology to justify unrestrained taking of the Earth's resources. Conservative pundit Ann Coulter quipped, "God gave us the earth. We have dominion over the plants, the animals, the trees. God said, 'Earth is yours. Take it. Rape it. It's yours.'"[42]

Max Weber once compared religious "world images"—a faith's fundamental understanding of its deities, morality, and the nature of people—to railroad "switchmen," saying that they "determined the tracks along which action has been pushed by the dynamic of [economic and political] interest."[43] Conservative theological ideas thus began to go hand in hand with conservative ideas about government and business. God was a free-market Republican. Capitalist society was a paragon of free choice, the perfect social order to fulfill what conservative Protestant theologians saw as God's desire for people to freely choose either righteous or sinful ways to live. Pat Robertson even claimed the Bible supported the disciplined pursuit of profit: "The enjoyment of life was God's plan. Enlightened self-interest was also obviously His plan." Socialism, on the other hand, was for La-Haye "a Babylonian [Satan-inspired] philosophy for the conduct of government, commerce and religion."[44] And liberal humanism was of course a variant of socialism.

Consequently, the far-right Christian evangelical leadership saw supporting conservative politicians as a religious obligation for the pre-Rapture period. LaHaye even came up with an ingenious name for this open-ended era, calling it the "pretribulation tribulation." "The tribulation is predestined and will surely come to pass," he wrote. "But pretribulation—that is, the tribulation that will engulf this country if liberal humanists are permitted to take total control of our government—is neither predestined nor necessary."[45]

The Republican Party eagerly reached out to take the hand the evangelicals offered. In the 2000 presidential election, a mobilized evangelical constituency made up at least 30 percent of Bush's total support, helping to put him into office. Plans for dismantling the federal government's environmental regulations began almost immediately. The September 11, 2001, attacks on the World Trade Center and the Pentagon further strengthened the Republican-Evangelical coalition. With the United States at war against "evil-doers," President Bush announced it was imperative for the country to obtain access to all possible natural resources, particularly oil and natural gas. At the same time, the pictures of the jets flying into the Twin Towers—the explosions, fires, and the collapse of the buildings, killing thousands—brought forth what religious studies scholar Glen Shuck calls "a palpable sense of apocalypse."[46] A CNN poll taken in 2002 showed 59 percent of Americans believing that the prophecies in the Bible's Book of Revelation—the primary source for dispensational premillennialism—would come true.[47]

By 2003, forty-five senators and 186 representatives received approval ratings of at least 80 percent from the three most influential conservative Christian lobbying groups—the Christian Coalition, Eagle Forum, and Family Resource Council. (Journalist Glenn Scherer noted that when these same officials had their voting records reviewed by the League of Conservation Voters, they earned average approval ratings of less than 10 percent.[48]) A number of these officials also publicly declared themselves to be evangelical Christians, including Senate Majority Leader Bill Frist (R-Tenn.), Senate Majority Whip Mitch McConnell (R-Ky.), House Majority Leader Tom DeLay (R-Tex.), and Senate Environment and Public Works Committee Chair James Inhofe (R-Okla.), who in 1997 had called the Environmental Protection Agency a "Gestapo bureaucracy." Inhofe is a member of Christian Zionists, an evangelical church with twenty million members whose theology says that the establishment of Israel signals the inexorable approach of the Rapture. DeLay also belongs to Christian Zionists, and has shown a similar appetite for the End Times. In 2002, for instance, when Pastor John Hagee proclaimed that "the war between America and Iraq is the gateway to the Apocalypse," DeLay endorsed the sermon as "the truth from God."[49]

Not every politician who received approval from conservative Christian groups necessarily read and agreed with Robertson and La-Haye. Some, like DeLay and Inhofe, clearly believed wholeheartedly in extreme doctrines, while others were prompted by more practical considerations: attracting fundamentalist voters, securing campaign donations from big businesses, and overturning environmental laws to give these businesses unlimited access to natural resources. George W. Bush himself proclaimed that he was born again, but the frequent gatherings of conservative Christian ministers and organizers at the White House struck some of his own staff members more as efforts to keep the Republican coalition together in support of his economic agenda than as expressions of faith.[50] But these various motivations—both "ideal" and "material," as Weber would say—all added up to the same thing: a potent Republican-Evangelical political machine, engaged in war on a grand scale against the nation's public lands and environmental laws.

THE FULL SCOPE of the Bush administration attack can be grasped only by examining it in detail. The first priority was to create a new national energy policy that would open most federal lands to oil and gas drilling. Executives from eighteen of the largest energy industry companies and trade associations had personally donated $16.6 million to Bush and to other Republican campaigns. During the four months leading up to the release of the Bush energy policy, they repeatedly met with Spencer Abraham, Bush's energy secretary.[51] In all, more than a hundred executives from the energy industry had meetings with Abraham. Only five environmental groups secured hearings.[52]

Bush, who as a candidate called for allowing oil and gas drilling in Alaska's Arctic National Wildlife Refuge, made ANWR the public focus of his new policy. He claimed that it could produce six hundred thousand barrels of oil a day: a figure that "happens to be exactly the amount we import from Saddam Hussein's Iraq."[53] Preserving ANWR, then, meant forcing America to buy oil from the devil himself, making the refuge a devil's landscape. Even after Hussein was overthrown in 2003, Bush and other Republican politicians, such as Alaska senator Ted Stevens, repeatedly argued that drilling in ANWR was essential for America's national security. At the same time, the Republican leadership clearly saw getting into ANWR as a crucial battle in the war to destroy the environmental movement. In August 2001, House Majority Leader Tom DeLay announced that Republicans "feel very, very confident we will be able to crack the back of radical environmentalists."[54] By implication, if the Republicans succeeded in opening up the refuge, then they could successfully win permission to drill anywhere, including near the California and Florida coasts, or in 297 other national wildlife refuges identified by the United States Geological Survey as having oil and gas potential.[55] As Governor Bill Richardson (D-N.Mex.) framed the struggle, "ANWR is the Holy Grail" for both parties: for Democrats because of their environmentalism, and for Republicans because they are oil and gas stalwarts.[56]

Opening up ANWR for drilling could be done only through new legislation from Congress. But Bush's national energy policy changed drilling rules on many other public lands by executive order. Following requests from energy companies and trade associations, the Bush administration told officials at the Bureau of Land Management and other federal agencies to "streamline" and "expedite" the process of reviewing oil and gas lease applications. Jerry Jordan, president of the Independent Petroleum Association of America, which represents 85 percent of domestic drillers, said that "the net effect, from our viewpoint, will be that things become more reasonable."[57] But, in fact, the changes that ensued were sometimes quite drastic. In Utah, for example, Bureau of Land Management supervisors ordered their field employees to ensure that "when an oil and gas lease parcel or when an application to drill comes in the door, that this work is their No. 1 priority."[58]

The National Petroleum Institute, an industry trade group, claimed that the Rocky Mountain states held 343 trillion cubic feet of natural gas, of which 137 trillion cubic feet could be found on some 470,000 square miles of public lands. Although the U.S. Geological Survey disputed those figures, estimating that federal lands in the West held only thirty-seven trillion cubic feet of gas, and that 90 percent of that was locked in rock formations that would make extraction prohibitively expensive, the NPI's estimates served as the basis for the new Bush energy policy.[59] Consequently, much of the West's public lands were made available for leasing to oil and gas companies. An additional 91,000 square miles of privately held Western lands also became open to oil and gas drilling, because these properties were once settled by homesteading: Their owners only possessed surface rights, while the Bureau of Land Management retained all rights to mineral extraction.[60]

In 2004, the Bureau of Land Management issued over six thousand oil and gas permits, roughly three times what the Clinton administration had granted a decade earlier—and Clinton's administration was more permissive than those of either Ronald Reagan or George H. W. Bush.[61] The West was to be transformed into an industrial grid of wells, roads, and pipelines. In New Mexico, the BLM proposed twenty thousand wells on over 7,800 square miles of the San Juan Basin.[62] Not to be outdone, BLM officials in Wyoming devised a ten-year plan for the region's Powder River Basin that would allow 51,000 methane gas wells on 12,500 square miles, including drilling in the 586-square-mile Bridger-Teton National Forest just south of Yellowstone National Park.[63]

In the Appalachian Mountains of Kentucky, Virginia, and West Virginia, coal mining during the Bush era turned hills and valleys into barren, rubble-filled flatlands. Author Erik Reece comments that the land left behind "looks like someone had tried to plot a highway system on the moon." The Environmental Protection Agency estimates that some five hundred square miles in the Appalachians have been stripped and leveled in a practice called "mountain-top removal." At 2005 rates, some twenty-two thousand square miles—nearly one-third of the entire Appalachian mountain range—will be leveled by 2010. Over seven hundred miles of streambeds have already been filled with the debris from coal mining, known as "valley fill."[64] In 2002 the Environmental Protection Agency decided that its customary practice of simply granting permits was no longer adequate legal protection for the mining industry, and issued new rules that made valley fill specifically exempt from the Clean Water Act (CWA). This was just the kind of ruling envisioned by the Bush administration's call for federal agencies to expedite energy production.[65] It was also an undisguised attack on the culture of enchantment. Judy Bonds, the organizer of an environmental group in West Virginia, explained, "It shows contempt for the people who live in these communities and don't want their lives destroyed by the coal industry. . . . God compels us to keep fighting. When these mountains go, our culture, our heritage and our identity are gone. This is a spiritual issue as well as an environmental issue."[66]

The Bush administration also moved to open all of the national forests to oil and gas drilling and timber harvesting. To accomplish this, the Republicans first had to undo a radical conservation measure enacted by the Clinton-Gore team, pushed through during its last days in office. In January 2001 the U.S. Forest Service had announced "the roadless rule": The Forest Service would no longer build roads in national forests to open them for logging and oil and gas exploration, abandoning a decades-long policy that had made some 141,000 square miles of national forests available for commercial use.[67] The roadless rule was intended to protect over 91,400 square miles of national forest—more land than in all the national parks. "Europe has its great castles and works of art. Africa has its ancient pyramids and cultures. Here in America we have our wild places," said Forest Service chief Mike Dombeck.[68] Prior to this last-minute 2001 proclamation, the Forest Service had spent years holding over six hundred public meetings on the proposal, and received some two million public comments—mostly in favor of stopping further road construction.[69]

Idaho's Republican governor, Dick Kempthorne, and the timber company Boise Cascade successfully challenged the "roadless rule" in an Idaho federal district court in May 2001. But in December 2002, environmental groups won a partial victory on appeal, reinstating the roadless rule while the full case underwent further review.[70] The Bush administration subsequently decided on an entirely different approach, delegating the decision to build new roads in national forests to the states.[71] No doubt the administration thought that state governments would be more readily susceptible to industry lobbying to open roadless areas.

Other last-minute efforts by the Clinton administration to protect the environment suffered a similar fate. In late 2001, the Bush administration reversed a rule that would have preserved small "backwoods" regions in the national forests, opening these areas for road building, timber harvesting, and oil and gas exploration.[72] Another Clinton directive, requiring Forest Service officials to evaluate possible commercial uses of national forests in terms of their impacts on forest sustainability, was similarly suspended by the Bush administration; even a Reagan-era requirement that the Forest Service manage the national forests to maintain wildlife populations was weakened.[73] And in 2003, Secretary of the Interior Gale Norton overturned the Clinton administration's designation of over four thousand square miles of federal land in Utah as protected wilderness, opening it to oil and gas exploration and other development.[74] She also announced that the Department of the Interior would no longer survey any public lands at all for possible protection under the 1964 Wilderness Act, which prohibits road building and subsequent commercial exploitation.[75]

Wildlife refuges and roadless forests were not the only targets of the Bush administration's quest to turn more land over to heavy industry. Right before Clinton left office, he designated areas totaling some 5,625 square miles as national monuments.[76] Under standard Department of the Interior regulations, such a designation does not put the land entirely off-limits: Relatively low-impact use, like cattle grazing, is still acceptable. Only more intrusive activities, such as oil and gas drilling, are prohibited. But the Bush administration rejected this traditional approach. Instead, Norton asked the governors of the Western states in which the newly designated monuments were located to complete a management plan for each one. The governors gave the task to notably business-friendly committees, which drastically shrank monument borders.[77] The Missouri Breaks National Monument in Montana, for example, lost over 80 percent of its protected land, diminishing it from more than 770 to roughly 140 square miles.[78]

Bush officials found yet another way to make more land open to economic development through a radical reinterpretation of the Clean Water Act. Ever since the act was first passed in 1972, successive administrations and the federal courts have interpreted it broadly, holding that—because the country's watersheds are ultimately connected—the federal government's right to protect "navigable waters of the United States" includes virtually all the nation's wetlands and streams. But in 2001 the U.S. Supreme Court ruled that an abandoned gravel pit in Illinois used as a pond by migratory ducks did not qualify as a protected wetland under the CWA and therefore could be filled for commercial development.[79] Bush administration officials saw this ruling as justification for a major policy shift. All wetlands not immediately adjacent to a river, stream, or lake, they declared, were "isolated" and thus no longer protected by the act.

It is estimated that, excluding Alaska, the United States originally had over 312,500 square miles of wetlands. By 2000, fewer than half remained, including 31,250 square miles that are seasonal wetlands: They appear during the rainy months and evaporate during the summer.[80] As a Texas Parks and Wildlife biologist explained, the new Bush policy made all seasonal wetlands "developable and hassle free."[81] Seasonal or ephemeral streams received the same treatment. In 2003 a new Environmental Protection Agency rule declared that CWA protection did not extend to any stream that ran less than six months a year, nor to any stream that did not have groundwater as its source. Under the new rule, some 80 to 90 percent of the streams in the Southwest could legally be paved over. A water policy expert from the National Wildlife Federation explained what was at stake: "It's like writing off the entire Southwest . . . where water is more precious than in any other region of the country."[82]

A similar mixture of deliberate neglect and drastic reinterpretation characterized the Bush efforts to destroy the 1973 Endangered Species Act (ESA), which governs the process of listing threatened and endangered species and designating as "critical habitat" areas that these species needed to survive. A critical habitat designation did not necessarily preserve a piece of land as wilderness, but it meant that development plans had to be reviewed for their impacts on threatened and endangered species. Many Republican officials hated the law, and Bush's assistant secretary of the interior declared the ESA "broken" because it prioritized the continued existence of plants and animals over economic growth.

The simplest way to undermine the ESA was just to stop adding new species to the threatened and endangered lists. During the first three years of the Clinton administration, the U.S. Fish and Wildlife Service added 211 species to these lists; by contrast, only twenty were added during the first three years of the Bush administration, and each of these additions came only after petitions and lawsuits by environmental groups.[83] In addition, the Bush administration stopped granting protection to regional populations of a species. For example, they removed the marbled murrelet of the Pacific Northwest from the threatened list—a status that had been influential in protecting old-growth forests in the area—because the Fish and Wildlife Service declared that there were healthy populations in Alaska and Canada.[84] In a similar move, administration officials declared that for the purposes of determining whether various salmon and steelhead stocks warranted listing under the ESA, any fish raised in hatcheries and released into streams would be counted the same as wild fish.[85] In a survey of U.S. Fish and Wildlife Service biologists, over half of the scientists who responded said that they had been ordered to deprioritize preservation.[86]

Besides refusing to protect additional species, the service began to chip away at critical habitat for threatened and endangered species already on the lists. Once a "threatened" or "endangered" determination is made, the Fish and Wildlife Service and the National Marine Fisheries Service are obligated by law to make a map of the habitats with the soil, vegetation, and temperature characteristics necessary for that species to survive and reproduce. Designated territories can encompass both public and private property, and there is evidence that the mandatory federal review of any commercial development on these lands makes a big difference: One 2005 study showed that species with critical habitats have twice the survival rate of those with no federally designated lands.[87] When Bush took office, over 234,000 square miles in the United States had been identified as critical habitat. By 2005, federal biologists working on plants and animals recently added to the threatened and endangered lists identified an additional 67,200 square miles requiring that designation.[88]

Their efforts were ignored. Instead of protecting more land, the Department of the Interior *reduced* critical habitat by some 25,600 square miles. For example, the endangered California red-legged frog, hero of Mark Twain's 1865 story "The Celebrated Jumping Frog of Calaveras County," saw its habitat reduced from 6,400 to less than 1,200 square miles. Fish and Wildlife Service officials said that protecting the frog would cost home builders $500 million, apparently more than a mere amphibian was worth. There are, of course, also quite a few benefits to preserving habitat—cleaner water and air, increased property values, and revenues brought in by hunters, fishers, and other tourists—but economists hired to do such studies are officially instructed that these may not be taken into account.[89]

IN ADDITION TO these assaults against America's lands, waters, and animals, perhaps the most drastic—and most symbolic—environmental attack was the Bush administration's campaign against the very air we breathe. Just fourteen months after his inauguration, President Bush renounced his presidential campaign pledge to regulate the emissions of carbon dioxide and list it as a pollutant under the 1970 Clean Air Act.[90] At the same time, lobbyists from the highest levels of the American Petroleum Institute, the Electrical Reliability Coordinating Council, and other energy industry groups began to advocate abandoning the New Source Review (NSR) program, one of the crucial components of Clean Air Act enforcement. Under NSR, any power plant undergoing significant upgrades was required to install new pollution control equipment to bring it into compliance with regulations. But Bush's national energy policy preferred a market-based system called "cap-and-trade" in which industry could buy and sell pollution credits. In 2001, Environmental Protection Agency director Christine Whitman told the Senate's Environmental and Public Works Committee that with the forthcoming cap-and-trade plan, "New Source Review is certainly one of those regulatory aspects that would no longer be necessary."[91]

Although never formally abandoned, New Source Review was effectively gutted by revisions of its most important rule: how much a utility company could spend on upgrading a power plant before triggering the requirement to install new pollution controls. In 2002, when the EPA initially announced plans to revise NSR, the head of the agency's enforcement division had suggested 0.75 percent of the plant's total value as a reasonable threshold. Nearly a year later, the agency finally announced its decision: 20 percent. In other words, owners of a power plant worth one billion dollars could spend two hundred million dollars per year in upgrades without worrying about the regulations. Frank O'Donnell, executive director of the Clean Air Trust, noted that this rendered the law essentially meaningless. "It's a moron test for power companies. It's such a huge loophole that only a moron would trip over it and become subject to NSR requirements."[92] For good measure, the EPA also dropped its investigations of fifty-one power companies accused of violating NSR under the Clinton administration.[93] (These companies accounted for just 10 percent of the nation's total number of power plants, but discharged 38 percent of the industry's sulfur dioxide and 30 percent of its nitrogen oxides.[94])

Meanwhile, the Clear Skies initiative, as the Bush administration's cap-and-trade proposal was formally known, proved to be a bitter mockery of its name. It allowed 50 percent more sulfur dioxide to escape into the air, nearly 40 percent more nitrogen oxide, and three times as much mercury as a rigorously enforced Clean Air Act with New Source Review would have permitted.[95] The mercury numbers soon became controversial, especially because in early 2004 EPA scientists announced that 15 percent of American babies had been exposed to dangerous levels of that neurotoxin in their mothers' wombs.[96] Coal-fired power plants, which put forty-eight tons of mercury into the air each year—40 percent of the country's total mercury pollution—are a major cause of this exposure.[97] But while the Clear Skies initiative was supposed to eliminate 70 percent of these emissions by 2018, the EPA's own data suggested that this claim was far from plausible.

The problem lay with the design of the cap-and-trade proposal. Under this system, each region of the country was given a "cap" for major pollutants (nitrogen oxide, sulfur dioxide, and mercury), and then power plants could choose either to install pollution controls themselves or buy "credits" from a company that did. This meant that companies that reduced mercury pollution in the early years of the program could save those credits for use later on when the pollution limit was stricter. Consequently, it would be at least 2025—and perhaps later than 2030, if ever—before a 70 percent reduction in mercury was obtained.[98] Moreover, because the cap-and-trade system did not require any specific plant to ever reduce its mercury emissions—it could just buy credits from those that did—mercury "hot spots" would accumulate across the country. After such concerns were expressed, EPA chief Michael O. Leavitt announced that the agency would investigate. A year later he proclaimed the proposal sound. The market would be trusted to solve all problems.

While the Bush administration was destroying New Source Review and hindering other efforts to control air pollution, it was also fighting virtually all efforts to reduce global warming. In early 2001, Bush rejected the Kyoto Treaty, which aimed to reduce worldwide emissions of greenhouse gases.[99] He denounced it as too expensive and contrary to American economic interests. The United States, with only 4 percent of the world's population, emitted 24 percent of its greenhouse gases, and it was not about to change its ways.

The administration was determined not only to avoid reducing $CO_2$ emissions but to censor or discredit any scientists who said global warming was dangerous. In the spring of 2002, energy industry lobbyists persuaded state department officials to fire Robert T. Watson, the United Nations chief of the Intergovernmental Panel on Climate Change. Watson's fault was in claiming that the burning of oil and other petroleum products was the principal reason for global warming.[100] That summer, the Environmental Protection Agency issued a report confirming Watson's conclusion: Global warming was mainly caused by fossil fuels. Within two days Bush rejected the research as meaningless, dismissively referring to it as "the report put out by the bureaucracy."[101] A White House spokesman instead argued that there was great scientific "uncertainty" about the causes of global warming.

The phrasing came straight from the American Petroleum Institute, which was fond of arguing that, because of uncertainty about the true causes of global warming, it was best to delay restrictions on emissions of carbon dioxide and other gases from smokestacks and tailpipes. In 2002, Philip A. Cooney, a former API lobbyist and "climate team leader," became head of the White House's Council on Environmental Quality. He immediately went to work editing the federal government's scientific reports.[102] In 2003, for example, the council changed an EPA report by eliminating all references to rapid temperature changes in the last decade. They also deleted references to many studies that pointed to smokestack and vehicle tailpipe emissions as causes of global warming and threats to human health and ecosystems. Instead, the report said that it "was a scientific challenge to document [climate] change"—another version of "uncertainty."[103]

Cooney and his associates similarly revised 2002–3 reports from the federal government's interagency Climate Change Science Program, a major initiative with a $1.8 billion annual budget. References to melting snow packs and retreating glaciers were deleted. Whenever possible, the Bush staff rewrote the work of scientists to emphasize uncertainty, such as by inserting "extremely" in the sentence, "The attribution of the causes of biological and ecological changes to climate change is extremely difficult."[104] Rick S. Piltz, a senior associate in the climate program office and a career government scientist, resigned in the summer of 2005, complaining of the Bush administration's intervention: "I have not seen a situation like the one that has developed under this administration during the past four years, in which politicization by the White House has fed back directly into the science program in such a way as to undermine the credibility and integrity of the program."[105]

The White House campaign to prevent any action against global warming also played out on the international stage. In 2005, the United States successfully lobbied the G8 group of nations (which includes the United States, Canada, France, Germany, Italy, Japan, Britain, and Russia) to modify its annual report by removing all language calling for prompt action to halt global warming.[106] That winter, when the 178 nations that signed the Kyoto Treaty met in Montreal to discuss new emissions targets for further reductions beyond 2012, the United States—while not a signatory—nevertheless lobbied for avoiding any discussion of specific targets, opposing even informal talks that might mention the subject.[107] Dr. James Hansen, director of NASA's Goddard Institute for Space Studies, protested that if "business as usual" continued, global warming would cause so much change that we would be living on a "different planet."[108] Senior NASA officials subsequently ordered Hansen to preclear all of his news media contacts, lectures, Web site postings, and even scientific papers with NASA public affairs officers.[109] In February 2006, NASA quietly changed its mission statement, removing the phrase "To understand and protect our home planet" that had served as the mandate for Hansen's and the Goddard Institute's global warming research.[110]

Although Bush administration policies were obviously rooted in a conventional Republican probusiness attitude, the all-out attack on the nation's public lands and environmental laws was unprecedented in its thoroughness and hostility. In the same way, the evangelical battle against the culture of enchantment was a hyperexaggerated version of conventional religious practices. This extreme fear of enchantment and environmental protection shows just how strongly the right felt that these movements were dangerous threats that had to be completely destroyed. In their own perverse way, the right's attacks were clear proof that environmental activism and the culture of enchantment had taken hold in mainstream America. And as it turned out, enchantment and environmentalism were strong enough to survive the assault.

# Part III

## HOPE RENEWED

# 9

## Fighting Back

With the culture of enchantment already weakened by its internal conflicts, the all-out attack on the environment waged by the Bush administration and its allies threatened to destroy the movement. But over time, proponents of enchantment learned to recognize and manage the movement's contradictions. Their passionate commitment helped achieve a string of significant environmental victories in the later Bush years, showing that even a combination of corporate lobbying and right-wing religious pressure could not overcome enchantment's popular appeal.

The balance began to tip in 2005, which at first looked like it would be another year of bitter disappointments. That March, the Senate voted for a budget bill authorizing oil and gas exploration in the Arctic National Wildlife Refuge's coastal plain. Advocates of drilling celebrated their triumph as proof that the culture of enchantment was irrelevant, even inane. Max Boot, a senior fellow at the Council on Foreign Relations, described the bill's opponents as "Democrats who couldn't tell the difference between a caribou and a cow."[1] The American Petroleum Institute proclaimed that "emotionalism won't power economic growth or create jobs."[2] The next month, the House of Representatives also passed a budget bill with a provision authorizing ANWR drilling. But that bill only passed by the slim margin of three votes, 214 to 211. And the two budget bills were different enough that further voting would have to be scheduled later in the year for a new, "reconciled" budget.

By this time, the movement to stop drilling in ANWR included virtually the entire spectrum of wilderness preservation organizations, several hunting and fishing groups, plus a wide range of religious communities—Quakers, Reform rabbis, the Episcopal Church, the National Council of Churches, and the Evangelical Environmental Network—and representatives from the Gwich'in Athabascan Indians and the Inuit Eskimos.[3] They lobbied the seven Democrats who had been absent from Congress on the day of the budget vote, and fervently pursued some thirty House Republicans who had expressed opposition to the drilling. By November, Tom DeLay and the other Republican leaders in the House of Representatives were forced to withdraw ANWR energy exploration from their new budget bill.[4] The next month, forty-four senators staged a filibuster against a reconciled budget bill with an ANWR drilling provision. Because ending a filibuster requires sixty votes and the Republican leadership only mustered up fifty-six, the proposal to open ANWR was defeated.[5]

A similar fate befell a proposal by Congressmen Richard Pombo (R-Cal.) and Jim Gibbons (R-Nev.) to resurrect an old provision of the 1872 Mining Law and sell up to 420,000 square miles of federal lands to private mining concerns, timber companies, and real estate developers. Their bill passed the House in November 2005 while environmentalists were focused on saving ANWR.[6] But sportsmen's groups persisted in their efforts to stop the legislation. Craig Sharpe, executive director of the Montana Wildlife Federation, asked: "How are you going to protect hunting and fishing access on our public land if it is no longer in public hands?"[7] After a coalition of hunting and fishing groups claiming fifty-five million members protested to Republican leaders, the proposal was removed from the budget bill.[8]

The following year, off-road vehicle advocates tried to get the National Park Service to change its historic mission of keeping the parks "unimpaired for future generations."[9] A revised mission statement, favoring recreation over preservation, would have made it easier to demand more park access for all-terrain vehicles, snowmobiles, and jet skis. But the off-roaders met with resistance from park service employees and wilderness groups, and failed to get the mission statement changed. The director of the National Park Service, Fran P. Mainella, a Bush administration appointee who had backed the revision, subsequently resigned.[10]

Meanwhile, the Republican coalition in Congress was weakened by the scandals surrounding lobbyist Jack Abramoff and his secret partner, Michael S. Scanlon, a former spokesperson for DeLay. In 2005 and 2006, under pressure from criminal and Senate investigators, Abramoff and Scanlon admitted swindling forty to eighty million dollars from Native American tribes over several years in the early 2000s.[11] Abramoff had told his clients—who hired him to keep Congress from taxing Indian casino profits and to secure favorable rulings from the Department of the Interior—that Scanlon needed to be brought in as a public relations consultant. Public relations expenses, unlike lobbying expenses, are not regulated, and so do not have to be disclosed to federal agencies. Scanlon was able to charge exorbitant fees, which he then split with Abramoff. The pair laundered the funds through nonprofit organizations, using the money for bribery, congressional junkets, and their personal gain. Partially as a result of the scandal, DeLay, who had worked with Abramoff since 1995, gave up his position as House Majority Leader and soon announced that he would not run for reelection.[12] The Abramoff case also proved to be the final straw for Gale Norton, Bush's strongly prodevelopment

Secretary of the Interior. Norton's former aide, Steven Griles, had had repeated contacts with the lobbyist, and Norton—already upset by the defeat of the ANWR drilling proposal—resigned in February 2006 as investigators pursuing Abramoff's bribery case probed her department.[13]

The following month, the Bush administration's program to undermine the Clean Air Act by gutting New Source Review also met with an unexpected setback: It was declared illegal by a panel of federal judges from the United States Court of Appeals for the District of Columbia. The judges wrote that the "plain language" of the Clean Air Act made it clear that Congress wanted to reduce air pollution. In contrast, procedures allowing a power plant owner to spend up to 20 percent of the plant's total worth annually on upgrades—thus increasing generating capacity without installing new pollution controls—meant that companies could increase emissions every year. "Only in a Humpty-Dumpty world" could the law be read as permitting this, and "we decline to adopt such a worldview," the judges concluded.[14]

More legal upsets followed. In September 2006, a federal district court in San Francisco rejected the Bush administration's effort to destroy the "roadless rule" that was enacted in the last days of the Clinton presidency. Judge Elizabeth D. Laporte concluded that the U.S. Forest Service's plan to allow state governors to decide whether to build roads within federal forests was fatally flawed. The Bush plan had been adopted without the Forest Service conducting any reviews of the potential environmental impacts of road building, as legally mandated by the National Environmental Policy Act (NEPA); nor had the Fish and Wildlife Service been asked to comment on the impacts that roads might have on threatened and endangered species, as required by the Endangered Species Act. The court brought back protection to 76,500 square miles of Forest Service land: "Defendants are enjoined from taking any further action contrary to the

Roadless Rule without undertaking environmental analysis consistent with this opinion."[15] Although further legislation and appeals were bound to follow, Judge Laporte's decision at the very least bought time for roadless areas, preserving them until political forces turned in their favor.

The decisive shift came on November 6, 2006, when voters ended Republican control of the House and Senate and installed slim Democratic majorities. While the Democratic gains were doubtlessly due in large part to public discontent over the war in Iraq, the election was still a stunning moment for environmentalists. The League of Conservation Voters had identified thirteen congressmen with the worst environmental voting records as the "Dirty Dozen"; of these, nine met defeat, in what Natural Resources Defense Council president Frances Beinecke called the "greenest day in American political history."[16] In a surprising and emblematic loss, Representative Richard Pombo—chair of the House Committee on Natural Resources, proponent of oil and gas drilling on public lands, advocate for selling fifteen national parks, and virulent opponent of the Endangered Species Act—was defeated by Jerry McNerney, an engineering consultant for companies building wind turbines.[17] McNerney got a critical boost from the Defenders of Wildlife, an organization with five hundred thousand supporters that stresses human-animal kinship by encouraging its members to symbolically adopt wild animals. The group raised six hundred thousand dollars for McNerney, and sent hundreds of volunteers to work for his campaign.[18]

Pombo's position as chair of the House Committee on Natural Resources was taken by Representative Nick J. Rahall (D-W.V.), who earned a 92 percent approval rating from the League of Conservation Voters.[19] In the Senate, James Inhofe (R-Okla.), the man who called the EPA a "Gestapo force" and said that "global warming is a hoax," lost the chair of the Environment and Public Works Committee. He was replaced by Senator Barbara Boxer (D-Cal.), who had frequently displayed Subhankar Banerjee's photographs of animals and the arctic landscape in her defenses of ANWR. She proclaimed the refuge to be "a God-given environment."[20]

AT THE SAME time as the Republican antienvironmental coalition collapsed, the right-wing evangelical movement also began to fall apart. Pat Robertson, the leader of the evangelical right who had vehemently denounced enchantment as Satan worship—and environmental protection as the Antichrist's stepping stone to world domination—horrified Americans with a series of even more bizarre pronouncements. In August 2005, he called for the assassination of Venezuelan president Hugo Chávez as a way to secure U.S. access to that country's oil. The next month, after Hurricane Katrina devastated New Orleans and the Mississippi coast, he called it "divine retribution" for legalized abortion. In early 2006, when Israeli premier Ariel Sharon suffered a stroke, Robertson declared this to be God's punishment of Sharon for giving up land to the Palestinians.[21] Other evangelical leaders began to pull away. Richard Land, president of the Southern Baptist Convention's Ethics & Religious Liberty Commission, said that "he speaks for an ever-diminishing number of evangelicals, and that process accelerates every time he makes a statement like this."[22] Robertson's decline was significant: His daily television show, "The 700 Club," had long been a crucial forum for conservative congressional leaders seeking to garner evangelical support for the Republican Party.[23]

While Robertson alienated many of his former allies, a broader theological shift away from his enchantment-as-Satanism doctrine was gaining momentum. A decade earlier, in the mid-1990s, the activist Jim Ball had founded the Evangelical Environmental Network (EEN), a collection of ministers and religious organizers seeking to unite evangelical theology and environment protection, to "declare the Lordship of Christ over all creation."[24] Their *Creation Care: A Christian Environmental Quarterly* published essays on God's sacred handiwork. Oceans and forests, fish and tigers, all reflected divine glory; what threatened them dishonored God and Jesus Christ. No longer were the harsh concepts of dominion and apocalyptic visions of Earth's destruction during the Tribulations the only evangelical vision of the environment.

In 2002, the Evangelical Environmental Network launched its "What Would Jesus Drive?" campaign, depicting energy conservation as a religious obligation for evangelicals. The campaign received extensive news coverage, and as EEN reached out to moderate evangelical leaders, it began to have tremendous influence. In 2004 the National Association of Evangelicals (NAE)—the evangelicals' most important organization—adopted a new program entitled "For the Health of the Nation: An Evangelical Call to Civic Responsibility." Although NAE leaders remained concerned about the sin of idolatry, taking pains to note that "we worship only the Creator and not the creation," they also emphasized that this creation needed evangelicals to be its stewards.[25] Citing Genesis 2:15, "watch out and care for it," the NAE called for sustainable practices that would "conserve and renew the Earth rather than . . . deplete or destroy it."[26]

In early 2006, some eighty-six NAE leaders formed the Evangelical Climate Initiative, and issued "Climate Change: An Evangelical Call to Action."[27] The report agreed with the scientific consensus that human-induced climate change is a threat, rejecting the Bush administration's denials. It stressed that the world's poor would be hit the hardest, and that Christians were morally obligated to respond and had to do so immediately. The initiative also cited polls showing that two-thirds of their constituents thought global warming was taking place, and about half agreed that measures to stop or slow the process would be worth it even if they incurred high economic costs.[28] Theologically, the evangelical leaders declared, "This is God's world, and any damage that we do to God's world is an offense against God Himself."[29]

The Evangelical Climate Initiative created a vision of science and theology, moral and political responsibility that can be characterized as a more traditional counterpart to the ecumenicalism of *Earth in the Balance*. (Like Al Gore's book, the initiative's report featured photographs of Earth taken from space flights, with the sun's light creating a new dawn.) Reverend Jim Ball told the *New York Times* that Gore's book had made him understand the connection between global warming and poverty, and helped inspire his green evangelical movement.[30] Reverend Richard Cizik, who would become president of the National Association of Evangelicals in 2007, in turn credits Jim Ball for introducing him to the scientific work on global warming (especially the studies done by John Houghton, a devout Christian) that made him a convert to "a cause which I believe every Christian should be committed to." The combination of global warming and Creation Care theology, Cizik says, leaves no room for doubt. "The climate change crisis that we believe is occurring is not something we can wait ten years, five years, even a year to address. . . . To deplete our resources, to harm our world through environmental degradation, is an offense against God."[31]

THE POLITICAL VICTORIES and the evangelicals' conversion were matched by progress in dealing with the unintended consequences of enchantment and with the culture's internal conflicts. The problems caused by exclusive emphasis on monumental landscapes, for example, were mitigated by renewed attention to less dramatic areas. When Thoreau celebrated swamps in 1862—"I enter a swamp as a sacred place, a *sanctum sanctorum*"—he was almost a lone voice.[32] Over eighty years later, Aldo Leopold's famous call for a new land ethic, inspired by attempts to restore the ecology of ordinary river-bottom lands in Wisconsin that had been abused by bad farming practices, took decades to gain an audience. Marjory Stoneman Douglas's famous 1947 ode, *The Everglades: River of Grass*, was similarly ahead of its time, all but ignored when it first came out.[33] South Florida residents mostly thought of the

Everglades as a wasteland, and many applauded when the U.S. Army Corps of Engineers began draining the area in the 1950s. But when *The Everglades* was republished in 1974, it inspired a movement to try to restore that ecosystem.

Subsequent generations of authors and activists have continued to evoke the great swamp's beauty and mystery while decrying its exploitation. Peter Matthiessen's trilogy—*Killing Mr. Watson* (1991), *Lost Man's River* (1997), and *Bone by Bone* (1999)—chronicled the destruction of Everglades wildlife in the early twentieth century by plantation farmers, railroads, hunters, and trappers.[34] Detective mystery writers Elmore Leonard and Carl Hiaasen routinely set their stories in the Everglades and other swamplands in Miami and south Florida, and what happens to the land and its creatures is a constant concern in their works.[35]

Likewise, more and more advocates have been speaking for the nation's grasslands, long thought fit only for plow and cattle. In 1991, William Least Heat-Moon published *PrairyErth*, his meditation on the Flint Hills of east-central Kansas, one of the nation's last intact tall-grass prairies.[36] A few years later, these hills received federal protection, becoming the Tallgrass Prairie National Preserve; by 2005, the *New York Times* travel section was extolling their beauty and historical significance, recommending a pilgrimage.[37] Also in 2005, the Nature Conservancy purchased Montana prairie lands to establish "grass banks," which allow ranchers to graze cattle on lands outside their own in return for practicing conservation of the prairie and the animals that live there.[38] Bit by bit, the tall-grass prairie is being restored. Although the acreage saved is still small, the change in attitude toward the grasslands marks a significant victory.

Even previously degraded and ignored urban rivers and harbors now appear as arteries of life, city dwellers' connections to nature. In New York City, the Hudson River was so polluted by sewage and industrial wastes in the middle of the twentieth century that author Joseph

Mitchell observed: "You could bottle it and sell it for poison."[39] Then came the 1972 Clean Water Act, and citizen lawsuits against industries and government agencies abusing the river eventually brought about marked improvements in water quality. Seeing that the Hudson had become clean enough for bluefish and striped bass to return, New Yorkers began to swim in its waters again, as they had done back in the early twentieth century.

One of these swimmers, a man named Teddy Jefferson, described his elation upon finally overcoming his fear of the river and diving in. "There I was, floating in green waves and looking over at the Empire State Building. The experience was so astonishing—walking to the edge of a huge metropolis and going for a swim."[40] Jefferson and his friends formed a group called Swim the Apple to spread the joy: Once "they realize the Hudson is swimmable . . . they want to go in, too."[41] Swim the Apple also lobbied the Hudson River Park Trust to include swimming and kayaking access in a planned four-hundred-million-dollar river park stretching from the southern tip of Manhattan to midtown. River rapture spread like magic through the city. In 2003 a *New York Times* editorial suggested that the park should be extended to two old thousand-foot-long industrial piers, which could be renovated for "sports or picnics, a place to read or simply sit and breathe"; the renovation could be paid for by federal money allocated to help New York recover from the 9/11 World Trade Center attacks.[42] Implicit in the *Times* piece was the cultural idea that the newly cleaned waters of the Hudson would help Manhattan heal.

In recent years, several other cities have decided to renovate their rivers by creating artificial white-water rapids. City planners hoped—rightly, as it turned out—that moving waters, a mesmerizing natural force, would keep people in the cities after the end of their workdays, and attract tourists from afar. But restored rivers mean more than dollars for the local economy. One Olympic-level kayaker marveled at being able to train right after work, thanks to Fort Worth's engineered rapids on the formerly placid Trinity River. He also noted that when he kayaked on the new Trinity, he saw beaver, birds, nutria, and fish of all kinds—some actually jumped on his boat. The presence of these creatures made the river even more compelling. "Everybody's first preference would be to have a beautiful, natural white-water river running through the middle of their town," he said. "But where that does not exist, this is the next best thing."[43] Fort Worth officials now plan on building a lake north of downtown, and are contemplating creating more rapids on the Trinity. Dallas, thirty miles downstream, is following Fort Worth's lead as it plans its own rapids and riverside parks for a Trinity renewal. In 2007, even Los Angeles announced a fifty-year, two-billion-dollar plan to remake the concrete-entombed Los Angeles River into a real waterway, with parks and rapids and meandering bends along thirty-one miles.[44]

Some coastal cities, meanwhile, have focused on cleaning their harbors. One-hundred-acre Spectacle Island, three miles from Boston, served as the city's dump for most of the twentieth century. The area was almost literally a hellhole: So much methane gas was produced by the landfill that underground fires ignited in 1960 and smoldered for years. Boston Harbor itself was a sewage pit, considered by many to be the dirtiest harbor in the country. But after federal courts ordered a cleanup, work commenced in the 1990s on transforming Spectacle Island into a national park. Three million cubic yards of dirt were brought in from "The Big Dig," the tunnel for a new underground Boston highway—enough to cover the island with sixty feet of soil. Upon this base, the island was replanted with trees, bushes, flowers, and grasses. New sand was brought in to make beaches. The United States Department of Transportation granted the park one million dollars for solar power and electric cars to be used by rangers and cleanup crews. "To see it, in twelve years, go from a very bad landfill to a zero-emission park," said Sheila Lynch, chairwoman of the park's advisory committee, "is like seeing a phoenix rising from the ashes."[45]

THE RESTORATION OF polluted waterways accompanies renewed awareness of the cities' native wildlife. Among those who live in the nation's densely populated areas, there is an aching desire to know that they exist alongside other species, to feel kinship and solidarity with them. The news media are now acutely attuned to stories about the survival of wild creatures in urban and suburban lands, and even the presence of potentially dangerous animals like mountain lions and bears is more often celebrated than feared.

In the summer of 2004, for instance, a mountain lion was reported in Los Angeles's six-square-mile Griffith Park. While many people worried about possible attacks, park officials decided not to hunt the animal, and instead posted warning signs on the trails. One city councilman captured the public ambivalence by saying that if he encountered the lion he would "stand tall, raise my hands, and yell, 'Welcome to Los Angeles. Now go back to the Angeles National Forest.'"[46] But just a few months later, when the last remaining pair of mountain lions in the Santa Monica Mountains gave birth to four cubs, the city celebrated. "Four Lion Cubs Are Born Free," one headline cheered.[47] Activists began to promote the Mountain Lion Project, a plan to create a network of tunnels, greenbelts, and corridors through property easements that would allow the lions (and other creatures) to move from one habitat area to another in search of food and mates. The activists explicitly said that bringing back the lions—and other mammals like coyotes, foxes, and bobcats—is necessary for "re-enchanting the city."[48]

When people rescue wild animals, or help restore species long lost to a region, their actions are now routinely recognized as heroic. In 1989, Meeri Zetterstrom, a recently widowed Vermont woman, assuaged her grief by constructing a lakefront nest for endangered osprey. Buoyed by the birth of young birds, she began a fifteen-year campaign to build and protect osprey nests around the entire state, in rural and urban areas alike. She became famous as "Grandma Osprey."[49] In Salt Lake City, Utah, a group of retirees guards the city's peregrine falcons each spring, alert for any juveniles that might fall from their nests or land in dangerous places while learning to fly. "If a bird flies into the street, Bob will try and catch it, and I'm supposed to throw myself in front of the cars," says one seventy-five-year-old volunteer.[50] And in 2004, when a wildlife rescue organization in Southern California's Orange County lost its office lease, the center's director took dozens of ailing brown pelicans into her home. "What choice do I have?" she asked. "All of these birds would die."[51]

Owls, peregrine falcons, and eagles have gained prominence in surprising settings. In New York City, a count of all the new chicks is announced every year as workers reintroduce them to parks, bridges, and other habitats, and follow-up stories appear on their fates. In 2004, when the governing board of a luxurious co-op on Fifth Avenue removed the nest of Pale Male and Lola, two well-known redtailed hawks, from the building's twelfth-floor cornice, protesters immediately picketed. The *New York Times* put Pale Male on the front page, and even featured a full family genealogy—detailing his arrival on Fifth Avenue in 1991, the names of all his mates, and how many chicks they'd had each year.[52] The co-op's governing board soon backed down. An architect designed a new stainless steel container for the nest that would help keep waste off the building's facade, and the birds eventually moved back. It was front-page news again when Lola laid eggs the following spring.

The resurgence of urban wildlife means that cities will no longer be removed from the drama of predators hunting prey—whether it's hawks swooping after pigeons and rats, striped bass jumping after shad, or mountain lions killing their own cubs over deer carcasses and territorial rights. While brutal and messy, the urban hunt means that life has come back. And although news stories never say so explicitly, the sheer volume and intensity of the coverage indicates a connection between the renewal of animal life and our hopes for a better human future. If the mountain lions and red-tailed hawks can live again, maybe other parts of nature can be restored, too; and if the rifts between society and nature can be healed, perhaps other societal problems are also not intractable, after all.

MAJESTIC MOUNTAIN LIONS and photogenic hawks are not the only beneficiaries of the newly vibrant culture of enchantment. Over the course of recent decades, visionary scientists have developed theories that are pushing enchantment toward a more encompassing embrace of life. As the world's economy expands, agricultural, industrial, and residential development has been devastating all kinds of natural habitats—farmlands, forests, prairies, deserts, mountains, and coasts. Consequently, the rate of species extinction has radically increased. For biologist Edward O. Wilson, the loss of genetic and species diversity through the destruction of natural habitats is "the one process now going on that will take millions of years to correct. . . . The one folly our descendents are least likely to forgive us."[53] To emphasize the importance of preserving all of the planet's inhabitants, no matter how ordinary or insignificant they might initially seem, Wilson and his colleagues developed the concept of "biodiversity"— "the variety of life across all levels of organization from genetic diversity within populations, to species, which have to be regarded as the pivotal unit of classification, to ecosystems."[54] Biodiversity became the goal of a new discipline, conservation biology.

Central to conservation biology is Wilson's idea that "we are literally kin to other creatures."[55] While Wilson is fond of discussing our links to the chimpanzee, our closest living relative, other scholars have stressed the breadth of human-animal-plant kinship. Cross-species kinship "is literally true in evolutionary time," notes biologist and philosopher Scott McVay. "All higher eukaryotic organisms, from flowering plants to insects and humanity itself, are thought to have descended from a single ancestral population that lived about 1.8 billion years ago."[56]

Pointing to the relationship among humans, animals, and plants, Wilson further argues that humans are genetically programmed to love nearly all living things—a drive he and his colleagues call biophilia. Biologist Hugh Iltis explains, "We are genetically programmed to be stimulated by biodiversity! . . . We're genetically programmed to explore the environment. I mean just watch a cat go into the woods. Watch a rat or a mouse go sniffing around in the woods. We're the same way."[57]

By the 1980s, conservation biology had become a hybrid discourse combining scientific study and poetic reenchantment. Two of the discipline's founders, Paul and Anne Ehrlich, called the goal of preserving biodiversity "fundamentally a religious argument" that was also "a natural and necessary extension of the cultural evolution of *Homo sapiens*."[58] In the late 1990s, Edward O. Wilson even went so far as to proclaim that the sciences, especially evolutionary studies, had simultaneously rendered religion obsolete and become its successor. "If the sacred narrative cannot be in the form of religious cosmology," he said, "it will be taken from the material history of the universe and the human species. That trend is in no way debasing. The true evolutionary epic, retold as poetry, is as intrinsically ennobling as any religious epic."[59]

The discussion of biodiversity and the renewed emphasis on evolution has had a profound influence—both on scientists, and on the broader public. Some saw Wilson's "evolutionary epic" not as an alternative to religion but as its complement. The new ideas coming from the field of conservation biology were part of what prompted many religious scholars to blend evolutionary theory and the notion of the universe as God's creation. As Catholic theologian Leonardo Boff argued, "All creatures bear within themselves traces of the divine hand, even if evolution was the way in which it happened. This means that creatures are sacramental."[60]

Both the science of biological diversity and the theology of a sacramental universe pointed toward the importance of saving *all* species and preserving *all* ecosystems. By the 1990s, these ideas provided the adherents of enchantment with rhetorical weapons to argue against those who disdained efforts to save noncharismatic creatures. In Mammoth, California, state conservation officers limited condo development in order to protect populations of chub, a fish no bigger than a minnow, proclaiming it part of "the long-term future of its community."[61] And in Tucson, Arizona, where the pygmy owl faced extinction from development pressures, the chief county official presented the endangered bird as an icon of a larger ecosystem problem: "The pygmy owl, frankly, is what you might characterize as a canary in the coal mine—an indicator that whatever we're doing is not quite balancing economic development and growth with natural resource protection and conservation."[62]

The promotion of biological diversity hasn't been limited to professional scientists. Ordinary people, too, have increasingly reached out to previously ignored animals and plants—becoming, in a sense, "lay" practitioners of conservation biology and creation theology. Twenty years ago, roughly half the bat species in the United States were in trouble, and few people cared: Bats were feared as vicious little creatures that carried rabies. But in the 1990s, when Bob Wisecarver, a retired man in his eighties, learned how much bats do for the broader environment—they eat thousands of mosquitoes and other insects every day, they are crucial pollinators of plants, and their guano makes great organic fertilizer—he began to build housing for bat colonies around the country.[63] Wisecarver's work, together with the efforts of professional naturalists and other lay practitioners of conservation biology, has led to increases in most bat species. By 2002, only six of the forty-five bat species in the United States remained endangered.[64]

Tim Watts, a Massachusetts janitor, has spoken for the American eel. He had used eels for bait his whole life, and eventually became fascinated with them. Watts noticed that eels couldn't make it over many of the dams on Massachusetts and Maine rivers, and consequently couldn't get back to the Atlantic Ocean to breed. "The eel is one of those species that seems to fall through the cracks because it isn't so pretty," he explained to an Associated Press reporter. "They don't have a voice. They don't have anyone to speak for them." In 2004, Tim and his brother, Doug, filed a petition with the U.S. Fish and Wildlife Service to get the American eel protected as an endangered species.[65] The service has so far declined to grant this protection, but the Watts brothers continue their rescue efforts, helping baby eels over dams despite arrest threats from state officials.[66] In 2008, a Maine environmental coalition announced that it had raised $25 million to remove two dams on the state's Penobscot River and build a bypass around a third, helping to restore migratory routes for nearly a dozen species of sea-run fish—including shad, sturgeon, striped bass, and American eel.[67]

Tom Aley, a Missouri spelunker, is another one of these "lay" defenders who has been in the news. Aley found a population of strange-looking snails—without eyes or mouths—living in a deep cave in the Ozarks, and used his life savings to buy land containing most of the cave. He sent some of the snails off to be identified. When scientists told him that he had discovered a new species, Aley's life acquired a new focus. "After that, it was official. The snail was special," he told the *Los Angeles Times*. "I felt responsible for them. This was their home and I owned it. It was my job to take care of them." By 2004, only 150 of the creatures remained; the rest had died because of polluted runoff from nearby cow pastures. But Aley persevered, buying up the pasture land and planting 52,000 trees to renew the land, clean up a stream, and save the snails.[68] Three years later the snail population seems to have stabilized, and Aley hopes that with additional environmental protection it will eventually increase.[69]

Long-neglected, ordinary kinds of plants have also gained advocates. In California, a retired construction worker and self-taught naturalist named Kerry Knudsen has spent decades researching lichens, becoming a nationally recognized expert in the field. Knudsen extols the lichens' beauty and their significance as an early warning system: Lichens take water from the air, and when the air is polluted they die. Today, there are very few lichens left in Southern California, Knudsen points out. "People should be worried."[70]

There is even hope that the culture of enchantment will transform what many Americans see literally outside their front doors. Over 31,250 square miles in the United States are devoted to lawns, more than are allotted to any single crop. Historically, these lawns have been the opposite of wilderness: highly controlled, manicured monocultures planted with a single type of grass. But a movement for "backyard biodiversity" says that wilderness should begin at home.[71] A lawn of native plants that offers shade and food can bring animals back to the suburbs, and bird boxes could attract owls that will hunt mice and other vermin. Holes cut along the bottom of fences would allow animal movement between yards and into any undeveloped lands that remain nearby.[72] Although building backyard biodiversity occurs one house at a time, it is part of a larger vision: Over time, each small yard transformed into a wild land will convert another neighbor to the cause. As the years go by, the yards along a street will merge into one another, creating contiguous wildlife habitats, and whole streets and communities will form a new kind of suburb, a better way of dwelling on the land.

THE GROWING SENSE of human-animal connections has meant that keeping wild animals in captivity no longer has the unquestioned appeal that it did in the mid-twentieth century. As late as 1962, John Wayne could star in *Hatari!*, which achieved great box-office success. Wayne played the leader of a company that captured wild game on the

African savannah for shipment to zoos. No questions were raised about the ethics of removing the animals from the land for lives in confinement, or splitting up animal families. Instead, Wayne and his crew simply romped across the plains, like cowboys riding jeeps. A romantic subplot and goofy secondary characters completed the picture.

But four years later came *Born Free*, the first of many animal films to emphasize that humans have a moral responsibility to help animals return to the wild. Based on Joy Adamson's bestselling memoir, the film tells the story of Elsa, a lion cub that Adamson and her husband adopted after the cub's mother had been killed. Rather than send Elsa to a zoo, Adamson decides to raise the cub herself, hoping to teach her the hunting skills she needs to live on the land. After much effort, Elsa returns to the savannah—coming back the next year to visit her human mother and father with cubs of her own. In this model of a human-animal family, the nurturing humans reach full maturity only by helping animals live in the wild. And healthy interspecies kinship comes only with recognition of the essential need for wild animals to be physically separate from the human world.

The most startling animal freedom movement of all began with the 1993 release of *Free Willy*, the story of an orca whale held captive in an amusement park and a twelve-year-old orphan boy's struggle to return him to the ocean. *Free Willy* was made for around twenty million dollars, and its producers thought that the film would do well to turn a modest profit. Instead, it grossed $154 million. Over three hundred thousand of those who saw the film accepted an invitation screened at its end to learn about whale protection. The number they dialed belonged to Earth Island Institute, a radical environmental group. Many of the callers asked Earth Island a question they hadn't anticipated: When was the whale that played Willy—an orca named Keiko—himself going to be freed?

In 2002, after nine years of work and twenty million dollars spent to restore Keiko's physical and mental health, the whale finally swam free from a kind of halfway house on the Icelandic coast. He joined up with a pod of orcas, and went on to Norway. Every phase of Keiko's journey from captivity through rehabilitation and release made national and international news.[73] Although Keiko never lived exclusively among whales at sea, but stayed in Norway's fjords and interacted with humans until his 2003 death from pneumonia, he remained an icon. To this day, he still inspires efforts to end whale captivity.[74] The effort to return Keiko wasn't just about saving one whale, but about the possibility of redemption, preserving the ocean and all its creatures.

It was a hope shared by Richard O'Barry. O'Barry had gained fame and fortune as the trainer of the dolphins that appeared in the 1963 movie *Flipper* and the popular spinoff television show of the same name. But in 1970, O'Barry returned from months of overseas travel to find his favorite dolphin, Kathy, covered with big black blisters. She died in his arms. O'Barry blamed himself for keeping her captive—"Why are we doing this?" he asked himself and his colleagues at Miami's Seaquarium—and realized that most of the dolphins he had helped capture in the past ten years were dead.[75] In his sorrow O'Barry flew to Bimini and tried to release a dolphin he had helped capture years ago. The effort failed (the dolphin wouldn't leave his pen), and O'Barry was arrested and spent a week in jail.

On the first Earth Day—April 22, 1970—O'Barry and his colleague Fred Neil founded the Dolphin Project to track the captive dolphin industry and educate the public about the harm done to the animals. In 2002, O'Barry estimated that some one thousand dolphins were at the center of a billion-dollar-per-year industry that included swim-with-dolphins resorts and cheap roadside amusement parks featuring dolphins bouncing balls and jumping through hoops.[76] O'Barry didn't want people to stop interacting with dolphins, but rather to understand that humans have no right to capture and own them. "Dolphins are like the ocean itself," he concluded, their nature as wild animals inseparable from the sea.[77]

It was slow, difficult work. Over thirty years, the Dolphin Project only managed to rehabilitate and successfully release fourteen dolphins. But in the early 2000s, as news stories began to focus on aquatic theme parks and swim-with-dolphins resorts, O'Barry's stature increased. As a consultant to the World Society for the Protection of Animals, he has been able to keep the treatment of dolphins in the public eye. "Think about what has happened to those dolphins," he said to a *Los Angeles Times* reporter. "They were abducted by aliens and transported here in a UFO. They are traumatized."[78] O'Barry continues to challenge the dolphin industry's image as a source for innocent encounters with animals who are happy to perform.

FINALLY, THERE HAVE been signs in the Native American community of a renewed environmental sensitivity—counterbalancing, to some extent, the moves toward gambling and entrepreneurship. Many Native American tribes have used casino revenue to buy lands they lost to whites in the nineteenth and twentieth centuries. In other cases, tribes that rely on gaming have avoided the industry's worst impacts by using casino revenues to protect what lands they have from pollution and reinforce their traditional culture. In the Florida Everglades, the Miccosuke have used casino profits to finance extensive lawsuits against the South Florida Water Management District, claiming that the district has violated the Clean Water Act by pumping water with excessive phosphorus (from fertilizers used on nearby sugarcane plantations) into the Miccosuke reservation. They want the water detoxified because, as tribal elder Buffalo Tiger explained to a reporter, "It is simply the right thing to do."[79] Across the country, in the deserts surrounding the Colorado River along the California-Arizona border, the Fort Mojave tribe has used its casino revenue to sue Pacific Gas and Electric for locating a water detoxification plant on the tribe's most sacred site, the Topock Maze. According to tribal tradition, the maze is the site for the soul's final atonement, part of "the essence of what it means to be Mojave." While no one doubts that a treatment plant is needed to remove toxins from groundwater before it reaches Southern California's aquifers, the Mojave contend that the choice of the treatment site ignored their cultural concerns.[80]

Some tribes have rejected gambling altogether and are fighting to regain lost tribal lands and protect existing reservations from devastation by mining and energy drilling. The Lakota Sioux, for example, remain steadfast in their determination to recover ownership of the Black Hills. According to the tribe's creation myth, both the Sioux people and the Pte Oyate (buffalo nation) emerged on Earth in the Black Hills; it is the Sioux's most sacred land, the site of crucial ceremonies and vision quests. Both the 1851 Sioux treaty with the U.S. government and the 1868 Fort Laramie Treaty, which included several Plains tribes, guaranteed Sioux ownership. But after the discovery of gold in the Black Hills in 1874, and Custer's defeat by Sitting Bull in 1876, the U.S. Congress retaliated against the Sioux, seizing the land in 1877 via eminent domain.[81]

In 1980, more than a century later, the U.S. Supreme Court ruled in favor of a Sioux lawsuit brought against Congress, declaring the 1877 land seizure a "ripe and rank case of dishonorable dealing." But the Court declared that it did not have authority to return the land (only Congress could do that), and offered $105 million in compensation instead. Led by Johnson Holy Rock, a self-taught legal expert and tribal elder whose father had fought Custer at the Little Big Horn, the Sioux spurned cash settlement, which by 1999 was worth over four hundred million dollars.[82] More than money, they wanted the two thousand square miles of sacred tribal lands in the Black Hills—now managed by the U.S. Forest Service—returned to them.

In 2005, after thirty-five years of struggle, Navajo and Hopi activists finally succeeded in ending Peabody Energy's draining of the aquifer under Black Mesa mountain, a place sacred to both tribes. Since 1970, Peabody had used about 3.3 million gallons of water each day to pump coal in a slurry 273 miles north to a power plant in Laughlin, Nevada. This went directly against Hopi cultural values:

According to Vernon Masayesva, an activist who founded Black Mesa Trust, the Hopi have a religious obligation to preserve groundwater. Their mythology says that the divine ancestor of the Hopi told the tribe to beware "a waterless world" with "no forests, no flowing water or lakes. . . . But if you take care of this land and use its resources in the best possible way, you will be here a long time."[83] Navajo activist Nicole Horseherder explained that her people share a similar cosmology. The "earth is female and the sky male. They are counterparts and keep everything in balance. . . . It is the relationship of the earth drawing water from the sky and the sky drawing water back from the earth that creates the harmony."[84] Taking groundwater from Black Mesa disrupted this harmony. It was not surprising that drought and dry springs followed.

Combining these traditional spiritual understandings with new studies on the aquifer's depletion, the Hopi and Navajo peoples persuaded their tribal councils to shut down water pumping at the end of 2005. Stopping the water pumping in turn led to the end of coal mining on Black Mesa until another source of water is found—which could take years, if it ever happens. The Nevada power plant, which had already been facing a lawsuit over its air pollution, was shut down as well. This extraordinary environmental victory will cost the Navajo and Hopi several hundred jobs and millions in revenues. Even so, the Hopi also voted down a proposal to build a casino that would bring in twenty-four million dollars in annual profits. As tribal vice chairman Caleb Johnson explained, "Gaming is making money off other people's bad habits, and the Hopi way says we should not use other people's bad habits to benefit."[85]

Other tribes have also staunchly protected their cultural heritage. In Tennessee, the Alliance for Native American Indian Rights fought developers who wanted to dig up a graveyard dating back to 1100 AD to build a new shopping center for Lowe's and Wal-Mart. "Great Spirit, we pray for the sacredness of our ancestors' graves," intoned the group's ceremonial leader in a protest. "Without them we would not be here. . . . We pray, grandfather, that our actions will touch the hearts and change the minds of the people who run Wal-Mart."[86] Similarly, Tongva leaders protested against the massive Playa Vista residential and commercial project in Los Angeles when its developers removed over one thousand bodies from one of the largest Tongva cemeteries ever discovered in order to dig a drainage ditch. Like many other Native American peoples, the Tongva believe that both the soul's spiritual journey and the well-being of the whole tribe are connected to the body's decay and mixing with the Earth.[87] Native Hawaiians are also fighting local developers. "They were bulldozing through the bones of our ancestors, then offering us jobs like they were doing us a favor," said Molokai activist Walter Ritte, indignant about the way nearly eighty-five square miles of the island were being given over to a resort complex and vacation homes.[88] That many tribes are standing up to powerful developers in order to protect their traditional culture and lands reaffirms the importance of Native American spirituality to the culture of enchantment.

# 10

## The Journey Ahead

In 2005, the United Nations released the Millennium Ecosystem Assessment, the result of a five-year study of the world's environment
involving some 1,360 scientists. Its executive summary, "Living Beyond Our Means: Natural Assets and Human Well-Being," portrays
the Earth as a giant business rapidly approaching bankruptcy: "Human activity is putting such strain on the natural functions of Earth
that the ability of the planet's ecosystems to sustain future generations
can no longer be taken for granted. . . . Nearly two-thirds of the services provided by nature to humankind are found to be in decline
worldwide. In effect, the benefits reaped from our engineering of the
planet have been achieved by running down natural capital assets."[1]

The report reads like a recitation of doom. Global warming looms
ominously, with the climate changing faster than anything seen since
the end of the last ice age some ten thousand years ago. The rapid
rise in temperature is endangering countless animals.[2] In the oceans,
populations of the fish species most prized by people—the larger,
meatier ones such as tuna and swordfish, and even the more humble
cod—have been reduced by 90 percent since the onset of industrialized

fishing sixty years ago. Roughly 30 percent of the world's coral reefs are dead and another 20 percent degraded from warming waters and polluted, turbid runoff. More than a third of the world's mangrove forests or swamps have been destroyed to make way for development.[3] Wild, open lands are rapidly being transformed into farms: People converted more forests and prairies to cropland from 1950 to 1980 than in the century and a half between 1700 and 1850.[4] The destruction of habitat leaves animals with nowhere to go: "Some 12% of birds, 25% of mammals, and at least 32% of amphibians are threatened with extinction over the next century," the scientists conclude. The current animal extinction rate is already roughly a thousand times greater than the long-term average rate as measured by the fossil record, and if present trends continue, the future extinction rate is projected to be ten times greater yet.[5]

Confronted with the diminishment of Earth's natural "services"— the regulation of the climate, the provision of food and freshwater, the supply of renewable resources such as wood—the report's authors call for the creation of much better accounting systems to measure just what the Earth provides. The implication is that businesses and governments need to see costs and profits differently, that forests and grasslands might be saved because "the total economic value associated with managing ecosystems more sustainably is often higher than the value associated with the conversion of the ecosystem through farming, clear-cut logging, or other intensive use."[6] It's as if everyone is a businessman, and thus will act rationally to save the Earth once it's made clear that this is what's profitable.

But another argument emerges from the study as well. "We must learn to recognize the true value of nature—both in terms of an economic sense and in the richness it provides to our lives in ways much more difficult to put numbers on," write the Millennium Assessment's board of directors. "Appreciation of the natural world is an important part of what makes us human."[7] With these words, the United Nations report becomes another text in the culture of enchantment.

The loss of so much of the world around us, it argues, also threatens humans with a loss of meaning. Sacred forests and mystical animals vanish. "Culturally valued ecosystems" deteriorate. Disfigured, diminished landscapes can less readily serve as a source of inspiration for art, folklore, and national symbolism. The assessment reads like a kind of funeral oratory, another hybrid discourse in which science and economics are mixed together with the ritual processes of grief and mourning.

Funerary rhetoric marks what is irretrievably gone, of course, but it also reveals a people's fundamental moral values—what the deceased meant to those still living, and what their hopes are for the future. As earlier chapters have noted, such rhetoric is now routinely featured in thousands of news reports. In a growing public acknowledgment of kinship, laments for the deceased are now given on behalf of wild animals and places of all kinds. Such oratory also serves as a kind of reveille, a call to make amends for creatures' wrongful deaths by acting to save those who are still left: Outlaw lead bullets, so the few remaining California condors won't die from lead poisoning when they eat carcasses left by hunters. Use rat poison with extreme care, so that coyotes, bobcats, and mountain lions won't die after eating poisoned rats. Urgently study the mysterious deaths of whales, and put the U.S. Navy's testing of powerful sonar systems under stringent government regulation.

Increasingly, for every funeral story or call for action there is also a tale of resurrection and renewal. Searches for "ghost" species, for instance, are holy pilgrimages, mythic quests to bring back life from death's grasp. If one near-extinct creature can be restored to a healthy population, then possibly others can, too, along with their habitats. When researchers finally announced in 2005 that they had videotaped an ivory-billed woodpecker in a forested Arkansas swamp, the first sighting since 1944, government agencies and the Nature Conservancy bought more forested river-bottom lands near the location of the sighting to increase the bird's chances for survival.[8]

The response to the sighting shows a new covenant between society and nature taking shape. As novelist and bird-watcher Jonathan Rosen commented, the return of the ivorybill offers hope: "It somehow suggests that we have found more than just a missing bird and that God, whom we invoked when we conquered the wilderness, is also present in our effort to get it back."[9] And even zoologist Jerome A. Jackson, who questioned the sighting, calling it "faith-based ornithology," points to the "grandeur of old-growth forests and the importance of those forests to migrant songbirds, wintering waterfowl, black bears . . . and a multitude of less-charismatic plants and animals."[10] He hopes that the search for the "Lord God" bird will lead people back to the Southern swamps, and that they will fall in love there with these forgotten lands and all their creatures.

The intense desire to connect human life to the broader natural world is influencing not just the sciences but every domain of culture. The art world, for instance, has seen an unprecedented number of artists over the past thirty-five years pursuing "Earth art," which attempts to change people's perceptions of nature through sculpture, photography, film, and ritual actions. In the Arizona desert north of Flagstaff, James Turrell has been working since 1977 to transform Roden Crater, the impact site of a meteorite, into a place for the contemplation of the heavens, like Stonehenge might have been. Underneath the crater, Turrell is boring out tunnels and special rooms to collect the light from stars. "The gathered starlight will inhabit that space," he says, "and you will be able to feel the physical presence of the light."[11]

Gregory Colbert's "Ashes and Snow" project, a photography exhibit of people and wild animals interacting freely, also celebrates human-animal kinship.[12] A boy sits with a cheetah nearby. A young girl and an orangutan hold hands while drifting down a river in a dugout canoe. A woman dances while an eagle flies by, grazing her as if they are dancing together. Colbert's traveling exhibition space is a dimly lit, cathedral-like structure encompassing 125,000 square feet, built out of shipping containers and translucent membranes—a twenty-first-century version of an itinerant preacher's tent. All the humans in the photographs appear with their eyes closed, as if praying or meditating.

Industrial designers are also showing the influence of the culture of enchantment. British engineer Graham Dorrington has designed a hot air balloon to look like a fish, uniting the arts and sciences through what he calls "organic design." The balloon carries a small gondola from which scientists can study the canopies of tropical rain forests. Just as a fish hovers above a coral reef, Dorrington and his colleagues hover above the rain forest, collecting data to help further understand the ecosystem.[13] Engineers from DaimlerChrysler, meanwhile, have unveiled a concept car design based on the body of the boxfish. The four-inch-long boxfish became a model because its squarish yet streamlined shape minimizes drag and its honeycomb-like frame provides high strength and low weight. The concept car gets seventy miles per gallon, and has vastly reduced emissions.[14]

No doubt the boxfish car is an engineering marvel, as is Dorrington's airship. But these engineering efforts, called "biomimetics," are also motivated by deeply held romantic impulses.[15] The artist-engineers are practicing what anthropologist James George Frazer called "homoeopathic" or "imitative" magic, meaning they design their creations through the magical principle of "like produces like."[16] They make machines that move within the natural world, and whose very shape and look remind people of their connections and moral obligations to the planet. One day, these designs imply, we all might learn to move along the Earth's surface like fish swimming harmlessly above an ocean reef.

ROMANTIC ATTITUDES TOWARD nature are a critical inspiration for the culture of enchantment, but they can also be an obstacle if they lead to unrealistic expectations of "purity" in ecological restoration. For example, if the program for rehabilitating the Everglades goes forward with full funding, then—after many years or even decades of work—much of south Florida will eventually be remade, with formerly straight canals turned back into meandering waterways, and a river of grass once again moving water from Lake Okeechobee southward to the park. But this task will require new dams, lakes, and pumping stations, and perhaps even scattered water-treatment plants to maintain water quality. Restoration doesn't mean that the Everglades will look exactly the way it did before south Florida's development.

A similar problem sometimes surfaces when naturalists try to restore endangered animal populations. By the late 1880s, commercial hunters had virtually exterminated the American buffalo; just a few dozen animals were saved by a handful of ranchers and Native American tribes. This remnant eventually became the basis for rebuilding the buffalo population, and by 2007 that population had reached over three hundred thousand animals. Biological studies report that, surprisingly enough, today's buffalo herds show remarkable genetic diversity; the pitfalls of inbreeding have been avoided. But these same genetic studies show that only a small portion of contemporary buffalo (the herd at Yellowstone and a few scattered groups elsewhere, totaling about ten thousand animals) are 100 percent buffalo. Instead, the vast majority of buffalo now carry cattle genes: They look and act like buffalo, but genetically are buffalo-cattle hybrids.[17] If a large part of the Great Plains becomes a buffalo-filled prairie reserve, then such hybrids would surely form the core of the herds.

With endangered predators, the genetic issues are even more complex. "Pure" subspecies often simply no longer exist. Florida panthers, for example, declined to such dangerously low levels—and showed signs of deterioration through inbreeding—that fish and game officials brought in mountain lions from Texas (also known as pumas) to help rejuvenate their cousins. And all across the United States, scores of Central American pumas either captured or bred for the exotic pet industry have been released by their owners into the wilds. Mountain lion populations are thus often mixed hybrids between formerly distinct subspecies or breeding groups. Even substantially increased habitats and improving public attitudes toward coexisting with lions can't change that biological reality.

Some conservation biologists have stopped trying to focus on purity, finding hope in a different approach. As global warming and expanding human populations create serious problems for wilderness areas in Africa and Asia, one proposed solution is to export some animals to the United States and other countries where they might survive. Evolutionary biologist Josh Donlan and his colleagues argue that threatened species such as African elephants and cheetahs could survive and prosper in massive "ecological history parks" on America's Great Plains, where they would serve as "proxies" for the wooly mammoths and saber-toothed tigers that roamed across North America thirteen thousand years ago.[18] While this is certainly part of the culture of enchantment, such "re-wilding" would not be a return to a lost golden age, but the creation of something distinctly new.

Even the very meaning of "wild" is becoming a vexed question. By definition, wild animals—especially predators like lions and bears—are not under human control: They flee or sometimes attack when they encounter humans. But what if bears and lions learn to change their behavior? Naturalist and journalist David Quammen visited India's Gir Wildlife Sanctuary and National Park, one of the last remaining areas where "African" lions roam. People live in and near the reserve, but the lions neither charge nor flee when humans are simply standing or sitting some one hundred feet away. While some lions do attack livestock, the herders can readily scare them off with sticks, so the lions are rarely killed.[19] The conventional distinctions between wild animals versus domesticated species no longer describe these lions, who seem to belong to neither category. Nor do we know what to call this kind of human-animal relationship.

All of these "compromises" point to the same challenge: We have to accept that even the grandest, boldest, most imaginatively conceived programs will not be able to restore many places and species to the way they once were. But while there is indeed a risk that people will become disappointed with an "imperfect" restoration, widespread disillusionment is not inevitable. It's worth remembering that the primary value of cultural mythologies is not that they provide a perfect account of the world but that they give meaning to life, a feeling of belonging to a specific place and a larger cosmos.

Moreover, enchantment gives mythic resonance to the great difficulties facing grand-scale environmental restoration. The Yahwist narrative in Genesis, for example, says that God placed Adam and Eve in the Garden of Eden to "cultivate and care for it" (Genesis 2:15). Doesn't the work of saving nearly extinct creatures and preserving the world's remaining undeveloped spaces parallel the caretaking tasks of Adam and Eve, even if the lands in question are degraded and the animals are "mongrels" or refugees from another continent? As the seventeenth-century English poet and theologian Thomas Traherne wrote, "By Love our Souls are married and solder'd to the creatures and it is our Duty like God to be united to them all." Surely this ethical prescription of human stewardship for all living things extends to cover buffalo-cattle hybrids, African elephants relocated to the Great Plains, and lions and bears that have adjusted to the presence of people.[20]


THE CULTURE OF enchantment is flowering now because it meets a human need for transcendence and connection to the natural world. Over a century ago, William James examined religious conversion experiences and their consequences for both individuals and society. James defined religion broadly to include whatever people consider divine or sacred, including mystical experiences. Conversion, he argued, releases energy and changes people's perceptions, creating "a new zest which adds itself like a gift to life, and takes the form either of lyrical enchantment or of appeal to earnestness and heroism."[21] This new zest also has a pragmatic function. In the case of enchantment, religious or quasi-religious conversion helps give people the vision and the will to act—to support social changes necessary to save the planet. Consequently, it is not necessary to pass judgment on whether or not Luna the redwood tree actually "spoke" to Julia Butterfly Hill during her two-year tree-sit, or whether Richard Nelson literally "became" an island by eating its fish and berries and drinking its waters. Whatever their literal truth, these boundary-shifting experiences with nature clearly enrich people's lives and make them more protective of the land and its creatures.

Historically, new ways of understanding and relating to nature have preceded actual political changes. Sometimes the lag is measured in decades: Neither Thoreau nor Melville lived to see their works lead to conservation. In other cases, however, the effect of reimagining nature is felt quickly. The writings of John Muir and Aldo Leopold and the photographs of Ansel Adams helped persuade Congress to save wilderness and create national parks. More recently, Subhankar Banerjee's photographs of the Arctic National Wildlife Refuge helped defeat the Bush administration's repeated efforts to "crack the back of radical environmentalists" and open the sanctuary to oil and gas drilling. And Al Gore's enormously successful film, *An Inconvenient Truth*, a classic hybrid discourse that combines scientific evidence with a spiritual drama of how creation has been damaged by human recklessness and how good works can bring renewal, made millions conscious of the need to address global warming.

Despite periodic losses and setbacks, the momentum behind this cultural transformation continues to build, and it suggests that anyone who cares about the Earth should take heart. The culture of enchantment has kindled people's interest in other creatures, helped them empathize with animals, made them want to see lands and oceans preserved. It has opened people's imaginations, and in doing so it has changed the political climate. The spread of enchantment means that the environmental movement and its allies can now shift their strategy from defense to offense. Such an offensive strategy will require a strong proactive agenda for environmental reform, one in which unambiguous legal mandates against drilling in ANWR and road construction in national forests are only the beginning. The reenchantment of nature—if coupled with political courage to act—offers a chance to remake the world.

# Notes

## Introduction: Call of the Wild

1. Interview with John Quigley, Los Angeles, March 2005.

2. Freeman House, *Totem Salmon: Life Lessons from Another Species* (Boston: Beacon Press, 1999), 141.

3. Ibid., 169.

4. John Daniszewski, "Hanging with the Cranes," *Los Angeles Times*, September 5, 2002, sec. A.

5. Myrna Oliver, "Jacques Mayol, 74: Set Record in 'Free Dive,'" *Los Angeles Times*, December 26, 2001, sec. B.

6. Jacques Mayol, *Homo Delphinus: The Dolphin Within Man* (New York: Idelson-Gnocchi Publishers, 1999), 355–56.

7. Rosemary McClure, "The Day Cinderella Vanished," *Los Angeles Times*, March 11, 2004, sec. A.

8. Eric Schlosser, *Fast Food Nation* (New York: Houghton Mifflin, 2001).

9. Matthew Scully, *Dominion: The Power of Man, the Suffering of Animals, and the Call to Mercy* (New York: St. Martin's Press, 2002), 260.

10. Ibid., 289.

11. Willett Kempton, James S. Boster, and Jennifer A. Hartley, *Environmental Values in American Culture* (Cambridge, Massachusetts: The MIT Press, 1996), 113.

12. Karl Marx and Friedrich Engels, *The Communist Manifesto*, trans. Samuel Moore (New York: Simon and Schuster; Pocket Books, 1964), 65–66.

13. Weber used the concept of disenchantment in much of his work in the sociology of religion and the rise of modernity, but never fully developed the idea. The

quote here is from the first volume of Weber's 1922 work, *Gesammelte Aufsatze zur Religionssoziologie*, 564. Cited by Arthur Mitzman, *The Iron Cage: An Historical Interpretation of Max Weber* (New York: Grosset and Dunlap, 1971), 221.

14. Carl G. Jung, *Psychological Reflections: An Anthology of Jung's Writings, 1905–1961*, ed. Jolande Jacobi (London: Routledge, 1971), 264.

15. The Center for Biological Diversity, Greenpeace, and the Natural Resources Defense Council filed suit in 2005, requesting that the Fish and Wildlife Service begin an investigation into the health of the polar bear population. Secretary of the Interior Dick Kempthorne announced the investigation in January 2007, but the department failed to meet the legal requirement of announcing a final resolution within a year. In March 2008, the three environmental groups filed another suit against the Department of the Interior for its failure to meet the deadline. A federal judge ruled in their favor, and in May 2008 the department listed the polar bear as threatened, while simultaneously asserting that oil and gas drilling in the region did not constitute a threat to the bears.

## Chapter 1: Modernity and Its Discontents

1. Karl Marx and Friedrich Engels, *The Communist Manifesto*, trans. Samuel Moore (New York: Simon and Schuster; Pocket Books, 1964), 63.

2. Friedrich Engels, *The Condition of the Working Class in England*, 1892 English edition (Moscow: Progress Publishers, 1973), 89.

3. Max Weber, *The Protestant Ethic and the Spirit of Capitalism*, trans. Talcott Parsons (New York: Charles Scribner's Sons, 1958), 26.

4. Max Weber, "Science as a Vocation," in *From Max Weber: Essays in Sociology*, trans. and ed. Hans H. Gerth and C. Wright Mills (New York: Oxford University Press, 1946), 155.

5. Weber, *The Protestant Ethic and the Spirit of Capitalism*, 182.

6. Shepard Krech III, *The Ecological Indian: Myth and History* (New York: W. W. Norton, 1999), 125–37.

7. Winona LaDuke, *All Our Relations: Native Struggles for Land and Life* (Cambridge, Massachusetts: South End Press, 1999), 141.

8. Dan O'Brien, *Buffalo for the Broken Heart: Restoring Life to a Black Hills Ranch* (New York: Random House, 2001), 67–68.

9. Barry Holstun Lopez, *Of Wolves and Men* (New York: Simon and Schuster, 1978), 178–81.

10. Krech, *The Ecological Indian*, 177.

11. Augustin Macdonald, "Decline of the Sea Otter," in *Green Versus Gold: Sources in California's Environmental History*, ed. Carolyn Merchant (Washington, D.C.: Island Press, 1998), 77.

12. Matthew Scully, *Dominion: The Power of Man, the Suffering of Animals, and the Call to Mercy* (New York: St. Martin's Press, 2002), 142.

13. Ralph Waldo Emerson, *Nature and Selected Essays*, ed. Larzer Ziff (New York: Penguin Books, 1982; Penguin Classics, 2003), 38.

14. Ibid.

15. Dick Russell, *Eye of the Whale: Epic Passage from Baja to Siberia* (New York: Simon and Schuster, 2001), 65.

16. Henry David Thoreau, "From *Journals,* February 16, 1860," in *Nature Writing: The Tradition in English,* ed. Robert Finch and John Elder (New York: W. W. Norton, 2002), 216–17.

17. Emerson, "Thoreau," in *Nature and Selected Essays,* 406.

18. Herman Melville, *Moby-Dick* (New York: Barnes & Noble Classic Edition, 1993), 67.

19. Melville, *Moby-Dick,* 451.

20. Witold Rybczynski, *A Clearing in the Distance: Frederick Law Olmsted and America in the Nineteenth Century* (New York: Simon and Schuster, 1999), 238.

21. Roderick Nash, *Wilderness and the American Mind* (New Haven: Yale University Press, 1967), 112.

22. Peter B. Hales, *William Henry Jackson and the Transformation of the American Landscape* (Philadelphia: Temple University Press, 1988), 141–73.

23. Philip G. Terrie, *Forever Wild: A Cultural History of Wilderness in the Adirondacks* (Syracuse, New York: Syracuse University Press, 1994), 85.

24. Nash, *Wilderness and the American Mind,* 131.

25. John Muir, "The Wild Parks and Forest Reservations of the West," in *The American Wilderness: Essays by John Muir, Photographs by Ansel Adams,* ed. John Thaxton (New York: Barnes & Noble Books, 1993), 4.

26. Muir, "The Sequoia and General Grant National Parks," in *The American Wilderness,* 69.

27. Muir, "The Approach to the Valley," in *The American Wilderness,* 96.

28. Muir, "Hetch Hetchy Valley," in *The American Wilderness,* 196.

29. Modern social and cultural theorists call this relation between a theory and the object being theorized "reflexivity." The theory is not simply descriptive, but has a transformative impact on the very subject under scrutiny.

30. Environmental historian Aaron Sachs argues that Emerson, Thoreau, Melville, and Muir were all influenced by the early nineteenth-century work of German naturalist and explorer Alexander von Humboldt. Humboldt's books, particularly *Views of Nature* (1808) and the three volumes of *Personal Narrative of Travel to the Equinoctial Regions of America, 1799–1804* (published between 1814 and 1825), included both scientific descriptions of regions and lyrical passages extolling their beauty and spirit. Humboldt in turn embraced Indian spirituality. "'Your God,' said they to me, 'keeps himself shut up in a house, as if he were old and infirm; ours is in the forests, in the fields, and on the mountains of Sipapu, whence the rains come.'" See Aaron Sachs, *The Humboldt Current: Nineteenth-Century Exploration and the Roots of American Environmentalism* (New York: Viking Press, 2006), 66.

31. Muir, "The Sequoia and General Grant National Parks," in *The American Wilderness,* 73.

32. Ibid., 88.

33. Nash, *Wilderness and the American Mind,* 186–87.

34. Aldo Leopold, "Thinking Like a Mountain," *A Sand County Almanac* (New York: Oxford University Press, 1949; New York: Ballantine Books, 1970), 138.

35. Ibid., 140.

36. Leopold, "The Land Ethic," *A Sand County Almanac*, 239.

37. Ibid., 240.

38. Ibid., 262.

39. Anne Hammond, *Ansel Adams: Divine Performance* (New Haven: Yale University Press, 2002), 142.

40. Ibid., 50.

41. François Leydet, *Time and the River Flowing: Grand Canyon*, ed. David Brower (San Francisco: Sierra Club, 1964). Also see Nadine Brozan, "Philip J. Hyde, 84, Conservation Photographer, Dies," *New York Times*, April 18, 2006, sec. C.

42. James William Gibson, *The Perfect War: Technowar in Vietnam* (New York: Atlantic Monthly Press, 1986), 13.

43. Ulrich Beck, *Risk Society: Towards a New Modernity*, trans. Mark Ritter (Thousand Oaks, California: Sage Publications, 1992).

44. Grace Thorpe, "Our Homes Are Not Dumps," in *Defending Mother Earth: Native American Perspectives on Environmental Justice*, ed. Jace Weaver (Maryknoll, New York: Orbis Books, 1996), 47; "Report Links Nuclear Tests, Cancer," *Los Angeles Times*, February 12, 2003, sec. A.

45. Steve Kroll-Smith and H. Hugh Floyd, *Bodies in Protest: Environmental Illness and the Struggle over Medical Knowledge* (New York: New York University Press, 1997), 25.

46. Rachel Carson, *Silent Spring* (New York: Houghton Mifflin, 1962).

47. Beck, *Risk Society*, 59.

48. Ibid., 70.

49. Richard Slotkin, *Regeneration Through Violence: The Mythology of the American Frontier, 1600–1860* (Middletown, Connecticut: Wesleyan University Press, 1973).

50. Old-style Western movies and television shows died out by the end of the 1960s. Films like *The Wild Bunch* (1969) and *Butch Cassidy and the Sundance Kid* (1969) killed off their stars in ways that said the cowboy hero was obsolete. Others, such as *Soldier Blue* (1970) and *Little Big Man* (1970) undercut America's cultural celebration of the Indians' decimation by showing the U.S. Cavalry attacking Indian villages. As old conceptions about the Indian conquest became discredited, interest grew in learning more about Western history.

51. Donald A. Grinde and Bruce E. Johansen, *Ecocide of Native America: Environmental Destruction of Indian Lands and Peoples* (Santa Fe, New Mexico: Clear Light Publishers, 1995), 44–49; Krech, *The Ecological Indian*, 93.

52. Ward Churchill, *Struggle for the Land: Native American Resistance to Genocide, Ecocide, and Colonization* (San Francisco: City Lights, 2002), 48.

53. Ibid.

54. Winona LaDuke, *All Our Relations*, 143.

55. Robert McG. Thomas Jr., "Thomas Banyacya, 89, Teller of Hopi Prophecy to World," *New York Times*, February 15, 1999, sec. A; "An Address by Thomas Banyacya, Kykotsmovi, Arizona, to the United Nations," December 11, 1992, http://www.welcomehome.org/rainbow/prophecy/hopi.html.

56. Peter Matthiessen, *Indian Country* (London: Collins/Harvill, 1985; Fontana Paperbacks, 1986), 86–91.

57. Ibid., 91.

58. Matthiessen, *The Birds of Heaven: Travels with Cranes*, paintings and drawings by Robert Bateman (New York: North Point Press, 2001), 261.

59. Susan Keese, "Early History," in *Free Land: Free Love: Tales of a Wilderness Commune*, ed. Don Monkerud, Malcolm Terence, and Susan Keese (Aptos, California: Black Bear Mining and Publishing Company, 2000), 21.

60. Black Elk, *Black Elk Speaks: Being the Life of a Holy Man of the Oglala Sioux*, ed. John G. Neihardt, illus. Standing Bear (New York: William Morrow and Company, 1932; New York: Pocket Books, 1972), 8.

61. Arthur F. McEvoy, *The Fisherman's Problem: Ecology and Law in the California Fisheries* (Cambridge, England: Cambridge University Press, 1986), 31.

62. John (Fire) Lame Deer and Richard Erdoes, *Lame Deer: Seeker of Visions* (New York: Simon and Schuster, 1972; Pocket Books, 1976), 31–32.

63. Jace Weaver, "Preface," *Defending Mother Earth: Native American Perspectives on Environmental Justice*, ed. Jace Weaver (Maryknoll, New York: Orbis Books, 2001), 10.

64. Grinde and Johansen, *Ecocide of Native America*, 31.

65. Ibid., 25.

66. Vine Deloria Jr., *God Is Red* (New York: Dell Publishing, 1973), 166–67.

67. Ibid., 269–70, 294.

68. Lame Deer, *Lame Deer*, 10.

69. Ibid., 145–46.

70. Luther Standing Bear, *Land of the Spotted Eagle* (New York: Houghton Mifflin, 1933; Lincoln: University of Nebraska Press, 1978), 38.

71. At Reed College in 1951, Snyder wrote his senior thesis on a Haida Indian myth tale; following literary critics Paul Radin and I. A. Richards, he argued that modern poets were essentially tribal shamans who can articulate intense inner experiences for their society. See Gary Snyder, *He Who Hunted Birds in His Father's Village: The Dimensions of a Haida Myth* (Bolinas, California: Grey Fox Press, 1979), 92–96.

72. Snyder's account of being influenced by Native American messengers is in his essay "The Rediscovery of Turtle Island," in *Deep Ecology for the 21st Century: Readings on the Philosophy and Practice of the New Environmentalism*, ed. George Sessions (Boston: Shambhala Publications, 1995), 457. The quote is from Snyder's 1969 essay "Four Changes," included in his collection of poetry, *Turtle Island* (New York: New Directions, 1974), 108.

73. Snyder, "Four Changes," *Turtle Island*, 105.

74. Snyder, "Tomorrow's Song," *Turtle Island*, 77.

75. Carlos Castaneda, *The Teachings of Don Juan: A Yaqui Way of Knowledge* (Berkeley, California: University of California Press, 1968).

76. Deloria, *God Is Red*, 7, 64.

77. LaDuke, *All Our Relations*, 12–20.

78. Peter Matthiessen, *In the Spirit of Crazy Horse* (New York: Viking Press, 1983).

79. For one AIM leader's account of that era, see Russell Means with Marvin J. Wolf, *Where White Men Fear to Tread: The Autobiography of Russell Means* (New York: St. Martin's Griffin, 1995).

80. Victor W. Turner, *The Ritual Process: Structure and Anti-Structure* (Ithaca, New York: Cornell University Press, 1969).

81. Run periodically for the rest of the 1970s, the Crying Indian (as the campaign was called in the advertising industry) made an impression on some fifteen billion people. See Krech, *The Ecological Indian*, 15.

82. Chief Seattle's original 1854 speech was translated by Dr. Henry Smith and published on October 29, 1887, in the *Seattle Sunday Star*, http://www.suquamish .nsn.us/seattle.html.

83. *Brother Eagle, Sister Sky* sold 280,000 copies within eight months. See Grinde and Johanesen, *Ecocide of Native America*, 24–25.

## Chapter 2: Animals Who Speak to Us

1. David Abram, *The Spell of the Sensuous* (New York: Pantheon, 1996), 87.

2. Barry Holstun Lopez, *Of Wolves and Men* (New York: Simon and Schuster, 1978), 112.

3. Peter Matthiessen, *The Birds of Heaven: Travels with Cranes*, paintings and drawings by Robert Bateman (New York: North Point Press, 2001), 17–18.

4. Claude Lévi-Strauss, *The Savage Mind* (Chicago: University of Chicago Press, 1966), 126–28.

5. James Cowan, "On Savage Art," in *The Soul of Nature: Visions of a Living Earth*, ed. Michael Tobias and Georgianne Cowan (New York: Continuum Publishing Company, 1994), 169.

6. Emile Durkheim, *The Elementary Forms of the Religious Life*, trans. Joseph Ward Swain (New York: The Free Press, 1965), 364.

7. Rachel Carson, *Lost Woods: The Discovered Writing of Rachel Carson*, ed. Linda Lear (Boston: Beacon Press, 1998), 91.

8. Alan Tennant, *On the Wing: To the Edge of the Earth with the Peregrine Falcon* (New York: Alfred A. Knopf, 2004), 4.

9. Ibid., 139.

10. Dan O'Brien, *Buffalo for the Broken Heart: Restoring Life to a Black Hills Ranch* (New York: Random House, 2001), 4.

11. Ibid., 9.

12. Paul Watson (as told to Warren Rogers), *Sea Shepherd: My Fight for Whales and Seals* (New York: W. W. Norton, 1982), 68–70.

13. Paul Watson tells this story—a creation myth—in almost all his works. This version comes from an interview with Dick Russell, *Eye of the Whale: Epic Passage from Baja to Siberia* (New York: Simon and Schuster, 2001), 119.

14. Watson, *Sea Shepherd*, 40–41.

15. Peter Heller, *The Whale Warriors: The Battle at the Bottom of the World to Save the Planet's Largest Mammals* (New York: The Free Press, 2007), 98, 227–29.

16. Raffi Khatchadourian, "Neptune's Navy: Paul Watson's Wild Crusade to Save the Oceans," *The New Yorker*, November 5, 2007.

17. Russell, *Eye of the Whale*, 147.

18. Ibid.

19. Ibid., 44.

20. Terry Tempest Williams, "Undressing the Bear," in *The Soul of Nature*, 109.

21. Peter Steinhart, *The Company of Wolves* (New York: Alfred A. Knopf, 1995), xiii.

22. Paul Shepard, *The Tender Carnivore and the Sacred Game*, drawings by Fons Van Woerkom (New York: Charles Scribner's Sons, 1973), 143.

23. Ibid., 169.

24. John (Fire) Lame Deer and Richard Erdoes, *Lame Deer: Seeker of Visions* (New York: Simon and Schuster, 1972; Pocket Books, 1976), 108–9.

25. Richard K. Nelson, *The Island Within* (San Francisco: North Point Press, 1989), 26.

26. Ibid., 31.

27. José Ortega y Gasset, *Meditations on Hunting*, trans. Howard B. Wescott (New York: Charles Scribner's Sons, 1972), 111.

28. Lopez, *Of Wolves and Men*, 94–95.

29. Freeman House, *Totem Salmon: Life Lessons from Another Species* (Boston: Beacon Press, 1999), 67–68.

30. Ibid., 70.

31. Nelson, *The Island Within*, 249.

32. Benjamin Kilham and Ed Gray, *Among the Bears: Raising Orphan Cubs in the Wild* (New York: A John Macrae Book/Henry Holt, 2002), 5.

33. Sy Montgomery, *Search for the Golden Moon Bear: Science and Adventure in Pursuit of a New Species* (New York: Simon and Schuster, 2002), 19.

34. Ibid., 20.

35. Ibid., 21.

36. Ibid., 153.

37. Ibid.

38. Claudia Dreifus, "A Biologist Decries Strip Mining of the Deep Sea" (Interview), *New York Times*, March 5, 2002, sec. F.

39. Friends of Animals, "One Fur Coat" (Advertisement), *Harper's*, July 2003.

40. Vicki Hearne, *Adam's Task: Calling Animals by Name* (New York: Alfred A. Knopf, 1986), 168.

41. Matthew Ebnet, "Samson the Bear Dies a Celebrity's Death," *Los Angeles Times*, May 16, 2001, sec. B.

42. Quentin Hardy, "The Deer Departed, So Larry Jones Hunts Elvis and Lost Souls," *Wall Street Journal*, May 18, 1999, sec. A.

43. Steve Hymon, "A Cruel End for a Great Elk," *Los Angeles Times*, February 8, 2005, sec. A.

44. Jacques Mayol, *Homo Delphinus: The Dolphin Within Man* (New York: Idelson-Gnocchi Publishers, 1999), 32.

45. Ibid., 14.

46. Elaine Morgan, *The Aquatic Ape: A Theory of Human Evolution* (New York: Stein and Day, 1982), 77.

47. Roger Payne, *Among the Whales* (New York: Charles Scribner's Sons, 1995), 218.

48. Mayol, *Homo Delphinus*, 64–79.

49. Ibid., 15.

50. Charles Darwin, *The Origin of Species*, ed. Richard E. Leakey (New York: Hill and Wang, 1979), 223.

51. Charles Darwin, *The Descent of Man, and Selection in Relation to Sex*, 3rd ed. (New York: Penguin Group, 2004), 151.

52. Charles Darwin, *The Expression of the Emotions in Man and Animals* (New York: Oxford University Press, 1998).

53. Paul Ekman, "Introduction to the Third Edition," *The Descent of Man*, xxix.

54. Mark Derr, "Brainy Dolphins Pass the Human 'Mirror' Test," *New York Times*, May 1, 2001, sec. F.

55. Laura Tangley, "Natural Passions," *International Wildlife*, Journal of the National Wildlife Federation, September–October 2001, 30, http://findarticles.com/p/articles/mi_m1170/is_2001_sept-oct/ai_77627999.

56. Louis Sahagun, "Far More Than Creatures of Habit," *Los Angeles Times*, November 28, 2005, sec. B.

57. Claudia Dreifus, "Ode with a Nightingale, and a Thrush, and a Lyrebird," *New York Times*, September 20, 2005, sec. D.

58. Edward O. Wilson, *Biophilia* (Cambridge, Massachusetts: Harvard University Press, 1984), 130.

59. David Suzuki, "Listening to Elders," *New Dimensions*, tape no. 2359 (Ukiah, California: New Dimensions Foundation, undated), quoted in Paul H. Ray and Sherry Ruth Anderson, *The Cultural Creatives: How 50 Million People Are Changing the World* (New York: Three Rivers Press, 2000), 314.

60. Steinhart, *The Company of Wolves*, 21.

61. Ibid., 27.

62. Ibid., 252–53.

63. Ibid.

64. House, *Totem Salmon*, 19.

65. David Petersen, *Ghost Grizzlies: Does the Great Bear Still Haunt Colorado?* revised and updated edition (Boulder, Colorado: Johnson Books, 1998), 7, 105–7.

66. Rick Bass, *The Lost Grizzlies: A Search for Survivors in the Wilderness of Colorado* (Boston: A Mariner Book/Houghton Mifflin, 1995), 22.

67. Ibid., 5.

68. Ibid., 51.

69. Ibid.

70. Ibid., 169.

71. Ibid., 95.

72. Ibid., 225.

73. Ibid., 219.

74. Ibid., 225.

75. James Gorman, "In the Shadow of Extinction," *New York Times*, February 8, 2002, sec. B.

76. Gorman, "Listening for the Call of a Vanished Bird," *New York Times*, March 5, 2002, sec. D.

77. Gorman, "In the Shadow of Extinction."

78. Gorman, "Listening for the Call of a Vanished Bird."

79. Gorman, "Faint Hope for Survival of a Woodpecker Fades," *New York Times,* June 10, 2002, sec. A.

80. Durkheim, *The Elementary Forms of the Religious Life,* 398.

81. Kirk Johnson, "So You Hate a Crowded Beach? So Do These Shy Terrapins," *New York Times,* July 13, 2003, sec. YT.

82. Gary Polakovic, "Deaths of the Little Bighorns," *Los Angeles Times,* August 29, 2001: A1, 12.

83. Deborah Schoch, "Five Condors Released into Wild at Big Sur," *Los Angeles Times,* April 6, 2001, sec. A.

84. David Kelly, "Condor Is Free to Roam After 15 Years in Protective Custody," *Los Angeles Times,* May 2, 2002, sec. B.

85. David Kelly, "Welfare State for Vultures," *Los Angeles Times,* July 24, 2002: Aa.25.

86. Ibid.

87. Zanto Peabody, "Condors Hang Out with Gliders over Valley," *Los Angeles Times,* March 27, 2002, sec. B.

88. Jonathan D. Glater, "Condor Rescuers Lose a Most Valued Teammate," *New York Times,* April 26, 2003, sec. A.

89. James Barron, "A Coyote in Central Park Proves That He, Too, Can Run a Marathon," *New York Times,* March 22, 2006, sec. A.

90. Kareem Fahim, "Rat Poison Cited in Coyote's Death," *New York Times,* April 8, 2006, sec. A.

91. Kelefa Sanneh, "Stretching from the Heavens to the Deep Sea, the Songs of a Bird-Watcher," *New York Times,* July 8, 2006, sec. A.

92. Sonya Geis, "Woman Traumatized by Failed Rescue of Impaled Deer," *Pasadena Star News,* December 21, 2004, sec. A.

93. Mary Jonilonis, "A Gentle Reminder," *Los Angeles Times,* May 5, 1993, sec. C.

94. William Wan, "Protecting Bears by Targeting Humans," *Los Angeles Times,* July 19, 2004, sec. B.

95. Mircea Eliade, *Myth and Reality,* trans. Willard R. Trask (New York: Harper Colophon Books; Harper and Row, 1963), 30.

96. Richard Nelson, *The Island Within,* 276.

97. Carl Safina, *Song for the Blue Ocean: Encounters Along the World's Coasts and Beneath the Seas* (New York: A John Macrae Book/Henry Holt, 1997), 77.

98. Abram, *Spell of the Sensuous,* 22.

99. Paul Shepard, *Nature and Madness* (San Francisco: Sierra Club Books, 1982), 34.

100. Shepard, *The Tender Carnivore,* 203.

101. Steinhart, *The Company of Wolves,* xv.

102. Shepard, *The Tender Carnivore,* 188.

103. Kilham, *Among the Bears,* 254.

104. Ibid., 274.

105. Daniel Quinn, *Ishmael* (New York: A Bantam/Turner Book, 1993), 242–43.

106. Ibid., 262.

## Chapter 3: Holy Lands

1. Mircea Eliade, *The Sacred and the Profane: The Nature of Religion*, trans. Willard R. Trask (San Diego, California: Harcourt Brace Jovanovich, 1959), 116.

2. Richard K. Nelson, *The Island Within* (New York: North Point Press, 1989), 52.

3. Eliade, *The Sacred and the Profane*, 151.

4. Karl Polanyi, *The Great Transformation* (Boston: Beacon Press, 1957).

5. Tony Hiss, *The Experience of Place* (New York: Alfred A. Knopf, 1990; Vintage Books, 1991), 116.

6. James Howard Kunstler, *The Geography of Nowhere: The Rise and Decline of America's Man-Made Landscape* (New York: Simon and Schuster, 1993), 26.

7. John R. Logan and Harvey L. Molotch, *Urban Fortunes: The Political Economy of Place* (Berkeley, California: University of California Press, 1987).

8. David Harvey, "The Geopolitics of Capitalism," in *Social Relations and Social Structures*, ed. Derek Gregory and John Urry (New York: St. Martin's Press, 1985), 150.

9. John Wesley Powell, *The Arid Lands*, ed. Wallace Stegner (Lincoln: Bison Books/University of Nebraska Press, 2004), xvi–xviii.

10. Ibid., xxxiv.

11. Robert Pogue Harrison, *Forests: The Shadow of Civilization* (Chicago: University of Chicago Press, 1992), 73.

12. Ibid., 170.

13. Chatsumarn Kabilsingh, "Early Buddhist Views on Nature," in *This Sacred Earth: Religion, Nature, Environment*, ed. Roger S. Gottlieb (New York: Routledge, 1996), 149.

14. David R. Brower (with Steve Chapple), *Let the Mountains Talk, Let the Rivers Run: A Call to Those Who Would Save the Earth* (San Francisco: HarperCollins West, 1995), 32–33.

15. Ibid., 37.

16. David Quammen, "Saving Africa's Eden," *National Geographic*, September 2003, 50–77.

17. Rick Bass, *The Lost Grizzlies: A Search for Survivors in the Wilderness of Colorado* (Boston: A Mariner Book/Houghton Mifflin, 1995), 102.

18. Hank Fischer, *Wolf Wars: The Remarkable Inside Story of the Restoration of Wolves to Yellowstone* (Helena and Billings, Montana: Falcon Press Publishing, 1995), 12–19.

19. Douglas W. Smith and Gary Ferguson, *Decade of the Wolf: Returning the Wild to Yellowstone* (Guilford, Connecticut: The Lyons Press, 2005), 14–15.

20. Anne Matthews, *Where the Buffalo Roam: The Storm over the Revolutionary Plan to Restore America's Great Plains* (New York: Grove Press, 1992).

21. Dan O'Brien, *Buffalo for the Broken Heart: Restoring Life to a Black Hills Ranch* (New York: Random House, 2001), 14–15.

22. Stephanie Brown, "In Midwest, Prairies Have Become Grasslands of Opportunity," *Los Angeles Times*, May 25, 1999, sec. A.

23. Kenneth R. Weiss, "The Man Behind the Land," *Los Angeles Times*, October 27, 2004, sec. A.

24. The Wildlands Conservancy, "About Us: Mission Statement," http://www.wildlandsconservancy.org/twc_about.html.

25. Bettina Boxall, "A Quiet Broker of the Wild," *Los Angeles Times*, April 24, 2002, sec. A.

26. Deborah Schoch, "Bold Dream for America's Wildernesses," *Los Angeles Times*, September 13, 1999, sec. A.

27. Maria Mudd Ruth, *Rare Bird: Pursuing the Mystery of the Marbled Murrelet* (New York: Rodale Press, 2005), 202–3.

28. Kenneth R. Weiss, "Fishing Permanently Banned Around the Channel Islands; A Reserve, Encompassing 175 Square Miles, Takes Effect Jan 1 and Is One of the Largest in the U.S.," *Los Angeles Times*, October 24, 2002, sec. A.

29. Dick Russell, *Eye of the Whale: Epic Passage from Baja to Siberia* (New York: Simon and Schuster, 2001), 85–88.

30. Ibid., 86.

31. Ibid., 140.

32. Ibid., 527.

33. Ibid., 12.

34. Peter Matthiessen, "In the Great Country," in *Arctic National Wildlife Refuge: Seasons of Life and Land, A Photographic Journey* by Subhankar Banerjee (Seattle, Washington: Mountaineers Books, 2003), 43.

35. Kim Murphy, "2 Villages, 2 Views of the Dynamics of Oil," *Los Angeles Times*, April 16, 2001, sec. A.

36. Matthiessen, "In the Great Country," 41.

37. Norma Kassi, "A Legacy of Maldevelopment: Environmental Devastation in the Arctic," in *Defending Mother Earth: Native American Perspectives on Environmental Justice*, ed. Jack Weaver (Maryknoll, New York: Orbis Books, 1996), 81.

38. James Gertenzang, "Bush Gets Union Allies in Arctic Drilling Drive," *Los Angeles Times*, January 18, 2002, sec. A; Richard Simon, "Bush Plan Calls for Increase in Oil Production," *Los Angeles Times*, February 24, 2002, sec. A.

39. Jimmy Carter, "Make This Natural Treasure a National Monument," *New York Times*, December 29, 2000, sec. A.

40. Kim Murphy, "Caribou's Plight Intersects Oil Debate," *Los Angeles Times*, July 5, 2001, sec. A.

41. Richard Simon, "Senate Rejects Oil Drilling in Arctic Refuge," *Los Angeles Times*, March 20, 2003, sec. A.

42. David Firestone, "Drilling in Alaska, a Priority for Bush, Fails in the Senate," *New York Times*, March 20, 2003, sec. A.

43. At the time, an exhibition of Banerjee's ANWR photographs was on display at the Smithsonian Institution. In an act of revenge, administration officials pressured the Smithsonian to relocate the exhibit downstairs to a less prestigious room near the cafeteria, with short captions replacing Banerjee's lyrical descriptions. "Some Scary Pictures," *Los Angeles Times*, May 2, 2003, sec. A.

44. Subhankar Banerjee, *Arctic National Wildlife Refuge*, 11.

45. Eliade, *Sacred and Profane*, 131.

46. Michael Engelhard, *Where the Rain Children Sleep: A Sacred Geography of the Colorado Plateau* (Guilford, Connecticut: The Lyons Press, 2004), 82.

47. Tim Palmer, *Endangered Rivers and the Conservation Movement* (Berkeley, California: University of California Press, 1986), 91.

48. Richard T. Cooper, "Future of Hydropower Must Navigate Crosscurrents of Competing Interests," *Los Angeles Times*, September 7, 2001, sec. A.

49. Sam Howe Verhovek, "Returning River to Salmon, and Man to the Drawing Board," *New York Times*, September 26, 1999, sec. A.

50. Ibid.

51. Ibid.

52. Kim Murphy, "U.S. Salmon Recovery Plan Could Mean Removing Dams," *Los Angeles Times*, December 22, 2000, sec. A.

53. Sam Howe Verhovek, "Army Decides Not to Back Breaching of Four Dams," *New York Times*, December 5, 2001, sec. A.

54. David James Duncan, "Salmon's Second Coming," *Sierra*, vol. 85, no. 2, March/April 2000, 40–41.

55. Sandra Blakeslee, "Panel O.K.'s Plan to Flood Part of River in Canyon," *New York Times*, April 26, 2002, sec. A.; Sandra Blakeslee, "Restoring an Ecosystem Torn Asunder by a Dam," *New York Times*, June 11, 2002, sec. D.

56. Associated Press, "Put Parts of Missouri River Back as We Found It, Panel Says," *Los Angeles Times*, January 10, 2002, sec. A.

57. Christopher Hallowell, "Letting the River Run," *New York Times*, May 4, 2001, sec. A.

58. Cornelia Dean, "Time to Move the Mississippi, Experts Say," *New York Times*, September 19, 2006, sec. D.

59. Kenneth R. Weiss, "Deal Struck to Restore Salt Ponds in S.F. Bay," *Los Angeles Times*, May 29, 2002, sec. B.

60. Andrew C. Revkin, "Stockpiling Water for a River of Grass," *New York Times*, March 26, 2002, sec. D.

61. Mireya Navarro, "Everglades Comeback Threatens Way of Life," *New York Times*, December 5, 2002, sec. A; Elizabeth Shogrin, "Bush Brothers Agree to Plan for Everglades," *Los Angeles Times*, January 10, 2002, sec. A.

62. John H. Cushman Jr., "Clinton Backing Vast Effort to Restore Florida Swamps," *New York Times*, February 18, 1996, sec. A; Revkin, "Stockpiling Water for a River of Grass."

63. Critics have raised doubts about whether the Everglades plan would actually return water to the swamp or would primarily be used to provide Florida cities with water. Water pollution from the region's sugar industry is also a major concern. As of May 2008, the river of grass has not been rehydrated. Damien Cave, "Everglades Park Counts the Good and Bad After a Blaze," *New York Times*, May 23, 2008, sec. A. However, in June 2008, the state of Florida announced that it was buying nearly three hundred square miles of United States Sugar property located south of Lake Okeechobee and north of Everglades National Park to restore the river of grass. See Damien Cave, "Florida Buying Big Sugar Tract for Everglades," *New York Times*, June 25, 2008, sec. A. For a good history of the conflicts surrounding the restoration plan, see Michael Grunwald, *The Swamp: The Everglades, Florida, and the Politics of Paradise* (New York: Simon and Schuster, 2006).

64. Hector Tobar, "Where the Forests Are Foes," *Los Angeles Times*, March 12, 2003, sec. A.

65. Hector Tobar, "Two Firms in Chile to Save Some Trees," *Los Angeles Times*, November 13, 2003, sec. A.

66. Wendell Berry, "The Making of a Marginal Farm," in *Nature Writing: The Tradition in English*, ed. Robert Finch and John Elder (New York: W. W. Norton, 2002), 735.

67. Clifford Geertz, *Local Knowledge: Further Essays in Interpretive Anthropology* (New York: Basic Books, 1983).

68. Hiss, *The Experience of Place*, 40–41; Arthur F. McEvoy, *The Fisherman's Problem: Ecology and Law in the California Fisheries* (Cambridge, England: Cambridge University Press, 1986), 25–26.

69. Yi-Fu Tuan, *Topophilia: A Study of Environmental Perception, Attitudes, and Values* (Minneapolis: University of Minnesota Press, 1974), 101.

70. Christopher Y. Tilley, *A Phenomenology of Landscape: Places, Paths, and Monuments* (Oxford, England: Berg, 1994), 31, 40.

71. Barbara Kingsolver, Camille Kingsolver, and Steven L. Hopp, *Animal, Vegetable, Miracle* (New York: HarperCollins, 2007).

72. Daniel Duane, *Caught Inside: A Surfer's Year on the California Coast* (New York: North Point Press/Farrar, Straus and Giroux, 1996), 122.

73. Ibid., 176.

74. Carl Safina, *Song for the Blue Ocean: Encounters Along the World's Coasts and Beneath the Sea* (New York: A John Macrae Book/Henry Holt, 1997), 435.

75. David Abram, *Spell of the Sensuous* (New York: Pantheon, 1996), 69.

76. William James, *A Pluralistic Universe*, in *William James: Writings 1902–1910*, ed. Bruce Kuklick (New York: Library of America, 1987), 702.

77. John M. Gionna, "Dam Dispute Looses a Flood of Emotions," *Los Angeles Times*, August 11, 2002, sec. B.

78. Dean E. Murphy, "Conservationists Try to Undo Large Reservoir in Yosemite," *New York Times*, October 15, 2002, sec. A.

79. Ibid.

80. Eric Bailey, "A Hefty Price Tag on Hetch Hetchy," *Los Angeles Times*, July 20, 2006, sec. B.

81. Marjory Stoneman Douglas, *The Everglades: River of Grass* (St. Simons Island, Georgia: Mockingbird Books, 1947), 290.

82. Brower, *Let the Mountains Talk, Let the Rivers Run*, 25.

83. John McPhee, *Encounters with the Archdruid: Narratives About a Conservationist and Three of His Natural Enemies* (New York: Farrar, Straus and Giroux, 1971), 240.

## Chapter 4: Space Exploration, Gaia, and the Greening of Religion

1. John McPhee, *Encounters with the Archdruid: Narratives About a Conservationist and Three of His Natural Enemies* (New York: Farrar, Straus and Giroux, 1971), 166.

2. David Brower (with Steve Chapple), *Let the Mountains Talk, Let the Rivers*

*Run: A Call to Those Who Would Save the Earth* (San Francisco: HarperCollins West, 1995), 52.

3. Ibid.

4. McPhee, *Encounters with the Archdruid*, 80.

5. Association of Space Explorers, "ASE History," http://www.space-explorers .org/association/history.html.

6. Kevin W. Kelley, ed., *The Home Planet* (New York: Addison-Wesley, 1988), 24.

7. Ibid., near plate 82, "The Atlantic Coast of Argentina."

8. Ibid., near plate 70, "Indonesia."

9. Ibid., near plate 110, "Lake Powell in Arizona and Utah, USA."

10. Ibid., near plate 60, "The Atlantic Coast of South Africa."

11. Ibid., near plate 24, "Astronaut Using Hand-held Maneuvering Unit."

12. Ibid., near plate 38, "A Nearly Full Earth."

13. Ibid., near plates 42–45, "Earthrise as Seen from the Moon," and near plate 52, "Africa, Europe, and Western USSR."

14. Ibid., near plate 138, "Andros Island, Bahamas."

15. Ibid., near plate 137, "Cumulonimbus Clouds over the Congo Basin, Zaire."

16. Theodore Roszak, *The Voice of the Earth: An Exploration of Ecopsychology*, 2nd ed. (Grand Rapids, Michigan: Phanes Press, 2001), 144–45.

17. James Lovelock, *Gaia: A New Look at Life on Earth* (Oxford and New York: Oxford University Press, 1979; reprinted with a new preface by the author, 2000), 8. Page references are to the 2000 edition.

18. Ibid.

19. Ibid., 10.

20. Ibid., 120.

21. Ibid., 10.

22. Ibid., 9–10.

23. James Lovelock, *The Ages of Gaia: A Biography of Our Living Earth* (New York: W. W. Norton, 1988; updated and revised edition, 1995), 39. Page references are to the 1995 edition.

24. Ibid., 19.

25. Ibid., 194.

26. Ibid., 193.

27. Ibid, 199.

28. Ibid., xiv.

29. Ibid., xv.

30. Lovelock, *Gaia: A New Look at Life on Earth*, xiii.

31. Roszak, *The Voice of the Earth*, 304–5.

32. Ibid., 308.

33. Ibid., 157–58.

34. Václav Havel, "The Need for Transcendence in the Post-Modern World," delivered at Independence Hall, Philadelphia, Pennsylvania, July 4, 1994, http:// www.gaianation.net/org/vaclav.html.

35. Carolyn Merchant, *The Death of Nature: Women, Ecology, and the Scientific Revolution* (New York: Harper and Row, 1980; HarperSanFrancisco paperback edition, 1990), 2–3.

36. Susan Griffin, *Women and Nature: The Roaring Inside Her* (New York: Harper and Row, 1978), 1.

37. Paula Gunn Allen, "The Woman I Love Is a Planet; the Planet I Love Is a Tree," in *Reweaving the World: The Emergence of Ecofeminism*, ed. Irene Diamond and Gloria Feman Orenstein (New York and San Francisco: Sierra Club Books, 1990), 52.

38. Ibid., 57.

39. Diann L. Neu, *Return Blessings: Ecofeminist Liturgies Renewing the Earth* (Cleveland: The Pilgrim Press, 2002), 22.

40. Marija Gimbutas, *The Language of the Goddess* (London and New York: Thames and Hudson, 2001), quoted in Neu, *Return Blessings*, 90.

41. Riane Eisler, *The Chalice and the Blade: Our History, Our Future* (New York: Harper and Row, 1987), 28.

42. Ibid.

43. Starhawk, *Dreaming the Dark: Magic, Sex, and Politics* (Boston: Beacon Press, 1982), 4.

44. Ibid., 53.

45. Ibid., 172.

46. Ibid., 179.

47. Clarissa Pinkola Estés, *Women Who Run with the Wolves: Myths and Stories of the Wild Woman Archetype* (New York: Ballantine Books, 1992), 1.

48. Ibid.

49. Ibid., 15.

50. Ibid., 26.

51. Jean M. Auel, *The Clan of the Cave Bear*, vol. 1, Earth's Children (New York: Crown Publishers, 1980; Bantam Books, 1981), 433.

52. Jean M. Auel, *The Valley of the Horses*, vol. 2, Earth's Children (New York: Crown Publishers, 1982; Bantam Books, 1983), 118.

53. Ibid., 259.

54. Ibid., 258.

55. Ibid., 401.

56. Ibid., 132.

57. Jean M. Auel, *The Shelters of Stone*, vol. 5, Earth's Children (New York: Crown Publishers, 2002; Bantam Books, 2003), 540.

58. Harvey Cox, *The Secular City: Secularization and Urbanization in a Theological Perspective* (New York: Collier Books, 1965; repr. 1990).

59. Lynn White, "The Historical Roots of Our Ecological Crisis," *Science*, vol. 155, no. 3767, March 10, 1967, 1203–7. White's work has been widely reprinted.

60. Lynn White, "The Historical Roots of Our Ecological Crisis," in *The Sacred Earth: Religion, Nature, Environment*, ed. Roger S. Gottlieb (New York: Routledge, 1996), 185.

61. Norman Wirzba, *The Paradise of God: Renewing Religion in an Ecological Age* (New York: Oxford University Press, 2003), 13.

62. Roderick F. Nash, *The Rights of Nature: A History of Environmental Ethics* (Madison: The University of Wisconsin Press, 1989), 90; Theodore Hiebert, "Rethinking Dominion Theology," *Direction*, vol. 25, no. 2, Fall 1996, 4.

63. The King James Version of the Bible translates the shrines of Asherah as

270 · *Notes*

"sacred groves," while the New Revised Standard Version translates them as "sacred poles." Biblical scholar Tilde Binger argues that the evidence suggests both living trees and carved wooden columns served her, along with small clay idols. See Tilde Binger, *Asherah: Goddess in Ugarit, Israel, and the Old Testament*, (Sheffield, England: Sheffield Academic Press, 1997), 141.

64. Wirzba, *The Paradise of God*, 26.

65. David Kingsley, *Ecology and Religion: Ecological Spirituality in Cross-Cultural Perspectives* (Englewood Cliffs, New Jersey: Prentice-Hall, 1994), 107–14.

66. Ibid., 107.

67. H. Paul Santmire, *The Travail of Nature: The Ambiguous Ecological Promise of Christian Theology* (Philadelphia: Fortress Press, 1985), 125.

68. John F. Haught, *The Promise of Nature* (New York/Mahwah, New Jersey: Paulist Press, 1993), 99.

69. Theodore Hiebert, *The Yahwist Landscape: Nature and Religion in Early Israel* (New York: Oxford University Press, 1996), 5.

70. Wirzba, *The Paradise of God*, 20.

71. Ibid., 67–69.

72. Ibid., 81.

73. Morton discusses his role in helping launch Lovelock's first book in an interview with Alan Atkisson, "The Green Cathedral: An Interview with Reverend James Parks Morton," *In Context: A Quarterly of Human Sustainable Culture*, no. 24, Late Winter 1990, 16, www.context.org/ICLIB/IC24/Morton.htm.

74. Charles M. Murphy, *At Home on Earth: Foundations for a Catholic Ethic of the Environment* (New York: Crossroad, 1989), 126.

75. Evangelical Lutheran Church in America Environmental Task Force, "Basis of Our Caring," in *The Sacred Earth*, ed. Roger S. Gottlieb, 245. In 1993 the Evangelical Lutheran Church voted in favor of a "Creation Care theology and policy." See *Caring for Creation: Vision, Hope, and Justice* (Minneapolis: Augsberg Fortress, 1993).

76. Hiebert, *The Yahwist Landscape*, 24.

77. Ibid., 63.

78. Ibid., 72–73, 109, 132.

79. In contrast, the Priestly Writer portrays God as ordering highly ornate altars, to be made from acacia wood and bronze (Exodus 27:1–6).

80. Hiebert, *The Yahwist Landscape*, 110.

81. Wirzba, *The Paradise of God*, 44.

82. David Kinsley, *Ecology and Religion* (Englewood Cliffs, New Jersey: Prentice-Hall, 1994), 119.

83. Ibid., 120.

84. Ibid., 122.

85. Pope John Paul II, "The Ecological Crisis: A Common Responsibility" (Washington, D.C.: United States Conference of Catholic Bishops, 1990), 11–12.

86. Thomas Traherne, *Centuries of Meditations* 1:3, ed. Bertram Dobbell (London, 1908), http://www.spiritofprayer.com/o1century.php.

87. Traherne, *Centuries of Meditations* 2:66, http://www.spiritofprayer.com/o2century.php.

88. James A. Nash, *Loving Nature: Ecological Integrity and Christian Responsibility*

(Nashville: Abingdon Press and The Churches' Center for Theology and Public Policy, 1991), 129.

89. Haught, *The Promise of Nature*, 94.

90. United States Conference of Catholic Bishops, *Renewing the Earth: An Invitation to Reflection and Action on Environment in Light of Catholic Social Teaching* (Washington, D.C., 1992), 6.

91. Evangelical Lutheran Church in America, *Caring for Creation*.

92. Annecy Report, "Liberating Life: A Report to the World Council of Churches," in *This Sacred Earth: Religion, Nature, and the Environment*, ed. Roger S. Gottlieb (New York and London: Routledge, 1996), 257.

93. American Baptist Churches, USA, "Creation and the Covenant of Caring," in *This Sacred Earth*, ed. Roger Gottlieb, 240.

94. Wirzba, *The Paradise of God*, 51.

95. National Religious Partnership for the Environment, "NRPE History," http://www.nrpe.org/whatisthepartnership/founding_intro02.htm.

96. National Religious Partnership for the Environment, "NRPE Partners," http://www.nrpe.org/whatisthepartnership/partners_intro01.htm.

97. Willett Kempton, James S. Boster, and Jennifer A. Hartley, *Environmental Values in American Culture* (Cambridge, Massachusetts: The MIT Press, 1996), 91–95.

98. John C. Green, "The American Religious Landscape and Political Attitudes: A Baseline for 2004" (Akron, Ohio: Bliss Institute, University of Akron), 22–23.

99. Patriarch Bartholomew I, *Cosmic Grace & Humble Prayer: The Ecological Vision of the Green Patriarch Bartholomew I*, ed. Friar John Chryssavgis (Grand Rapids, Michigan: William B. Eerdmans, 2003), 55.

100. Environmental Task Force, Evangelical Lutheran Church of America, "Basis for Our Caring," in *This Sacred Earth*, ed. Roger Gottlieb, 249.

101. Nash, *Loving Nature*, 123.

102. Gary Snyder, *Turtle Island* (New York: New Directions Books, 1974), 108.

103. Roszak, *The Voice of the Earth*, 137.

104. Rodney Barker, *And the Waters Turned to Blood* (New York: Simon & Schuster, 1997), 174.

105. Ibid., 179.

106. Jon Krakauer, *Into Thin Air: A Personal Account of the Mt. Everest Disaster* (New York: Villard Books, 1997), 45.

107. Ibid., 51–52.

108. Ibid., 128.

109. Ibid.

110. Ibid., 286–87.

111. James Powlik, *Sea Change* (New York: Island Books, 1999), 249.

112. Carlos Fuentes, "When Nature Punishes Us," *Los Angeles Times*, January 16, 2005, sec. M.

113. "Mangrove Forest Saved Lives in 2004 Tsunami Disaster," World Conservation Union, December 19, 2005; "Healthy Mangroves Protected Communities Hit by Tsunami, Survey Says," Associated Press, December 21, 2005, http://www.wildsingapore.com/news/20051112/051219-5.htm.

114. Simon Winchester, "The Year the Earth Fought Back," *New York Times*, December 29, 2004, sec. A.

115. Abby Goodnough, "Survivors of Tsunami Live on Close Terms with Sea," *New York Times*, January 23, 2005, sec. A.

116. Paul Watson, "Swept into the World," *Los Angeles Times*, February 3, 2005, sec. A.

117. Ashley Powers, "Surfers Paddle Out for Victims of Tsunamis," *Los Angeles Times*, January 16, 2005, sec. B.


## Chapter 5: Eco-Warriors and Blood Sacrifice

1. Susan Zakin, *Coyotes and Town Dogs: Earth First! and the Environmental Movement* (Tucson: University of Arizona Press, 2002), 41–42.

2. Ibid., 47–51.

3. Ibid., 55.

4. Ibid.

5. Ibid., 53.

6. Ibid., 57.

7. Edward Abbey, *The Monkey Wrench Gang* (Philadelphia and New York: J. B. Lippincott Company, 1975), 23.

8. Richard Slotkin, *Regeneration Through Violence: The Mythology of the American Frontier, 1660–1860* (Middletown, Connecticut: Wesleyan University Press, 1973).

9. James William Gibson, *Warrior Dreams: Paramilitary Culture in Post-Vietnam America* (New York: Hill and Wang, 1994).

10. Peacock's experience in Vietnam was not unique. For an analysis of the U.S. mode of warfare in Vietnam, see James William Gibson, *The Perfect War: Technowar in Vietnam* (New York: Atlantic Monthly Press, 1986).

11. Doug Peacock, *Grizzly Years: In Search of the American Wilderness* (New York: Henry Holt, 1990), 51.

12. Ibid., 64.

13. Ibid., 24–25.

14. Ibid., 211–12.

15. Ibid., 17.

16. Ibid., 26.

17. Ibid., 61.

18. Paul Watson, as told to Warren Rogers, *Sea Shepherd: My Fight for Whales and Seals* (New York: W. W. Norton, 1982), 153.

19. Edward Abbey, *Hayduke Lives!* (Boston: Little, Brown, 1990).

20. Paul Watson, *Ocean Warrior: My Battle to End the Illegal Slaughter on the High Seas* (Toronto: Key Porter Books, 1994), 217.

21. Zakin, *Coyotes and Town Dogs*, 95.

22. Rick Scarce, *Eco-Warriors: Understanding the Radical Environmental Movement* (Chicago: The Noble Press, 1990), 24.

23. Zakin, *Coyotes and Town Dogs*, 93–98.

24. Ibid., 133.

25. Ibid., 194.

26. Ibid., 67.

27. Dave Foreman, *Confessions of an Eco-Warrior* (New York: Harmony Books/ Crown Publishing Group, 1991), 34.

28. Scarce, *Eco-Warriors*, 74.

29. Zakin, *Coyotes and Town Dogs*, 60–61.

30. Ibid., 196.

31. Ibid., 296.

32. Ibid., 142.

33. Foreman, *Confessions of an Eco-Warrior*, 22.

34. Ibid. Since 2005, drought conditions in the Southwest have lowered the water level in Lake Powell to one-third of capacity. Glen Canyon has literally resurfaced, further popularizing the goal of restoring the Colorado from a stagnant lake to a river running through a magnificent 186-mile gorge. See Susan Spano, "Exposing Utah's Depths," *Los Angeles Times*, April 3, 2005, L1, 13; Ward Graham, "Houseboat Heaven: Flush It," *Los Angeles Times*, June 19, 2005, M1, 2.

35. Zakin, *Coyotes and Town Dogs*, 252–53.

36. At its peak strength in the 1980s, The *Earth First! Journal* had roughly six thousand annual subscribers, and another four thousand issues were either bought in bookstores or given away at promotional events each year. Personal communication from Dave Foreman, April 4, 2008.

37. Steve Chapple, "Laws of the Jungle," *Los Angeles Times Magazine*, August 8, 2004, 11.

38. Zakin, *Coyotes and Town Dogs*, 149.

39. Steve Chapple, "Running the Green Machine," *Los Angeles Times Magazine*, August 8, 2004, 10.

40. Ibid., 29–30.

41. Ibid.

42. Zakin, *Coyotes and Town Dogs*, 218.

43. Dave Foreman and Bill Haywood, eds., *Ecodefense: A Field Guide to Monkey-wrenching* (Tucson: Ned Ludd Books, 1985). Although Dave Foreman and Bill Haywood are listed as the book's editors, *Ecodefense* is not an edited reader, but a narrative written in a single voice.

44. Michael A. Lerner, "The FBI vs. the Monkeywrenchers," *Los Angeles Times Magazine*, April 15, 1990, 6; Zakin, *Coyotes and Town Dogs*, 440–41.

45. Dave Foreman and Nancy Morton, "Good Luck, Darlin'. It's Been Great," in *The Earth First! Reader: Ten Years of Radical Environmentalism*; ed. John Davis (Salt Lake City: Peregrine Smith Books, 1991), 264.

46. In the late 1990s and early 2000s, Craig Rosebraugh served as spokesperson for ELF at the North American Earth Liberation Front Press Office. Interviews with him appear on the Internet at Web sites such as http://www.animalrights.net and http://www.nocompromise.org and in videos such as "Igniting the Revolution: An Introduction to the Earth Liberation Front."

47. Craig Rosebraugh, *Burning Rage of a Dying Planet* (New York: Lantern Books, 2004), 20.

48. Ibid., 213. The property damage estimate cited by Rosebraugh came from Congressman Scott McInnis.

49. Julie Cart and Monte Morin, "Eco-Terrorism Suspected as Fire Levels Construction Site," *Los Angeles Times*, August 2, 2003, sec. B; Tony Perry and Jia-Rui Chong, "Six Homes Torched in Protest Act," *Los Angeles Times*, September 20, 2003, sec. B.

50. Brian Carnell, "Craig Rosebraugh Responds to House Subcommittee," March 15, 2002, http://www.animalrights.net/archives/year/2002/000089.html.

51. Rosebraugh, *Burning Rage of a Dying Planet*, 214.

52. David Samuels, "Notes from Underground: Among the Radicals of the Pacific Northwest," *Harper's*, May 2000, 41.

53. Sam Howe Verhovek, "S.U.V.'s, Golf, and Even Peas Join Growing Hit List of Eco-Vandals," *New York Times*, July 1, 2001, sec. Y.

54. Henry Chu, "Activists Hope Nun's Slaying in Amazon Is Catalyst for Change," *Los Angeles Times*, February 16, 2005, sec. A.

55. Associated Press, "Brazil Carves Out Two Vast Preserves in the Amazon Rain Forest," *New York Times*, February 18, 2005, sec. A.

56. Douglas Burton-Christie, "The Wild and the Sacred," *Anglican Theological Review*, vol. 85, no. 3, Summer 2003, 502.

57. Dean E. Murphy, "Book on Environmentalist Creates Storm," *New York Times*, January 28, 2005, sec. A.

58. Lee Romney, "That Tree Stood for So Much," *Los Angeles Times*, July 6, 2005, sec. A.

59. Tim Reiterman, "Strapped Pacific Lumber Plans to Sell 60,000 Acres," *Los Angeles Times*, February 11, 2006, sec. C.

60. Eric Bailey, "A Truce Amid the Redwoods," *Los Angeles Times*, August 24, 2008, sec. A.

61. Patrick E. Tyler, "Peace Prize Goes to Environmentalist in Kenya," *New York Times*, October 9, 2004, sec. A.

62. The film was based on Fossey's memoir, *Gorillas in the Mist* (New York: Houghton Mifflin, 1983). Fossey's murder has never been solved, and she might have been killed for reasons other than her efforts to protect the gorillas from poachers. Still, she was murdered in the mountain preserve, and would not have died if she had not gone to Africa to study and defend the animals. See Harold T. P. Hayes, *The Dark Romance of Dian Fossey* (New York: Simon and Schuster, 1990).

63. *Mountain Patrol* has been broadly distributed to art house theaters in various countries by National Geographic Worldwide Films.

64. Peter Heller, *The Whale Warriors: The Battle at the Bottom of the World to Save the Planet's Largest Mammals* (New York: The Free Press, 2007), 216.

## Chapter 6: Loving It to Death

1. Mark Owens, *Marine Tourism: Development, Impacts, and Management* (New York: Routledge, 1999), 58.

2. Douglas Frantz, "Alaskans Choose Sides in Battle over Cruise Ships," *New York Times*, November 29, 1999, sec. A.

3. Kim Murphy, "Alaska Seeks to Clean Up Cruise Ships," *Los Angeles Times*, May 10, 2001, sec. A, 24.

4. Douglas Frantz, "Gaps in Sea Laws Shield Pollution by Cruise Lines," *New York Times*, January 3, 1999, sec. A.

5. Hans Greimel, "Garbage Threatening Beauty of 'Paradise' Islands," Associated Press, March 30, 2004.

6. Tourism scholar R. W. Butler first discussed this problem in his famous 1980 theory of the "tourist area life cycle," in which every resort is postulated to have a "carrying capacity" that must not be exceeded to avoid eventual decline. See David A. Fennell, *Ecotourism: An Introduction* (London and New York: Routledge, 1999), 120–23.

7. Philip G. Terrie, *Forever Wild: A Cultural History of Wilderness in the Adirondacks* (Syracuse: Syracuse University Press, 1994), 44.

8. Ibid., 69–75.

9. Paul S. Sutter, *Driven Wild: How the Fight Against Automobiles Launched the Modern Wilderness Movement* (Seattle: University of Washington Press, 2002), 24.

10. Zbigniew Mieczkowski, *Environmental Issues of Tourism and Recreation* (Lanham, Maryland: University Press of America, 1995), 309.

11. Amy Kane, "National Parks Wrestle with Traffic Jams," Reuters, America Online, July 19, 2001.

12. Ibid.

13. Gary Polarkovic, "Accord Reached to Reduce Levels of Haze at National Parks," *Los Angeles Times*, August 20, 2003, sec. A.

14. Elizabeth Shogren, "More National Parks Fail New EPA Smog Ratings," *Los Angeles Times*, April 8, 2004, sec. A.

15. Janet Wilson and Seema Mehta, "Two Visions of the Countryside Clash," *Los Angeles Times*, May 6, 2005, sec. A.

16. Susan Sullivan, "L.A.'s Wild Fringe," *Los Angeles Times*, February 17, 2004, sec. F.

17. Scott Gold, "BLM, Wildlife Agency at Odds over Off-Roading at Dunes," *Los Angeles Times*, September 13, 2002, sec. B.

18. Scott Gold, "U.S. Seeks to Reopen Area to Off-Roaders," *Los Angeles Times*, March 28, 2002, sec. B.

19. Julie Cart, "Dust-Up over Off-Roaders Roars Across Backcountry," *Los Angeles Times*, September 21, 2003, sec. A.

20. Jason Tanz, "Making Tracks, Making Enemies," *New York Times*, January 2, 2004, sec. D.

21. Ibid.

22. Louis Sahagun, "No Happy Trail in Desert Tale," *Los Angeles Times*, March 25, 2004, sec. B.

23. Tanz, "Making Tracks, Making Enemies."

24. Nick Madigan, "California Dunes May Be Reopened to Off-Road Vehicles," *New York Times*, March 29, 2002, sec. A.

25. Cart, "Dust-Up over Off-Roaders Roars Across Backcountry."

26. Jason Brininstool, "Off-Road Emissions and Their Effects on Human Health," *Wildlands CPR.Road RIPorter*, Spring Equinox 2006, vol. 11, no. 1, http://www.wildlandscpr.org/biblio-notes/off-road-vehicle-emissions-and-their-effects-human-health.

27. Julie Cart, "Plan Backs Snowmobiles at Parks," *Los Angeles Times*, November 8, 2002, sec. A.

28. Jon Bilman, "Snowmobiles and Yellowstone: Sledheads vs. Greenies," *Outside Magazine* (online at outsidemag.com), December 30, 2001.

29. Cart, "Plan Backs Snowmobiles at Parks."

30. Associated Press, "Agency Again Seeks Snowmobiles Ban in 2 Parks," *New York Times*, April 30, 2002, sec. A.

31. Cart, "Plan Backs Snowmobiles at Parks."

32. Bilman, "Snowmobiles and Yellowstone: Sledheads vs. Greenies."

33. Personal Watercraft Industry Association, 2007, http://www.pwia.org.

34. Bluewater Network, "Personal Watercraft: Creating Havoc in their Wake," April 7, 2005, http://www.bluewaternetwork.org/campaign_pl_pwc.shtml.

35. Rone Tempest, "Off-Roading Mecca at a Crossroads," *Los Angeles Times*, July 5, 2002, sec. A.

36. Nick Madigan, "California Dunes May Be Reopened to Off-Road Vehicles," *New York Times*, March 29, 2002, sec. A.

37. Kenneth T. Jackson, *Crabgrass Frontier: The Suburbanization of the United States* (New York: Oxford University Press, 1985).

38. Joel Garreau, *Edge City: Life on the New Frontier* (New York: Anchor Books, Doubleday, 1991).

39. Timothy Egan, "Heat Invades Cool Heights over Arizona Desert," *New York Times*, March 27, 2007, sec. A.

40. Evan Halper, "Parkland Is Home to Planned Community," *Los Angeles Times*, March 31, 2002, sec. B.

41. Nick Madigan, "In a California Desert, Visions of Country Clubs," *New York Times*, April 1, 2002, sec. A.

42. Russell Boniface, "Log Home Popularity Booming," *AIArchitect This Week*, November 17, 2006, http://www.aia.org/aiarchitect/thisweek06/1117/1117p_log.cfm.

43. Matt Richtel, "A Return to Nature, Mostly by Cutting It Down," *New York Times*, April 12, 2002, sec. D.

44. John-Thor Dahlburg, "Hello, Dolly—and More Hurricanes That May Be Coming This Season," *Los Angeles Times*, June 6, 2002, sec. A.

45. Cornelia Dean, *Against the Tide: The Battle for America's Beaches* (New York: Columbia University Press, 1999).

46. Tom Horton, with photographs by Peter Essick, "Saving the Chesapeake," *National Geographic*, June 2005, 36.

47. Jesse McKinley and Kirk Johnson, "On Fringe of Forests, Homes and Wildfires Meet," *New York Times*, June 26, 2007, sec. A.

48. Dahlburg, "Hello, Dolly—and More Hurricanes That May Be Coming This Season."

49. Bettina Boxall and Julie Cart, "Nevada's Plan to Develop the Desert," *Los Angeles Times*, August 18, 2004, sec. A.

50. Julie Cart, "Grizzlies Losing Ground Around Yellowstone," *Los Angeles Times*, January 9, 2005, sec. A.

51. Anthony DePalma, "Crossing Their (Flight) Path," *New York Times*, January 31, 2004, sec. A.

52. Henry Fountain, "Fast-Food Nation Is Taking Its Toll on Black Bears, Too," *New York Times*, November 25, 2003, sec. D.

53. Bob Butz, *Beast of Never, Cat of God: The Search for the Eastern Puma* (Guilford, Connecticut: The Lyons Press, 2005), 183.

54. "When Cute Deer Go Bad," *New York Times*, March 20, 2005, sec. WK.

55. Donna Horowitz, "Marin Giving No Thanks for Tasty Visitor," *Los Angeles Times*, September 2, 2003, sec. B.

56. Dean E. Murphy, "Rooting for Rain and for Relief from Feral Pigs," *New York Times*, November 10, 2002, sec. YNE.

57. Peter Matthiessen, *Indian Country* (London: Collins/Harvill, 1985; Fontana Paperbacks, 1986), 112–15

58. Benett Kessler, "Tiny Fish Sparks Big Battle over Development," *Los Angeles Times*, July 6, 1993, A3, 13.

59. Douglas Jehl, "Rio Grande Choice: Take City Water or Let Minnow Die," *New York Times*, January 19, 2003, sec. A.

60. Sema Mehta, "Judge Overturns 'Critical Habitat' of Two Species," *Los Angeles Times*, February 26, 2002, sec. B.

61. Carl Safina, *Song for the Blue Ocean: Encounters Along the World's Coasts and Beneath the Seas* (New York: A John Macrae Book/Henry Holt, 1997), 278.

62. Cornelia Dean, "Earth's Uncanned Crusaders: Will Sardines Save Our Skins?" *New York Times*, November 23, 2004, sec. D.

63. Mary F. Pols, "Condor Conundrum," *Los Angeles Times*, April 28, 1996, sec. A.

64. Douglas Jehl, "Rare Arizona Owl (All 7 Inches of It) Is in Habitat Furor," *New York Times*, March 17, 2003, sec. A.

65. Associated Press, "Arizona: U.S. Moves to Delist an Endangered Owl," *New York Times*, August 3, 2005, sec. A.

66. Tim Gallagher, *The Grail Bird: Hot on the Trail of the Ivory-Billed Woodpecker* (New York: Houghton Mifflin, 2005), 238.

67. Richard B. Woodward, "A Sliver of Prairie Still Untamed," *New York Times*, June 10, 2005, sec. D.

68. Ann Vileisis, *Discovering the Unknown Landscape: A History of America's Wetlands* (Washington, D.C.: Island Press, 1997), 3.

69. Bruce Robertson (writer, producer, director), *Nature's Last Stand: Saving the Ballona Wetlands*, 2006, www.BallonaWetlands.org; Sheila A. Laffey (writer, producer, director), *The Last Stand: The Struggle for Ballona Wetlands*, 2000, www.ballona.com.

70. James William Gibson and Chester King, "Skeletons in Playa Vista's Closet," *Los Angeles Times*, June 20, 2004, sec. M. In 2004, the developer's archeologists announced that over four hundred human remains had been excavated. The 1,200 to 1,400 figure was revealed when the bodies were reburied at another location in Playa Vista on December 13, 2008.

71. John Balzar, "No Safe Arbor in the City," *Los Angeles Times*, March 8, 2004, sec. A.

72. Steve Lopez, "Big Bucks Support Befouling of Beach," *Los Angeles Times*, January 19, 2003, sec. B. These legal battles are ongoing. For example, in July 2008, a state court ruled in favor of the cities challenging the Los Angeles Regional Water

Control Board's 2005 regulations to reduce polluted runoff flowing into storm-water channels. The judge agreed with plaintiffs that the water control board had not considered the costs of compliance. See David Pierson, "Ruling Halts Building Permits; O.C. Judge's Striking Down of Pollution Rules Affects Work in Ventura, L.A. Counties," *Los Angeles Times*, July 18, 2008, sec. B.

## Chapter 7: Imitation Wildness and the Sacred Casino

1. Doug Peacock, *Grizzly Years: In Search of the American Wilderness* (New York: Henry Holt, 1990); Charlie Russell and Maureen Enns, *Grizzly Heart: Living Without Fear Among the Brown Bears of Kamchatka* (Toronto: Vintage Canada, 2003).

2. Timothy Treadwell and Jewel Palovak, *Among Grizzlies: Living with Wild Bears in Alaska* (New York: Ballantine Books, 1997), 10.

3. Ibid., 33.

4. Ibid., 139.

5. Ibid., 158.

6. Ibid., 22.

7. Charlie Russell, "Counterattack," *Outside Magazine*, January 2004, 22, http://outside.away.com/outside/news/200401/200401_russell_letter.html.

8. Richard Slotkin, *Regeneration Through Violence: The Mythology of the American Frontier* (Middletown, Connecticut: Wesleyan University Press, 1973).

9. Russell, "Counterattack"; Doug Peacock, "Blood Brothers," *Outside Magazine*, January 2004, http://outside.away.com/outside/news/200401/200401_blood_brothers_1.html.

10. "The Makah Whaling Conflict: Background," *Native Americans and the Environment*, http://www.cnie.org/nae/cases/makah/m1.html.

11. Robert Sullivan, *A Whale Hunt: Two Years on the Olympic Peninsula with the Makah and Their Canoe* (New York: Scribner, 2000), 32–35.

12. "The Makah Whaling Conflict," *Native Americans and the Environment*.

13. Sullivan, *A Whale Hunt*, 238.

14. Ibid., 15.

15. "The Makah Whaling Conflict: Background," *Native Americans and the Environment*.

16. Sam Howe Verhovek, "Reviving Tradition, Tribe Kills a Whale," *New York Times*, May 18, 1999, sec. A.

17. Mircea Eliade, *Myth and Reality*, trans. Willard R. Trask (New York: Harper Colophon Books; Harper and Row, 1963), 30.

18. Emile Durkheim, *The Elementary Forms of the Religious Life*, trans. Joseph Ward Swain (New York: The Free Press, 1965), 186.

19. Durkheim, *The Elementary Forms of the Religious Life*, 378.

20. Ibid., 384–85.

21. Ibid., 388.

22. Sullivan, *A Whale Hunt*, 215.

23. Ibid., 17, 92.

24. Dick Russell, *Eye of the Whale: Epic Passage from Baja to Siberia* (New York: Simon and Schuster, 2001), 113.

25. Ibid., 115.

26. Ibid., 114.

27. Sullivan, *A Whale Hunt*, 96.

28. Ibid., 166.

29. Durkheim, *The Elementary Forms of the Religious Life*, 348.

30. Sullivan, *A Whale Hunt*, 65.

31. Paul Watson, "Where Is the Whales' Manifesto? Sea Shepherd's Response to the Makah Manifesto," *Seattle Times*, September 10, 1998, sec. B.

32. Durkheim, *The Elementary Forms of the Religious Life*, 337–38.

33. Alan Green and The Center for Public Integrity, *Animal Underworld: Inside America's Black Market for Rare and Exotic Species* (New York: Public Affairs, 1999), 12.

34. Randal C. Archibold, "Poachers in West Hunt Big Antlers to Feed Big Egos," *New York Times*, December 9, 2006, sec. A.

35. Green, *Animal Underworld*, xxvii.

36. Bob Butz, *Beast of Never, Cat of God: The Search for the Eastern Puma* (Guilford, Connecticut: The Lyons Press, 2005), 211; Green, *Animal Underworld*, 121.

37. Peter Steinhart, *The Company of Wolves* (New York: Alfred A. Knopf, 1995), 301, 310.

38. Sam D. Gill, *Mother Earth: An American Story* (Chicago: University of Chicago Press, 1987), 8.

39. Shepard Krech III, *The Ecological Indian: Myth and History* (New York: W. W. Norton, 1999), 142.

40. Quoted in Donald A. Grinde and Bruce E. Johansen, *Ecocide of Native America: Environmental Destruction of Indian Lands and Peoples* (Santa Fe, New Mexico: Clear Light Publishers, 1995), 26.

41. Western Governors Association, "The Indian Gaming Regulatory Act and 'Off-Reservation' Indian Gaming Proposals: A Primer" (2005), 1. http://www.westgov .org/wga/meetings/gaming/Primer.pdf.

42. Ibid., 62.

43. Washington Research Council, "Untaxed and Lightly Regulated," November 14, 2002, 6–7, http://www.researchcouncil.org/publications_container/untaxed.pdf.

44. Western Governors Association, "The Indian Gaming Regulatory Act and 'Off-Reservation' Indian Gaming Proposals: A Primer," 7.

45. Charles V. Bagli, "Cayugas Closer to a Casino in the Catskills," *New York Times*, May 4, 2004, sec. A. In late 2004, New York State concluded negotiations for casino developments in the Catskills with four Indian tribes to settle their lawsuits over land claims. Kirk Semple, "Catskill Casino Politics: Game of Delicate Balance," *New York Times*, January 31, 2005, sec. B.

46. Raymond Hernandez, "Trump Among Those Named in Inquiry into Bankrolling of Would-Be Tribes," *New York Times*, May 6, 2004, sec. A.

47. Dan Morain, "Tribes Have Become Players in Sacramento," *Los Angeles Times*, September 20, 2003, sec. A.

48. Louis Sahagun, "Tribes Fear Backlash to Prosperity," *Los Angeles Times*, May 3, 2004, sec. B.

49. "Thirteenth Census of the United States Taken in the Year 1910," *United States Bureau of the Census* (Washington, D.C.: Government Printing Office, 1912–1914).

50. Karen Kaplan, "Ancestry in a Drop of Blood," *Los Angeles Times*, August 30, 2005, sec. B.

51. Joel Rubin, "Bloodlines Issue Divides Tribe," *Los Angeles Times*, November 30, 2003, sec. B.

52. Ibid.

53. Although the Agua Caliente lawsuit did not succeed in entirely erasing the critical habitat designation, the government's proposed settlement agreement would remove the seven square miles of the tribe's land from the sheep protection plan, and cut the overall protection area by more than 50 percent. Janet Wilson, "Lawsuit Pits Tribe Against U.S. and Endangered Bighorn Sheep," *Los Angeles Times*, April 11, 2005, sec. B; Jennifer Bowles, "Proposal Would Shrink Endangered Sheep Habitat," *Press Enterprise*, October 10, 2007; Department of the Interior, "Endangered and Threatened Wildlife and Plants: Designation of Critical Habitat for the Peninsular Bighorn Sheep (*Ovis canadensis nelsoni*) and Proposed Taxonomic Revision; Proposed Rule," *Federal Register*, 50 CFR (Code of Federal Regulations), part 17.

54. Louis Sahagun, "Point Man for Gaming Tribes Is Bold Leader," *Los Angeles Times*, January 18, 2004, sec. A.

55. Christopher Reynolds, "Pechangas Delay Pact with L.A. Museum," *Los Angeles Times*, May 20, 2002, sec. B.

56. Jeff Benedict, *Without Reservation: The Making of America's Most Powerful Indian Tribe and Foxwoods, the World's Largest Casino* (New York: HarperCollins, 2000), 340.

57. Ibid., 283.

58. Andy Newman, "Raising the Ante," *New York Times*, April 18, 2008, sec. F.

## Chapter 8: The Right-Wing War on the Land

1. Max Weber, "The Social Psychology of the World's Religions," *From Max Weber: Essays in Sociology*, ed. Hans Gerth and C. Wright Mills (New York: Oxford University Press, 1958), 270.

2. Gore book sales listed in "25 Most Influential Americans," *Time*, June 17, 1996.

3. Al Gore, *Earth in the Balance: Ecology and the Human Spirit* (New York: Houghton Mifflin, 1992; Plume/New American Library, 1993), 265.

4. Ibid. 384–85.

5. Ibid., 260.

6. Ibid., 305–6.

7. Bruce Barcott, "Changing All the Rules: How the Bush Administration Quietly—and Radically—Transformed the Nation's Clean-Air Policy," *New York Times Magazine*, April 4, 2004, 40–44.

8. "Timber and Other Loud Noises," *Wall Street Journal*, April 2, 1993, sec. A.

9. Glenn W. Shuck, *Marks of the Beast: The "Left Behind" Novels and the Struggle for Evangelical Identity* (New York: New York University Press, 2005), 30–37.

10. Paul S. Boyer, *Where Time Shall Be No More: Prophecy Belief in Modern American Culture* (Cambridge, Massachusetts: Harvard University Press, 1992), 254.

11. Hal Lindsey (with C. C. Carlson), *The Late Great Planet Earth* (Grand Rapids, Michigan: Zondervan Publishing, 1970; New York: Bantam Books, 1973), 168.

12. Frank Peretti, *Piercing the Darkness* (Westchester, Illinois: Crossway Books, 1989), 378.

13. Samantha Smith, *Goddess Earth: Exposing the Pagan Agenda of the Environmental Movement* (Lafayette, Louisiana: Huntington House Publishers, 1994), 18.

14. Ibid., 124.

15. Susan Friend Harding, *The Book of Jerry Falwell: Fundamentalist Language and Politics* (Princeton, New Jersey: Princeton University Press, 2000), 19, 126.

16. Ibid., 127.

17. Pat Robertson, *The Collected Works: The New Millennium; The New World Order; The Secret Kingdom* (New York: Inspirational Press, 1994).

18. Pat Robertson, *The Collected Works: The New Millennium*, 202.

19. Ibid.

20. Ibid.

21. Ibid., 203.

22. Pat Robertson, *The Collected Works: The Secret Kingdom*, 698.

23. Ibid., 699.

24. Ibid., 17.

25. Pat Robertson, *Collected Works: The New World Order*, 448–49.

26. Ibid., 460.

27. Ibid., 489–90.

28. Ibid., 497.

29. Tim LaHaye, *Revelation Illustrated and Made Plain*, revised edition (Grand Rapids, Michigan: Zondervan, 1973), 307.

30. Ibid., 216.

31. Tim LaHaye and Jerry B. Jenkins, *Are We Living in the End Times?* (Wheaton, Illinois: Tyndale House Publishers, 1999), 329.

32. Ibid., 215.

33. James William Gibson, *Warrior Dreams: Paramilitary Culture in Post-Vietnam America* (New York: Hill and Wang, 1994).

34. Shuck, *Marks of the Beast*, 10.

35. Tim LaHaye and Jerry Jenkins, *Apollyon: The Destroyer Is Unleashed* (Wheaton, Illinois: Tyndale House Publishers, 1999), 54.

36. LaHaye and Jenkins, *Are We Living in the End Times?*, 179–92.

37. Ibid., 193–208.

38. Ibid., 234.

39. Quoted without a source note in Barbara R. Rossing, *The Rapture Exposed: The Message of Hope in the Book of Revelation* (Boulder, Colorado: Westview Press, 2004), 6.

40. Amy Johnson Frykholm, *Rapture Culture: "Left Behind" in Evangelical America* (New York: Oxford University Press, 2004), 11.

41. Pat Robertson, *The Collected Works: The Secret Kingdom*, 568.

42. Cited in Rossing, *The Rapture Exposed*, 7. The quote appeared in "The Wisdom of Ann Coulter," *Washington Monthly*, October 2001, http://www.washingtonmonthly.com/features/2001/0111.coulterwisdom.html.

43. Weber, "The Social Psychology of the World's Religions," *From Max Weber*, 280.

44. LaHaye and Jenkins, *Are We Living in the End Times?*, 132.

45. Tim LaHaye, *The Battle for the Mind* (Old Tappan, New Jersey: Fleming H. Revell, 1980), 217–18.

46. Shuck, *Marks of the Beast*, 21.

47. Glenn Scherer, "The Godly Must Be Crazy," *Grist Magazine: Environmental News and Commentary*, October 27, 2004, http://www.grist.org/news/maindish/2004/10/27/scherer-christian/index.html.

48. Ibid.

49. Ibid., 5.

50. David Kuo, *Tempting Faith: An Inside Story of Political Seduction* (New York: The Free Press, 2006).

51. Don Van Natta Jr. and Neela Banerjee, "Documents Show Energy Officials Met Only with Industry Leaders," *New York Times*, March 27, 2002, sec. A.

52. Ibid.

53. President George Bush, "Excerpts from Bush's Speech Outlining a New Energy Policy," *New York Times*, May 18, 2001, sec. A.

54. Lizette Alvarez and Joseph Kahn, "House Republicans Gather Support for Alaska Drilling," *New York Times*, August 1, 2001, sec. A.

55. Mathew L. Wald, "Oil Drilling in Arctic Called Departure from Past Policy," *New York Times*, November 12, 2001, sec. A.

56. Elisabeth Bumiller and Jeff Gerth, "Ambitious Bush Plan Undone by Energy Politics," *New York Times*, August 20, 2001, sec. A.

57. David E. Sanger and Joseph Kahn, "Bush, Pushing Energy Plan, Offers Scores of Proposals to Find New Power Sources," *New York Times*, May 18, 2001, sec. A.

58. Timothy Egan, "Bush Administration Allows Oil Drilling Near Utah Parks," *New York Times*, February 8, 2002, sec. A.

59. Geoffrey Mohan, "Bush Oil, Gas Bid Skirts Key Issues," *Los Angeles Times*, August 12, 2001, sec. A.

60. Timothy Egan, "Drilling in West Pits Republican Policy Against Republican Base," *New York Times*, June 22, 2005, sec. A.

61. Ibid.

62. Associated Press, "Environmentalists, Ranchers Take on Oil and Gas Drillers," *Los Angeles Times*, November 15, 2002, sec. A.

63. Elizabeth Shogren, "Nation's Energy Needs Collide with a Way of Life," *Los Angeles Times*, May 19, 2003, sec. A.

64. Erik Reece, "Moving Mountains: Will Justice Have Its Day in Coal Country?" *Orion*, January–February 2006, 56–57.

65. Katharine Q. Seelye, "Rule Could Let Mine Debris Fill in Valleys and Streams," *New York Times*, April 26, 2002, sec. A. The new rule was overturned in

federal courts a month later. See Frances X. Clines, "Judge Takes on the White House on Mountaintop Mining," *New York Times*, May 19, 2002, sec. A.

66. Elizabeth Shogren, "Damage in Appalachia Trickles from the Top," *Los Angeles Times*, January 18, 2004, sec. A.

67. Douglas Jehl, "Clinton to Put New Restraints on U.S. Forests," *New York Times*, January 5, 2001, sec. A.

68. Bettina Boxall, "Winding Paths for Roadless Lands," *Los Angeles Times*, July 26, 2004, sec. B.

69. Rick Bass, "Lost in Space," *West* (Sunday magazine of the *Los Angeles Times*), April 16, 2006, 42.

70. Douglas Jehl, "Court Reinstates Ban on Building Forest Roads," *New York Times*, December 13, 2002, sec. A.

71. Boxall, "Winding Paths for Roadless Lands."

72. Elizabeth Shogren, "Some See Nature as a War Victim," *Los Angeles Times*, December 26, 2001, sec. A.

73. Elizabeth Shogren and Richard Simon, "New Forest-Thinning Policy Drops Safeguard for Wildlife," *Los Angeles Times*, December 4, 2003, sec. A.

74. Henry Weinstein, "A Changing Landscape: Recasting Wilderness as Open for Business: A Bush Administration Policy Reversal Ends Decades of Shielding the Nation's Untamed Areas," *Los Angeles Times*, October 25, 2004, sec. A.

75. Boxall, "Winding Paths for Roadless Lands."

76. Geoffrey Mohan, "Bush Oil, Gas Bid Skirts Key Issues," *Los Angeles Times*, August 12, 2001, sec. A.

77. Kim Murphy, "National Monument Dealt a Setback," *Los Angeles Times*, May 19, 2001, sec. A.

78. Jim Robbins, "Debate Over a National Monument Emphasizes Old West–New West Divide," *New York Times*, August 20, 2001, sec. A.

79. Tim Reiterman, "A Policy Showdown in Prairie Wetlands," *Los Angeles Times*, April 12, 2005, sec. A.

80. Douglas Jehl, "U.S. Could Ease Limits on Wetlands Development," *New York Times*, January 11, 2003, sec. A.

81. Douglas Jehl, "Changes in Defining Wetland Anger Critics of Army Corps," *New York Times*, February 11, 2003, sec. A.

82. Elizabeth Shogren, "Rule Drafted That Would Dilute the Clean Water Act," *Los Angeles Times*, November 6, 2003, sec. A.

83. Julie Cart, "Species Protection Act 'Broken,'" *Los Angeles Times*, November 4, 2003, sec. B.

84. Julie Cart and Kenneth R. Weiss, "Governors Seek Easing of Endangered Species Act," *Los Angeles Times*, December 4, 2004, sec. B.

85. Elizabeth Shogren and Kenneth R. Weiss, "Critics Call Fish Count a Whopper," *Los Angeles Times*, April 30, 2004, sec. A; Timothy Egan, "Shift on Salmon Reignites Fight on Species Law," *New York Times*, May 9, 2004, sec. A.

86. Julie Cart, "U.S. Scientists Say They Are Told to Alter Findings," *Los Angeles Times*, February 10, 2005, sec. A.

87. Julie Cart and Janet Wilson, "'Critical Habitat' About to Go on Endangered List," *Los Angeles Times*, September 28, 2005, sec. A.

88. Janet Wilson, "Habitats May Shrink by Leaps, Bounds," *Los Angeles Times*, November 4, 2005, sec. A.

89. Ibid. In September 2008, the U.S. Fish and Wildlife Service proposed to increase frog habitat in central and northern California to over 2,800 square miles on the grounds that Susan MacDonald, a former Interior Department official closely tied to developers, had altered scientists' conclusions about frog populations and so justified reducing their federally protected wetlands. Julie Cart, "Room to Stretch a Frog's Red Legs," *Los Angeles Times*, September 17, 2008, Sec. B.

90. Elizabeth Shogren, "U-Turn on Emissions Shows Big Energy Clout," *Los Angeles Times*, March 15, 2001, sec. A.

91. Gary Polakovic and Elizabeth Shogren, "Smog Rules May Be Eased," *Los Angeles Times*, July 27, 2001, sec. A.

92. Bruce Barcott, "Changing All the Rules," *New York Times Magazine*, April 4, 2004, 77.

93. Christopher Drew and Richard A. Oppel Jr., "Lawyers at E.P.A. Say It Will Drop Pollution Cases," *New York Times*, November 6, 2003, sec. A.

94. Katherine Q. Seelye, "Regulators Urge Easing U.S. Rules on Air Pollution," *New York Times*, January 8, 2002, sec. A.

95. Barcott, "Changing All the Rules," 75.

96. "Act Fast on Mercury Threat," *Los Angeles Times*, February 16, 2004, sec. B.

97. Tom Hamburger and Alan C. Miller, "Mercury Emissions Rule Geared to Benefit Industry, Staffers Say," *Los Angeles Times*, March 16, 2004, sec. A.

98. Jennifer 8. Lee, "E.P.A. May Tighten Its Proposal on Mercury," *New York Times*, March 16, 2004, sec. A.

99. Miguel Bustillo, "Kyoto Pact Takes Effect Without U.S.," *Los Angeles Times*, February 16, 2005, sec. A.

100. Andrew C. Revkin, "Dispute Arises over a Push to Change Climate Panel," *New York Times*, April 2, 2002, sec. A; Andrew C. Revkin, "U.S. to Back Scientist from India to Replace Global Warming Expert," *New York Times*, April 3, 2002, sec. A.

101. Katharine Q. Seelye, "President Distances Himself from Global Warming Report," *New York Times*, June 5, 2002, sec. A.

102. Andrew C. Revkin, "Top-Level Editing on Climate Issues," *New York Times*, June 8, 2005, sec. A.

103. Andrew C. Revkin and Katharine Q. Seelye, "White House Cuts Data on Warming in an E.P.A. Report," *New York Times*, June 19, 2003, sec. A.

104. Andrew C. Revkin, "Top-Level Editing on Climate Issues," *New York Times*, June 8, 2005, sec. A.

105. Ibid.

106. Andrew C. Revkin, "G-8 Draft on Global Warming Is Weakened at U.S. Behest," *New York Times*, June 18, 2005, sec. A.

107. Andrew C. Revkin, "U.S. Resists New Targets for Curbing Emissions," *New York Times*, December 8, 2005, sec. A.

108. Andrew C. Revkin, "Climate Debate: Incremental Gains," *New York Times*, December 11, 2005, sec. A.

109. Andrew C. Revkin, "Climate Expert Says NASA Tried to Silence Him," *New York Times*, January 29, 2006, sec. A.

110. Andrew C. Revkin, "NASA's Goals Delete Mention of Home Planet," *New York Times*, July 22, 2006, sec. A.

## Chapter 9: Fighting Back

1. Max Boot, "The 500-Mile-per-Gallon Solution," *Los Angeles Times*, March 24, 2005, sec. B.

2. Red Cavaney, president and chief executive, American Petroleum Institute, "Oil in Arctic Refuge," *New York Times*, March 20, 2005, sec. A.

3. Richard Simon, "Senate Votes for Drilling in Arctic Refuge," *Los Angeles Times*, March 17, 2005, sec. A.

4. Robert Pear, "Arctic Drilling Push Is Seen as Threat to Budget Bill," *New York Times*, November 3, 2005, sec. A; Natural Resources Defense Council, "Thank These Environmental Heroes for Forcing Arctic Drilling out of the House Budget Bill!," November 16, 2005. http://www.nrdcactionfund.org/arcticad/heroes.asp.

5. Carl Hulse, "Senate Blocks Arctic Drilling in Final Spending Bills," *New York Times*, December 21, 2005, sec. A.

6. Mike Dombeck, "Your Birthright, Up for Grabs," *Los Angeles Times*, November 18, 2005, sec. B.

7. Kirk Johnson and Felicity Barringer, "Bill Authorizes Private Purchase of Federal Land," *New York Times*, November 20, 2005, sec. A.

8. Janet Wilson and Bettina Boxall, "Revisions of Mining Law Put on Hold," *Los Angeles Times*, December 14, 2005, sec. B.

9. "Drafting the Future of the Parks," *New York Times*, July 10, 2006, sec. A.

10. "Beleaguered Director to Leave Park Service," *Los Angeles Times*, July 27, 2006, sec. A.

11. The forty-million-dollar figure comes from Chuck Neubauer and Richard B. Schmitt, "Abramoff's Charity Began at Home," *Los Angeles Times*, February 11, 2006, sec. A. The higher eighty-million-dollar total was reported by Susan Schmidt and James V. Grimaldi, "The Fast Rise and Steep Fall of Jack Abramoff," *Washington Post*, December 29, 2005, sec. A.

12. Ibid.

13. Peter Wallsten and Tom Hamburger, "Cabinet Official Norton Resigns," *Los Angeles Times*, March 11, 2006, sec. A.

14. Michael Janofsky, "Judges Overturn Bush Bid to Ease Pollution Rules," *New York Times*, March 18, 2006, sec. A.

15. Plaintiffs included the states of California, Oregon, New Mexico, and Washington, together with twenty environmental groups, among them The Wilderness Society, the Center for Biological Diversity, the Sierra Club, and the Defenders of Wildlife. *People of the State of California* ex rel. *Bill Lockyer, et al., vs. United States Department of Agriculture, Mike Johanns, Secretary of the Department of Agriculture, et al.*, United States District Court Northern District of California. Case 3:05-cv-03508-EDL Document 189. September 20, 2006, 52.

16. Frances Beinecke, president, Natural Resources Defense Council, "Greenest Day in American Political History," November 13, 2006.

17. Faye Fiore, "Unlikely New Lawmaker Rode Winds of Change," *Los Angeles Times*, November 20, 2006, sec. A.

18. Rone Tempest, "Pombo Race Is the Fight of His Career," *Los Angeles Times*, November 4, 2006, sec. A.

19. Cat Lazaroff, press secretary for policy and legislation, Earthjustice, "View from the Hill: Winds of Change," November 15, 2006, http://www.earthjustice.org /news/view_hill/page.jsp?itemID=29258026.

20. Sheryl Gay Stolberg, "Senate Supports Arctic Drilling," *New York Times*, March 17, 2005, sec. A.

21. Faye Fiore, "A Wholly Controversial Holy Man," *Los Angeles Times*, February 12, 2006, sec. A.

22. Laurie Goodstein, "Even Pat Robertson's Friends Are Wondering," *New York Times*, January 8, 2006, sec. WK.

23. Ibid.

24. Taken from the mission statement of the Evangelical Environmental Network, http://www.creationcare.org/welcome.php. For an example of a campaign, see "Healthy Families, Healthy Environment," *Creation Care: A Christian Environmental Quarterly*, no. 19, Fall 2002, 3.

25. In October 2004, the board of directors of the National Association of Evangelicals voted 42 to 0 to endorse a public agenda called "For the Health of the Nation: An Evangelical Call to Civic Responsibility." The environmental platform is on pages 11–12, http://www.nae.net/images/civic_responsibility2.pdf.

26. Ibid.

27. Laurie Goodstein, "86 Evangelical Leaders Join to Fight Global Warming," *New York Times*, February 8, 2006, sec. A. A full-page ad appeared the next day: "The Evangelical Climate Initiative," *New York Times*, February 9, 2006, sec. A. The signers included Dr. Duane Litfion, president of Wheaton College; David Neff, editor of *Christianity Today*; Richard Stearns, president of World Vision; Commissioner Todd Bassett, national commander of the Salvation Army; and Dr. Rick Warren, author of the bestselling book *The Purpose Driven Life*. Reverend Ted Haggard, then president of the National Association of Evangelicals, did not sign the initiative because he worried that it would be interpreted as an endorsement by the entire NAE, but he personally supported the measure.

28. Evangelical Climate Initiative, "Nationwide Study Shows Concerns of Evangelicals over Global Warming," February 2, 2006, http://www.christiansandclimate .org/polling.

29. Evangelical Climate Initiative, "Climate Change: An Evangelical Call to Action," January 2006, http://www.christiansandclimate.org.

30. Laurie Goodstein, "Living Day to Day by a Gospel of Green," *New York Times*, March 8, 2007, sec. F.

31. Cizik's comments appear in the 2006 documentary *The Great Warming*, which stresses both the scientific studies of global warming and the Evangelical Climate Initiative. Cizik describes his conversion to the cause of stopping climate change in terms of what Methodist founder John Wesley called "a warming of the heart."

32. Henry David Thoreau, "Walking," in *The Portable Thoreau*, ed. Carl Bode (New York: Viking Penguin, 1947; Penguin Books, 1982), 613.

33. Marjory Stoneman Douglas, *The Everglades: River of Grass* (St. Simons Island, Georgia: Mockingbird Books, 1947, 1974).

34. Peter Matthiessen's trilogy was published by Random House in New York.

35. See, for example, Carl Hiaasen, *Hoot* (New York: Alfred A. Knopf, 2002).

36. William Least Heat-Moon, *PrairyErth (a Deep Map)* (Boston: A Peter Davison Book/Houghton Mifflin, 1991).

37. Richard B. Woodward, "A Sliver of Prairie Still Untamed," *New York Times*, June 10, 2005, sec. D.

38. Jim Robbins, "Where the Cattle Herds Roam, Ideally in Harmony with Their Neighbors," *New York Times*, July 11, 2006, sec. D.

39. Barbara Stewart, "Come on In, the Hudson's Fine," *New York Times*, October 1, 2002, sec. A.

40. Ibid.

41. Ibid.

42. "Piers as Parks Downtown," *New York Times*, August 6, 2003, sec. A.

43. Kathryn Jones, "Big City, Big Water," *New York Times*, October 8, 2004, sec. D.

44. Steve Hymon, "Plan for L.A. River Okayed," *Los Angeles Times*, May 10, 2007, sec. B.

45. Carey Goldberg, "Stinking Heap in Boston Harbor Is Well on Its Way to Revival," *New York Times*, June 27, 1999, sec. A.

46. Steve Hymon and Jessica Garrison, "Puma Expert to Assess Situation in Griffith Park," *Los Angeles Times*, June 7, 2004, sec. B.

47. Nancy Wride, "Four Lion Cubs Are Born Free," *Los Angeles Times*, October 6, 2004, sec. B.

48. Veronique de Turenne, "Migrations: Free-Range Highways," *Los Angeles Times*, October 12, 2004, sec. F.

49. Helen O'Neill, "Widow Assuages Grief with Love for Rare Bird," *Los Angeles Times*, July 11, 2004, sec. A.

50. Melissa Sanford, "For Falcons as for People, Life in the Big City Has Its Risks as Well as Its Rewards," *New York Times*, June 28, 2004, sec. A.

51. Dave McKibben, "She Swoops In to Help Starving Pelicans Survive," *Los Angeles Times*, July 15, 2004, sec. B.

52. Thomas J. Lueck and Jennifer 8. Lee, "No Fighting the Co-op Board, Even with Talons," *New York Times*, December 11, 2004, sec. A.

53. Quoted by Scott McVay, "Prelude: A Siamese Connection with a Plurality of Other Mortals," in *The Biophilia Hypothesis*, ed. Stephen R. Kellert and Edward O. Wilson (Washington, D.C.: Island Press/Shearwater Books, 1993), 4.

54. Interviewed by David Takacs, *The Idea of Biodiversity: Philosophies of Paradise* (Baltimore: The Johns Hopkins University Press, 1996), 50.

55. Edward O. Wilson, *Biophilia* (Cambridge, Massachusetts: Harvard University Press, 1984), 130.

56. Scott McVay, "Biophilia and the Conservation Ethic," in *The Biophilia Hypothesis*, 39.

57. Interviewed by David Takacs, *The Idea of Biodiversity*, 221.

58. Paul R. and Anne H. Ehrlich, *Extinction: The Causes and Consequences of the Disappearances of Species* (New York: Random House, 1981; Ballantine Books, 1983), 58–59.

59. Edward O. Wilson, *Consilience: The Unity of Knowledge* (New York: Alfred A. Knopf, 1998), 265.

60. Leonardo Boff, *Ecology and Liberation: A New Paradigm*, trans. John Cumming (Maryknoll, New York: Orbis Books, 1998), 77.

61. Benett Kessler, "Tiny Fish Sparks Big Battle over Development," *Los Angeles Times*, July 6, 1993, sec. A.

62. Douglas Jehl, "Rare Arizona Owl (All 7 Inches of It) Is in Habitat Furor," *New York Times*, March 17, 2003, sec. A.

63. Demian Bulwa, "Bat Man Sheds Some Light on Maligned Animal," *San Francisco Chronicle*, November 15, 2002, Marin County sec.

64. Ibid.

65. Adam Gorlick, "American Eel Gains a Champion," *Fort Worth Star-Telegram*, The Associated Press, December 25, 2004, sec. A.

66. U.S. Fish and Wildlife Service, "Endangered and Threatened Wildlife and Plants: 12-Month Finding on a Petition to List the American Eel as Threatened or Endangered," *Federal Register*, vol. 72, no. 22, February 2, 2007, Proposed Rules, 4967–97. Timothy and Doug Watts, "What Is Right and Wrong?," http://www.glooskapandthefrog.org/benton%20falls.htm.

67. Katie Zezima, "Maine Conservationists Reach Milestone in Plan to Buy Three Dams," *New York Times*, August 22, 2008, sec. A. Penobscot River Restoration Trust, "Wide-Range Benefits," September 19, 2008, http://www.penobscotriver.org/content/4033/Widerange_Benefits/.

68. P. J. Huffstutter, "At One with the Snails," *Los Angeles Times*, October 30, 2004, sec. A.

69. Kevin Krajick, "Small Miracle of the Cave World," *On Earth: An Independent Publication of the Natural Resources Defense Council*, Summer 2007, http://www.onearth.org/article/small-miracle-of-the-cave-world-0?page=all.

70. Paul Pringle, "Lichen Lover Isn't Liking What He Sees," *Los Angeles Times*, May 2, 2004, sec. B.

71. "Backyard Biodiversity," *Greentips: Environmental Ideas in Action*. An e-newsletter from the Union of Concerned Scientists, April 2005.

72. John Johnson, "Making Out Like Bandits," *Los Angeles Times*, July 27, 2004, sec. A.

73. Philip Cousteau's foundation, Ocean Futures, organized Keiko's rehabilitation. The twenty million dollars came from Ocean Futures; Warner Brothers and New Regency, the two production companies that made the film; the Humane Society of North America; and Nextel Communications chief Craig McGraw. The press coverage of Keiko's release can be found on the Ocean Futures Web site, http://www.oceanfutures.org. Also see Susan Orlean's account of the organizational effort to free Keiko, "Where's Willy?," *The New Yorker*, September 23, 2002.

74. In 2007, for example, after an orca whale at San Diego's Sea World theme park attacked a trainer, the *Los Angeles Times* ran an editorial questioning "whether it's a fair thing for the whales to be confined to swimming pools. In the wild, pods of whales can travel more than 100 miles a day. Not so at Sea World. No wonder they

sometimes get ornery in captivity." "Save the Whale Guy," *Los Angeles Times*, March 4, 2007, sec. M.

75. Richard O'Barry (with Keith Coulbourn), *Behind the Dolphin Smile: A True Story That Will Touch the Hearts of Animal Lovers Everywhere* (Los Angeles: Renaissance Books, 1999), 250.

76. The Dolphin Project, "About Us," January 24, 2002, http://www .dolphinproject.org.

77. O'Barry, *Behind the Dolphin Smile*, 33.

78. Richard C. Paddock and Richard Boudreaux, "Any Way to Treat a Dolphin?," *Los Angeles Times*, October 17, 2003, sec. A. Also see David Gonzalez's two articles, "Flipper's Trainer in Crusade Against Dolphin Exploitation," *New York Times*, July 3, 2001, sec. A and "Cancun Journal: This Is Fun, but Did Anyone Ask the Dolphin?," *New York Times*, October 2, 2003, sec. A.

79. Felicity Barringer, "Water Pump Case Will Test the Limit of Clean Water Act," *New York Times*, January 14, 2004, sec. A.

80. Marc Lifsher, "In the Desert, a Soul's Journey vs. Water Risk," *Los Angeles Times*, June 21, 2005, sec. C.

81. Winona LaDuke, *Recovering the Sacred: The Power of Naming and Claiming* (Cambridge, Massachusetts: South End Press, 2005), 91–92.

82. Kevin Helliker, "Elder Statesman: Who Would Reject $400 Million? Listen to Johnson Holy Rock," *Wall Street Journal*, June 14, 1999, sec. A.

83. Sean Patrick Riley, "Gathering Clouds: Last Stand at Black Mesa," *Los Angeles Times Magazine*, June 6, 2004, 14.

84. Ibid., 27.

85. Steve Lopez, "Are Tribes Cashing In Their Heritage?," *Los Angeles Times*, September 24, 2004, sec. B.

86. Emily Yellin, "In Wal-Mart Plan, Indians See New Trail of Tears," *New York Times*, August 3, 1997, sec. A.

87. James William Gibson and Chester King, "Skeletons in Playa Vista's Closet," *Los Angeles Times*, June 20, 2004, sec. M.

88. Joe Kane, "Arrested Development," *Outside Magazine*, May 2001, 62.

## Chapter 10: The Journey Ahead

1. Board Members of the Millennium Ecosystem Assessment, "Living Beyond Our Means: Natural Assets and Human Well-Being," 2005, 5, http://www .millenniumassessment.org/en/index.aspx.

2. Ibid., 13.

3. Ibid., 10.

4. Millennium Ecosystem Assessment, *Ecosystems and Human Well-Being: Synthesis* (Washington, D.C.: Island Press, 2005), 2.

5. Board Members of the Millennium Ecosystem Assessment, "Living Beyond Our Means," 15.

6. Ibid., 6.

7. Ibid., 5, 9.

8. For the Nature Conservancy, the discovery of the bird represented a fulfillment of its historic mission. Back in the 1940s, the National Audubon Society sent researcher Richard Pough to look for the woodpecker on the Singer Track in Louisiana. The Singer family rejected the society's efforts to buy the forested swampland, instead selling logging rights to the Chicago Mill and Lumber Company. Pough saw only one bird after weeks of searching, and he never forgot that devastating experience. In the 1950s, he helped found the Nature Conservancy and formed its Land Preservation Fund to buy habitat for threatened species. See Tim Gallagher, *The Grail Bird: Hot on the Trail of the Ivory-Billed Woodpecker* (New York: Houghton Mifflin, 2005), 91–93.

9. Jonathan Rosen, "The Woodpecker in All of Us," *New York Times*, May 3, 2005, sec. A.

10. Jerome A. Jackson, "Ivory-Billed Woodpecker (*Campephilus principalis*): Hope, and the Interfaces of Science, Conservation, and Politics," *The Auk: A Quarterly Journal of Ornithology*, vol. 123, no. 1, January 2006, 15.

11. Suzi Gablik, *The Reenchantment of Art* (New York: Thames and Hudson, 1991), 83.

12. Kent Black, "Touched by Animals," *Los Angeles Times Magazine*, December 18, 2005, 22–25. Also see http://www.ashesandsnow.com.

13. Margaret Wertheim, "Lower, Slower, Nearer," *Los Angeles Times Magazine*, December 5, 2004, 15.

14. Bloomberg News, "Daimler Unveils a Fish-Inspired, Fuel-Efficient Diesel Concept Car," *Los Angeles Times*, June 8, 2005, sec. C.

15. Tom Mueller (with photographs by Robert Clark), "Biomimetics: Design by Nature," *National Geographic*, April 2008, 90.

16. James George Frazer, *The Golden Bough: A Study in Magic and Religion* (New York: Collier Books, 1922), 12–15.

17. Jim Robbins, "Out West, with the Buffalo, Roam Some Strands of Undesirable DNA," *New York Times*, January 9, 2007, sec. D.

18. Josh Donlan, et al., "Re-wilding North America," *Nature*, vol. 436, no. 18, August 2005, 913–14. Also see Dave Foreman, *Rewilding North America: A Vision for Conservation in the 21st Century* (Washington, D.C.: Island Press, 2004).

19. David Quammen, *Monster of God: The Man-Eating Predator in the Jungles of History and the Mind* (New York: W. W. Norton, 2003), 79–114.

20. Thomas Traherne, *Centuries of Meditations*, vol. 2, no. 66, http://www.spiritofprayer.com/o2century.php.

21. William James, *Varieties of Religious Experience: A Study of Human Nature*, Centenary Edition (London and New York: Routledge, 2002), 375.

# Index

# About the Author

JAMES WILLIAM GIBSON is the author of *Warrior Dreams: Paramilitary Culture in Post-Vietnam America* and *The Perfect War: Technowar in Vietnam*. A frequent contributor to the *Los Angeles Times* and winner of multiple awards, including a Guggenheim, Gibson is a professor of sociology at California State University, Long Beach. He lives in Los Angeles.